*"My earliest memory is of my father saying, 'Joey, get the broom,' or 'Joey, sweep the floor.' He owned an awning store below our three-bedroom apartment in Chicago. If the household chores were done, there was always useful work to do right downstairs in his shop."*

— Joe Selvaggio

D1521811

# MicroGrants

## *It's Working*

PREFACE BY JIM KLOBUCHAR

INTRODUCTION BY TONY BOUZA

FOREWORD BY JOE SELVAGGIO

NODIN PRESS

Library of Congress Cataloging-in-Publication Data

MicroGrants : it's working / foreword by Joe Selvaggio ; preface by Jim Klobuchar ; introduction by Tony Bouza.
    p. cm.
  ISBN 978-1-932472-94-3
  1.  MicroGrants (Program) 2.  Microfinance--United States--Case studies. 3.  Poverty--United States. I. Selvaggio, Joe.
  HG178.33.U6M53 2009
  332--dc22
                           2009023989

Nodin Press, LLC
530 North Third Street
Suite 120
Minneapolis, MN
55401

# Table of Contents

## The Entrepreneurs: Heroes You Have Never Met

## First Jobs

# 3 Bootstrappism Through Learning

# 4 Art

# 5 Altruism and Spunk

# 6 Single Parenting

## 7  Disabilities and Health

## 8  A Dog's Life and Other Tales

## 9  Hitting Bottom and Bouncing

## 10  Existentialists and Other Oddities

# 11 How Did It All Turn Out?

## Part II:Commentaries

# A Preface from the Community

## Jim Klobuchar

Somewhere in the mid- to late-twentieth century a handful of social entrepreneurs in widely separate parts of the world made a discovery that led to a radical conclusion about poor people. It attracted scant applause and even less visibility at the time.

Their names included Muhammad Yunus of Bangladesh, Pancho and Maria Otero of Bolivia, John and Bob Hatch of Wisconsin—and Joe Selvaggio of Minnesota.

Poor people with ambition, they said, poor people willing to dig in for a second chance, can be trusted.

It didn't matter whether they were poor in Tanzania or India, South America or in south Minneapolis. They might live in the bleakest poverty in Africa or without wheels or credit in America. They might live on the same block with predatory drug dealers in urban America. They are still worth a chance. If they make it, we all benefit.

This concept as described by its promoters like Yunus and Selvaggio initially startled the corporate and foundation rainmakers they were trying to recruit as funding partners.

They asked a question: Can poor people be trusted with money?

Yes.

A second question: When?

Well, how about now?

In Bangladesh, Yunus, the economics professor, created the model for what is now known and accepted internationally as microfinance or microcredit. The proposition is this: you can lend money to ambitious poor people, particularly women; you can charge interest to cover the administration of the loan; and the borrowers will use the loan to build tiny one-person enterprises. And they will repay the loan.

In the last 40 years, those loans have been repaid at the rate of 97 percent around the world. Hundred of millions of families now live better lives. Their kids can go to school. The self-respect and sustainable health it has brought to people who were trusted cannot be measured.

But in Minneapolis, Joe Selvaggio, a former priest and a longtime soldier in the never-ending struggle to uplift the poor, understood that in urban America the microcredit plan might not be as suitable as a direct grant that can inject immediate support into the lives of thousands in the underclass who are fighting to escape oblivion.

An accountant's course at a community college could qualify a mother of three for a decent job to support her children when she graduates. She has extricated herself from an abusive marriage. She might have experimented with drugs somewhere in the past, but now she is clean and wants out from that kind of life. She is serious, but where does she go and how? In our society, she's one more woman with a troubled life, on the lower rungs, hanging on. Their numbers run into the millions. Some have stopped trying. This one hasn't. The tuition isn't much compared with today's exploding fees at the major colleges. But she doesn't have anything close to the money for it, or at least she didn't until Joe Selvaggio and some of his partners organized a system called MicroGrants.

It works with organizations and prosperous people who understand the possibilities of the ambitious poor reclaiming their lives, and in the process lifting the community one more incremental but very necessary notch. It's one more person off dependency. A life now possible for the kids; people able to contribute far into the future; fewer calls at the police station, or to 911, or to the county coroner.

But also and beyond that, fundamentally it's the human thing to do. Those who have can share a little. When Selvaggio comes calling for donations, most of those prosperous folk or the institutional rainmakers have learned the virtue of easy and quick capitulation. The alternative is a fatherly but unsinkable 45-minute exposition on the benefits we receive when we save a life, or a hundred, or a thousand lives that are salvageable.

Joe Selvaggio's networks in this undertaking stretch back years, with

Minnesota organizations like WomenVenture, Summit Academy OIC, and Twin Cities Rise!, as well as the organizations he founded, Project for Pride in Living, and the One Percent Club.

And today that woman with three kids learns about WomenVenture. They help her get started, tell her about MicroGrants, and she applies. Then one day in the mail, she receives a check for $1,000.

It is a grant, she is told. There are no strings attached to it. You will repay with the work and study you do, reaching for your goal, for your children and for yourself. MicroGrants is saying it believes in her and her plan for her education. The money, it tells her, can be used free and clear to pay her tuition.

She weeps, and then figures out the quickest route to the college admissions office. She boards a bus. She applies and the tuition is paid.

And some time not all that long after her first class, she is hired by the third little company where she applies. She essentially does gopher work in the office for a while. But then she is assigned to some real bookkeeping. Her salary is increased. She rushes home to tell her growing kids. They hug her. Momma came through. They knew it all along.

How many lives are saved? What does it mean to the community?

You will learn some of those answers in this book by meeting scores of people like this woman. They're not all headed for the Hall of Fame. But somebody trusted them. They responded.

We grew up convinced America was a place where it could happen. Some have wavered about that in the past few years of jarring economics in this country.

This book, with its foreword by Joe Selvaggio, will reassure you that the American idea still flourishes.

*January 2009*
*Jim Klobuchar is a former columnist with the*
**Minneapolis StarTribune,** *and has authored 20 books,*
*including* **The Miracles of Barefoot Capitalism.**

# Introduction

## Tony Bouza

A million people left homeless in the
U.S. is a statistic.

One homeless person whose story and
name are splashed across the front page after
freezing to death under a bridge is a tragedy.

In these pages we encounter the faces and
learn the names of people who struggle
daily against odds stacked heavily against
them. These are the stories of the incredible
people involved with MicroGrants.

In the sagas we find the most eloquent testimony to the lofty heights
and abysmal depths scaled by the human animal in all his/her guises.

Folly, heroism, fear, courage, violence and Gandhi-like altruism all
make appearances in the lives of the members of the underclass depicted.
Mostly the exploration—like spelunking—involves emergence—or at
least heroic attempts to emerge—from the dark depths of human errors
and despair.

The incredible complexity and variety of causes leading to the travails
so graphically etched in the minds and hearts of the principals provide a
viewing perch into the lives of otherwise mostly invisible denizens of our
ghettos.

The courage to face and overcome prodigious odds seems worthy of
the highest recognitions we reserve for our honored heroes. Here the struggles occur mostly beyond our sight and knowledge.

Spunk—one of those archaic words reserved for those who endure, despite hideous blows—automatically suggests itself as a description of the behavior of so many on these pages.

Sisyphean struggle acquires concrete form and substance in the lives we explore. And the metaphor is apt for the many failures encountered and stumbles endured. The folks described are not involved in an uninterrupted march Onward and Forward, but rather, the zigzag and sometimes plummeting course of the lives actually led.

And, still, they keep on truckin'.

Hard work, devoted study, incredible altruism (despite the distractions of individual sufferings) ultimately prove not only inspiring but reflective of the indomitable spirit residing in so many human breasts. The unexpectedness only heightens the effect. The people here serve as Charons guiding us to the River Styx.

In these pages we have slice-of-life freeze frames that inform us of the messy, awful, terrifying reverses and privations afflicting so many human spirits. Yet these are mere words—abstractions. To explore the emotional meanings beyond the intellectual appreciations of facts and figures we have to study—much as scientists looking at the excitement and confusion in a petri dish—the real, actual lives and the true circumstances surrounding the struggles.

The human condition is a fine and useful description, but it does little to help us grasp how it is actually reflected in individual lives.

Failure or success move ephemeral, transient situations. The constant is the gritty determination to endure—to continue the fight—to move forward toward the light.

In these pages we encounter the truly needy and the deserving poor. We also meet the Welfare Queens, the grandiose and the hopelessly deluded. We learn anew that decisions bring consequences—some that seem unendurable.

The truth can be harsh and cruel. The young women who resisted the blandishments of seducers fared incomparably better than those who succumbed. Yet the latter invariably embraced the new responsibilities in ways we might be tempted to describe as in a manly fashion—except the male was usually the exploiter who abandoned his obligations, while the female faced the obstacles and fought to overcome them.

The pages describe folks who not only experienced many abject failures and stumbles but who—if we are honest and confront it—will fail again. Yet all the evidence shows they arise, dust off, and resume the thumping march that spells triumph.

The surprising strengths painted are nothing short of amazing. It is the amazement of which the unconquerable human spirit has—here and elsewhere—offered so many eloquent proofs.

The nature of poverty is not just lack of cash. It can be cultural and emotional as well as economic. Poverty leads to toothaches that go untreated and affect lives. Poverty produces misery, violence, and the desperate need to escape—often into addiction. Poverty smells bad, tastes awful, produces pain, and results in fruitless quests and avoidable overwork. Poverty is inefficient and costly—to everyone. In these pages we encountered folks whose middle-class upbringing enabled them to flourish even when transplanted into exotic, foreign environments. Their devotion to such values as education, family and even culture becomes a ladder up.

Poverty is a charnel house of suffering in which the residents arise and begin the cleanup every day. It is a place of unrelenting pain, where new and surprising setbacks rain down on the afflicted, who, numb with pain and agony, continue the struggle.

Illness, addiction, single motherhood, accidents, thefts, crimes, violence, betrayals, and the cruelty and indifference of the larger world abound and are the daily fare of the underclass. We meet them and give names and vivid descriptions of the sufferings—and conquests—here.

What the stories principally reveal are hard truths.

Money matters. It is the most useful tool of our civilization, and its presence or absence results in fearful or hopeful consequences. Gertrude Stein once said, "Those who say money can't buy happiness don't know where to shop."

The male libido is a powerful driving force for the continuation of the species—and for the abuse and exploitation of its targets. Yet, here, we also encounter surprisingly decent behavior.

The female's need for nurturing, family, and safety, can be turned into vehicles for her exploitation and defeat. Single motherhood, domestic violence, and similar handicaps are the abstractions masking the sometimes hideous realities behind the words.

Statistics matter. They enable us to understand the length and breadth of problems and opportunities. They permit us to prioritize and focus. They foster evidence for the adoption or abandonment of broad, sweeping policies and programs. They debunk myths while promoting knowing appreciations of the issues.

But statistical panoramas also conceal the human pain, suffering, and defeat, and also the victory of the individual amidst the mob.

To grasp the individual dilemmas we resort to anecdote: and that is what these pages contain.

In a real way the stories permit focus on the travails of the specific, which enable us to see the outlines and nature of the larger problem and opportunity they represent.

Victimization is a word that masks the agony of discovering that your last dollars have been taken from you by your neighbor—in church. Or that the loan so generously arranged is actually a trap.

Obstacles can take the form of lacking a drivers license, being impeded from working by a criminal record, encountering a foreign language and culture, and battling the disabilities of immigrant status.

The lack of education is a recurring theme. Illness, disability or addiction inflict merciless loss.

Poor judgment, bad choices, desperate options increase the losses. Mentors can provide guidance in life's minefield.

Failure is endemic among the underclass. But the human march continues and its soldiers are movingly etched in the details of the struggles described in these stories.

There are few whiners here. Few who blame life's unfairness. Few who reconcile themselves to self-pity or defeat.

The stories inspire because they reflect triumphs—of the spirit, of the human will to power. It's power to attack problems and solve them. It's the heroism of arising at an ungodly hour and trudging off to work. The devotion to just do—anything—to help and protect those you love—and sometimes even those you've never met.

The surprising allure of capitalism attests to the value of freedom to make choices, save, plan, and bring those schemes to fruition without roadblocks. And we encounter surprising capitalists among the many entrepreneurs (and entrepreneuses) described.

The strategic impact of a timely intervention in launching an educational, business, residential, or even medical initiative is hard to measure, but it must be pursued as an act of faith.

## Epiphanies Occur and They Matter

Often we can only evaluate the impact of an intervention—monetary, advisory, emotional, psychic, or experiential—in retrospect, but we all have felt them or seen them. And because of the usual absence of a clearly visible cause-and-effect relationship between intervention and outcome, we are forced to measure our approaches on the basis of the available evidence while hoping that the remedy takes.

We can "trust but verify," but we need to also acknowledge both the impossibility of ensuring success, or gauging the outcome specifically and accurately. Human interventions are slippery transactions and demand the acceptance of the possibility of failure. Indeed, like the ministrations of dedicated teachers, interventions are offered without guarantees of success. They are mystical acts of unknowing confidence taken within the context of as much evaluative information as can be garnered. Success is as much an ingredient as failure. Both must be accepted at the outset.

Catholic doctrine teaches the hope of redemption—even for the gravest sinner—if there is insight and genuine contrition, and the acceptance of salvation, even at the final moment. Redemption—after lives full of sin, in one form or another—is a central feature of these cases.

And we encounter the subtle, yet critical, difference in outlook between American blacks brought up amongst racism, and foreign blacks who, having grown up in black societies where racism is irrelevant (though not necessarily tribalism or other stupidities) perform within the frameworks of their inheritance. Americans suffer the incredible disability of racism, while foreigners see the opportunities and seize them. Thus can culture impact lives.

## JOE SELVAGGIO, THE FOUNDER OF MICROGRANTS

In order to understand MicroGrants it is essential that we talk of its founder. I will try to provide what is essentially an impressionistic, personal and unfortunately, probably flawed portrait.

Biographical accounts normally require thorough research, evaluation of facts, pretty faithful adherence to chronology and a real understanding of—and unusual affection for the hero.

Slavish devotion to facts sometimes leads to obscuring the essence of the human within, so I will adhere to furnishing insights, anecdotes, impressions, and observations, hoping thereby to reveal the actual person.

I first met Joe Selvaggio in 1980. He was then in his early forties. The reason is worth, I hope, describing. I had just been appointed Police Chief of Minneapolis and, through a long career had discovered that the real forces impinging on the existence of street crime were sociological. I had written that *Roe v. Wade* would, by around the late eighties, result in sharp drops in criminality because a large segment of the babies from incompetent, uneducated, poor, mostly Hispanic and black teenage mothers—the main source of street criminals—would have been aborted. A smaller cohort of drifting ghetto males meant less street crime. Unfortunately the benefits of *Roe v. Wade* (decided in 1973) would be too late for me to claim the fruits of victory. Other chiefs would be cited as geniuses for suppressing crimes.

Poverty, absent fathers, teen-age mothers, welfare, racism and related factors—not ignoring the thunderous indifference of the overclass (you and me, dear reader) were relevant. The number of cops was not.

I believe passionately in the role of cops in dealing with crime, responding to emergencies and regulating traffic, but not in the ability of the police to prevent muggings, burglaries, auto theft, drug crimes, assaults, rapes and such. When the cops arrived, the criminal had been formed and the crime had occurred.

This conviction made me very interested in the activities of organizations dealing with social problems—especially on the streets of the ghetto.

So I made informal little tours of these groups. I would drop in casually and just visit. I found a lot of feet on desks, music playing, even cigar smoking (the ultimate act of socially defiant triumphalism), laughter, shuckin' and swaying, jukin' and jivin'.

The big foundations had spiffy offices, immense bureaucracies, high salaries, first class travel and other emoluments—usually under the rubric of "administrative overhead." They seemed a more elegant version of the poverty pimps in the storefronts.

Yes, there were good ones too, here and there; doing useful work, and it is unfair and untrue to ignore their wonderful contributions. I saw some of these, too.

But two stood out—urban saints who were, as all saints must be, flawed, but performing miracles. The first, Mary Jo Copeland, fed, housed, clothed and medicated the street people and even washed a few feet on her road to salvation. A fervent Catholic, her devotion can only be understood within the context of that central fact. I became a fan. Her mission is called "Sharing and Caring Hands."

But Joe Selvaggio became a close friend—and I've only had a handful of those over the course of a long life. I think I must be a bit of a misanthrope.

Joe was then, in 1980, an ex-priest whose libido had conquered his calling. Having married, with a natural son and two adopted males (he later adopted a girl) who were fated to function only in low-level jobs, he'd evolved from activist priest to actually running programs for the underclass.

Joe founded Project for Pride in Living (PPL) in the seventies.

When I examined the operation in a series of drop-in visits, I found ex-cons working, single mothers housed, and armies of the poor being helped and trained to help themselves. All of this in a number of humble buildings housing clients turned into workers. Low overhead, low salaries, the employment of clients, and an absence of the panoply of "administrative overhead costs" gradually won me over. There were few suits in evidence.

Could Joe be for real?

I needed to understand the complexity behind the façade. Potemkin Villages were not for me. I needed to be sure.

My knowledge deepened as I befriended Joe, vacationing with him in Mexico and elsewhere, and generally spending a lot of time together. I was—and this is emblematic of the skeptical, cynical approach bred into all cops—actually reassured by his flaws. If I could discern the weaknesses, I could appreciate the humanity, plus convince myself I was not being taken.

Over the years I undertook a lot of chores for Joe, and had countless opportunities to observe him in myriad situations—and that is a thing cops absorb unconsciously—the need to observe. To us, society—our dish of bacteria—is to be scrutinized through a microscope. Cops often cannot afford error in sizing up people or situations, so they pay close attention.

Additionally my son Dominick—a born social worker—went to work for PPL. Another source of data for my scrutiny. Joe actually married Dom and Amy in my backyard.

All of it added up to my dubbing Joe an "Urban Saint," which found its way to a local magazine cover.

Saints are flawed. They are human. Yet most of us expect perfection.

Joe's humanness simply confirmed his sainthood. An active libido, a mischievous little boy's passion for potty jokes, and a fairly indifferent approach to his family's financial comfort (an admitted passion of mine) deepened the impression. He took minimal salaries and now, none at all, and lived in the ghetto. He drives used cars given to him by friends.

Joe had no compunction about taking a wonderful, simple, humble black lady to the elite Minneapolis Club, when he'd been given a free membership.

He maneuvers comfortably among the people reflected in these pages and the captains of industry at the country club.

Over the years Joe just kept on truckin'.

In the process he performed two of the many miracles I'd attribute to him.

First, he gained the trust of Minnesota's elite. They figured out he found deserving recipients, funneled the money to them and the programs without spillage, and gave a complete and honest accounting. He was not afraid to beg for the poor (priestly training), confident that his austerity gave him the moral authority.

Second, he found the people who needed help and, more importantly, who could use it constructively. No handouts. Only hands up.

And he made sure the givers saw all this and kept tabs on the takers.

These two factors made Joe only one of about six truly indispensable persons I'd ever met. Others were Mary Jo Copeland; Minneapolis' then-mayor, Don Fraser; the Police Commissioner in the NYPD from 1970-1973, Patrick V. Murphy, and an unheralded Princeton professor, George Kateb. As for the sixth, I'm waiting to meet him or her.

So over a quarter of a century, Joe had housed, fed, employed and helped thousands, while raising many millions for PPL. At seventy he could reflect in satisfaction.

Along the way, this slim, graying bespectacled Italian, divorced, characteristically amicable, plodded along.

Joe is a vague mumbler who seems the very model of the foggy wanderer. He exemplifies the peripatetic school, yet the miasma conceals a laser focus and intensity. He knows his objective, locks in on it, follows through, and doesn't let go. Amazing to watch, yet it is all done in a style so understated as to convey complete and utter casualness.

When his nonagenarian mother came to live with Joe and his wife Rose, he brought his usual, but effective, devotion to his ministrations. But humor plays a part, too, as he describes how, because of his lack of "upper body strength," his mother slipped slowly out of his arms as he attempted to lift her from the car seat. She slumped gently into a widowed black heap on the sidewalk. No harm done.

In the eighties Joe heard of a woman hiding in the Philippine mountains to escape the wrath of the dictator, Ferdinand Marcos. She'd been in opposition and they were closing in. The one way out was to have someone in the U.S. marry her to escape.

He asked friends for $100 each for the fare and expenses, and I kicked in. Sight unseen and unknown, Joe married her.

Rose Escañan was rescued.

A year later he sent me a check for $100 with a note explaining that they'd fallen in love, would stay together and he couldn't keep the money since romance had replaced altruism.

And over twenty-five years later they still live in the same house, in a dangerous neighborhood, where the sound of firearms and violence punctuate their existence. Joe can even show bullet holes in his home.

So it all now looked like a beautiful sunset to a useful life.

Only Joe handed over PPL to a successor and founded the One Percent Club, intended to get generous Minnesotans to give more (or, to be clear, one percent of their net worth annually) to either their favorite charity or to a program Joe would identify.

The Club flourished. Giving rose dramatically. Joe took no salary at first, and then just $500 per month. Some tiny amounts for such expenses as postage, printing and such are generally glommed. The rest comes from volunteers, free rent, and other cost cutters.

The years at the One Percent Club proved successful and he found a talented young attorney to devote her talents to continuing his work. As always, overhead was not the fiscal sponge normally associated with these ventures. Neither Joe nor his successor, Jennifer McDonald, took a salary.

All of this gets Joe's legion of buddies worrying about his retirement—should it ever come.

"I've got plenty of money," he confidently asserts as he describes assets any other person similarly situated would define as either very modest or ludicrously inadequate.

Joe has never been shy about accepting invitations to visit or use a vacation home or such similar favors, but he also pays his way. Money is really a way of expressing his philosophy. His approach is wonderfully reassuring.

After about a decade at the One Percent Club, Joe again let go. He founded his third major altruistic enterprise.

## MICROGRANTS

Having worked for the poor since emerging from the seminary, Joe understood the value of helping others to lift themselves from hideous problems. He believes totally that people must contribute—through effort, education, wiser choices and other disciplines—to their own worldly salvation. No free lunches.

Joe conceived—building, as ideas invariably do, on conceptions by others—the notion of a critical intervention in the form of a cash gift. He knew that human lives are charted with moments that decide fates—upward or down. Epiphanies occur. Words echo. Events can traumatize or inspire, and an infusion of wealth has the power to change things.

Joe was convinced that a loan simply burdened the poor with debt—

another obligation. But a gift might be just too facile an answer—what is today called enabling. So his challenge was to find people who had earned the right to be helped. Joe devised ways of vetting the bona fides of folks seeking help.

And so, the same issues segued into MicroGrants—finding generous donors willing to give money to people identified by Joe as not only deserving of it, but likely to use it constructively.

Inherent in all of this is the possibility of failure. There are reasons for the existence of so many needy folks, and they include fecklessness, stupidity, willfulness, or hedonism. The possibility of failure must not only be considered, but also confronted, admitted, and documented. No one is going to lead a perfect program, but every giver needs the assurance he/she ain't a pigeon either.

So Joe conceived a program where folks would give him money, and he'd find deserving people who'd get over a hump with about $1000 freely given. The strings attached were demonstration of merit and submitting to a follow-up that established the success or failure of the intervention.

The stories were compiled by really bright, dedicated Yale students who were willing to give up their summers.

The program occupies rent-free space and uses volunteers everywhere. Joe takes no salary. MicroGrants produces spiffy brochures, but all the costs are donated. A documentary was produced at a pittance. Joe knows how to beg, and dispenses great gobs of psychic income to those involved in his projects.

The stories in this book are the accounts of those helped, with no effort to cull the stars. In fact, many of the accounts will be of people who again stumbled after getting the help.

Joe has had no trouble raising the money and has devised effective ways of identifying folks who are not only in need, but who show promise that the help will be well used.

But it is the stories themselves that matter. If ever monuments to human heroism were aptly made, it is in these pages.

*– March, 2009*
*Tony Bouza is a former Chief of Police, Minneapolis*

# Foreword

## Joe Selvaggio

I have little doubt that my passion for launching people on self-sufficient careers started when I was a small boy. Every day I'd hear my mother talking on the telephone with her sisters. "How is Fran doing on his first job as an electrician? Is Tom going to finish college after he gets out of the Navy? And what have you heard about Billy? Anna told me a month or so ago that he was thinking of being a teacher." They never tired of talking about their children's successes on the road to adulthood. I learned early that work and education are the keys to a successful, self-supporting life.

When I started working with poor people over 40 years ago, I realized that one of the primary disadvantages they had was the fact that they rarely had a mother or aunt hovering over them as I had. It was unthinkable for me not to go to college, even though my parents' generation did not have a chance to go beyond high school.

Being lazy was not tolerated. My earliest memory is of my father saying, "Joey, get the broom," or "Joey, sweep the floor." He owned an awning store below our three-bedroom apartment in Chicago. If the household chores were finished, there was always useful work to do right downstairs in his shop.

In Barack Obama's wonderful book *Dreams of My Father,* he describes how the events of his life shaped him—from his childhood and adolescence in Indonesia and Hawaii, to his work in Chicago as a community organizer, and finally returning to his roots in Kenya. Similarly, my own vision developed from the path I followed and the roles I took on—from a priest in an inner city parish; to founder and executive director of two other nonprofits—first, Project for Pride in Living, then the One Percent Club—and finally to my work with MicroGrants.

As a 30-year-old priest in the days of Martin Luther King, Bobby Kennedy, and the War on Poverty, I had many profound experiences. I learned not only about the struggles of the poor, but also about how difficult it can be for the "haves" to help. Neither churches nor broad-based organizations like the Urban Coalition had much success moving the poor into middle class lives. We had riots, poor people marches on Washington, and civil rights legislation, but nothing seemed to help that much.

In 1968 I left the priesthood to work on the poverty issue more directly. I started a nonprofit corporation called Project for Pride in Living (PPL) in 1972. I had the good fortune to attract the attention of some of the wealthy folks in the community, and they helped me start the organization. One businessman, Ted Pouliot, insisted I use as a motto the now familiar, "Give me a fish and I eat for a day; teach me to fish and I eat for a lifetime." Right from the start, the PPL funders taught me not to expect them to do it alone. The people being helped had to do their part as well.

I am happy to say that PPL continues to be a thriving organization. It helps low-income individuals and families throughout the Twin City's metro area work toward self-sufficiency through housing, employment training, education, and support services. Over the years, PPL has created single and multi-family housing for low-income people and those who have suffered long term homelessness.

I retired from PPL after working as its executive director for 25 years. Then a conversation with a Minnesota philanthropist, Kenneth Dayton, became the catalyst for starting the "One Percent Club." Over the years, the generosity of families like the Daytons, the Bells, and the McKnights, has enhanced the quality of life in the Twin Cities in countless ways. However, Ken told me that many people of means were "under-giving" to charity. He felt that a person worth $5 million could easily contribute $50,000 per year, but that many were donating far less.

We came up with the idea of starting a "club" for local, wealthy people, whose members would pledge 1% of their net worth annually to charities of their choosing. Ken agreed to make a public statement on the condition that I find ten other peers to make the same pledge. I was able to find 37. And after the Minneapolis newspaper, the Star Tribune, ran a front-page story about the One Percent Club, it mushroomed. During my ten years with the organization, the club grew to over a thousand members.

My years with the One Percent Club taught me a great deal about how philanthropists think—a very valuable lesson if one is to work with the poor. For example, many prefer to fund people, rather than programs, who are promulgating values that are dear to their hearts.

My final job, now that I am 72 years old, is perfect for me because it allows me to continue working both with the poor and with philanthropists. At the end of 2005, after turning over the One Percent Club to a talented successor, I had another pivotal conversation. This time it was with a longtime friend and funder of my work, Tom Lowe, the CEO and primary owner of Lyman Lumber.

He said, "I would like to help the poor by investing directly in the hard work and resourcefulness of individuals. For example, if I gave you money to buy a power lawnmower or snow blower, could you find someone who would use these machines to make a living?"

This was the seed idea that got me going. With generous donations from Tom and from Angus Wurtele, former CEO of Valspar Paints, we were able to start MicroGrants. The organization is based on a simple concept: we give grants of $1000 to "poor people of potential" to help them take the next step toward stability and self-sufficiency. It is a program of investments in people who are willing to help themselves.

In the early days of the One Percent Club, one member told me the reason why so many families of means start family foundations: they want to have *control* of their money. The same concept is true when we give people grants of $1000. The recipient has input or control over how the money is spent.

Many people ask me whether MicroGrants is like the microcredit programs popularized by Nobel Peace Prize winner Muhammad Yunus and the Grameen Bank. Microcredit provides poor people—mainly women in third world countries—with small loans they use to start businesses to lift their families out of poverty. I was inspired by this straightforward, effective idea, as well as its spectacular success. The Grameen Bank and organizations modeled after it have enabled millions of people around the world to work their way out of poverty.

As it happens, I had tried something similar—on a very small scale—some 25 years ago. My wife Rose's relatives were struggling to make ends meet as farmers in the Philippine countryside. I gave each of them $50, as a gift, not a loan, to buy pregnant pigs. Although none of them turned out to be great entrepreneurs, it was a valuable learning experience for them to try to make money from our investment.

MicroGrants is similar to the Muhammad Yunus model in that we help people become self-sufficient through modest infusions of cash. But there are important differences. We decided at the outset that MicroGrants should be entirely a local organization, limited to the Twin Cities and surrounding areas. Grameen Bank, FINCA, Opportunities International, KIVA, and scores of other micro-lending programs were already flourishing overseas, and we have serious needs here in Minnesota. One of my contributors said, "If I can't see it from my office on the 49th floor of the IDS Center in Minneapolis, I don't want to fund it."

As we were designing the program, there were two vital questions that had to be answered:

1) How do you adapt the basic concept of microfinance to the economic realities in the United States? And,

2) How do you identify the needy people who can use a cash grant in a way that will make a long-term difference in their lives?

A key difference between our program and the micro-lending programs is that we give grants, not loans. In the United States, too many people—especially the poor—are saddled with immobilizing debt. We aim to teach our recipients about accumulating *equity, not debt.*

Some might be skeptical about the effectiveness of giving a cash grant to a poor person—especially to one who has a history of disadvantages and liabilities. But I have met so many people who have used timely opportunities to better their lives that I knew it could work.

One was Sheena Nguyen, a 16-year-old Vietnamese girl I met on a plane while traveling in Asia. She and her family later immigrated to Mobile, Alabama. Although they arrived with almost nothing, Sheena had impressed me as someone who was ambitious and who would work hard to succeed in her new environment. We kept in touch by letter and phone calls. I sent her occasional gifts of $25, and she confided her struggles to get through high school and find her first jobs.

She called me "Daddy Joe" and I guess I filled the role of a surrogate father and "investor" in her future. I suppose I provided the kind of encouragement that my mother and aunts did for me. I was someone who believed in her. Sure enough, by the time she was 30, she had a career and had bought a house and a car. She was married, and had accumulated almost $100,000. Now she has "paid it forward" and is a contributor to MicroGrants.

Another example is my own son Sam. When he was in college one of his aunts, on her deathbed, gave him $1,000. He was astounded by the "huge" gift. At that stage of his life, he could not have accumulated such a large sum of money on his own. Instead of spending it on short-term pleasures, he carefully invested it in his college education.

It's a terrible shame that thousands of poor people who have the potential to be successful, contributing members of their communities, remain in poverty. Business people are keenly aware of the tragedy of untapped resources. They like the idea of bringing out an individual's potential, as in the Army's slogan, "Be all that you can be." A man named Jesus put it a little differently. "I came to give life so you may have it more abundantly" (John 10:10). This may not be the King James version, but I think it's an accurate translation of intent.

Of course, not everyone has both the capabilities and discipline to use a cash gift constructively. It was a lesson I was slow to learn through years of experience. But many people have the innate qualities and drive to succeed. They just need someone to believe in them, and someone to give them that boost up. Someone to tell them we'll fund their *opportunities*, not their daily *needs* (e.g., rent and food.)

So how do you pick the winners? Even if you manage to choose talented individuals, how do you keep them motivated? Where can they get the guidance and encouragement they need when the inevitable setbacks occur? And how can you tell if they are succeeding?

What I needed for a successful program was an entity (or entities) that could do three things for me:
1) select the "winners," the people with potential,
2) mentor and coach recipients as they implement their plans, and
3) keep track of them, so we could monitor their progress.

Over the years I've worked with some excellent organizations that help people to become self-sufficient. They assist clients in defining goals, assessing resources, implementing plans, and they serve as mentors through the whole process.

I was not surprised to learn that these organizations are happy to work with me, by selecting promising individuals from their caseloads to receive MicroGrants. I am currently working with PPL, Summit Academy OIC, Twin Cities Rise!, WomenVenture, the Jeremiah Program, and Neighborhood Development Center.

*WomenVenture* provides classes, counseling, technical expertise and emotional support to women (and men) working to start or expand a business, find a new job, or develop a new career path.

*PPL Train to Work* prepares participants for employment by teaching "soft" and technical skills, and through job shadowing. Graduates are ready to move into jobs that pay $10-$14 or more per hour, plus benefits and opportunities to advance.

*PPL Health Careers Partnership* offers classroom training programs that help people from disadvantaged communities qualify for jobs that pay a living wage, offer benefits and opportunities for advancement in medical settings.

*Twin Cities RISE!* provides job training and job placement to low-income adults.

*Summit Academy OIC* is an educational and vocational training center for adults and youth residing in economically depressed neighborhoods in the Twin Cities. It helps them become educated, employed, and contributing members of their communities.

*The Jeremiah Program* provides safe, affordable housing for low-income, single mothers and their children. It gives the women the opportunity to complete their post-secondary education and build self-reliance through life skills training with a focus on education and employability.

*Neighborhood Development Center* (associated with Midtown Global Market) is a non-profit organization that works in the low-income communities of the Twin Cities to help emerging entrepreneurs develop successful businesses that revitalize their neighborhoods.

The arrangement works very well. Each week I receive the name of one person who is at the stage where a $1,000 grant will move them to a new level. The agencies know their clients—what their histories have been, and when they are ready to take the next step. Each of the organizations has the crucial mentoring/coaching role built into their programs, so that the recipients spend the money wisely and make good decisions along the way.

Monitoring the recipients' progress is an important element of the MicroGrants program. We need to know (and our funders do, too) whether the program is actually working. Does the recipient have a job after a year? Is the entrepreneur making any money? Have the families' situations improved? Does the progress of our recipients have any effect on the overall economy? Is there any "return on investment?" We also need to know if there are aspects of the program that need to be adjusted to make it more effective. The agencies we work with are required to keep records for the foundations and corporations that support them, and this is one source of our data.

In addition, John Mauriel, an emeritus professor from the Carlson School of Management, University of Minnesota, with assistance from a committee consisting of Dr. Rajni Shah, Phil Morton, Joanna Lees, and Marie Manthy, reviewed application data and follow-up information collected between January 2007 and June 2008 by the original four agencies whose clients were being funded by MicroGrants. Mauriel analyzed and organized the data and, with help from Dr. Shah in preparing tables and charts, wrote the narrative for chapter 11, the quantitave analysis chapter.

We gather baseline data at the time of application. Six months to a year after receiving a grant, the recipient gets a follow-up visit from a member of a team of college interns from Yale University and Macalester College.

The interns gather statistical data, and also write narrative reports that tell the story of the recipients' lives before receiving the grant, how they spent the money, and what changes took place as a result. These stories add detail and depth to the raw numbers. At the same time, for the students, meeting the people and hearing about their struggles is a valuable education. John Mauriel compiled the statistics for an analysis of the "return on investment" which is summarized in Chapter 11 of this book.

Working with MicroGrants has been a rewarding journey. I've met wonderful people—generous donors and volunteers, and courageous grantees. It has been deeply satisfying to see the positive changes in people's lives.

The program is eminently suited for replication. All that's needed are Givers, Receivers, and the agencies capable of choosing, coaching, and evaluating the grantees. It is my hope that others across the country will feel inspired to start their own programs. In that spirit, here are some guidelines and observations I've discovered along the way.

1) We should not assume that the recipient is powerless. An assertion made by my college ROTC officer has always bothered me. He said, "If the student fails to learn, the teacher failed to teach." This implies that the teacher has all the power and the student is just an empty vessel into which the teacher pours the content. This takes too much responsibility away from the student. The analogy I like better is of a baseball pitcher and a catcher. If the catcher fails to catch, it could be that the pitcher threw a wild pitch—or that the catcher took his eye off the ball. Both had responsibility. That's the way it is with MicroGrants. The "haves" need to invest, but the "have-nots" must perform.

2) I prefer giving MicroGrants to young people. We generally favor the young, not because we like them better than older people, but because we like efficiency. Young people have a longer time to work through their challenges—and pay it back, or "pay it forward" as some like to say. "More bang for the buck" is what a lot of business people say.

3) It is important to me that MicroGrants be as cost-effective as possible. I feel a responsibility to both the funders and recipients to make every dollar count. I don't take a salary, and because I work out

of my home office, MicroGrants doesn't have to pay rent or insurance. (It isn't really necessary to have a volunteer executive director. This is my choice. At the moment I am grooming a successor.) We also save money—and also enhance quality—by partnering with experienced self-sufficiency agencies, rather than taking on this part of the program ourselves.

4) Transparency is important. We send quarterly reports to all funders, plus a more detailed annual report. Several times a year, we also have box-lunch gatherings where funders and recipients can meet each other.

5) Microloans and MicroGrants are not "silver-bullets" that can lift all people from poverty. The world needs jobs, affordable housing, support for education, and food distribution systems to enable people to live self-sufficient, safe, and healthful lives. In its 3 years of existence, MicroGrants has helped more than a thousand people move toward greater long-term economic stability. The program has broad appeal to both liberals concerned about social issues, and to conservatives looking at the bottom line.

6) For any program to survive its founder, it's critical to find a successor. In the case of Microgrants, we've looked for someone with a strong commitment to empowering the poor, fearlessness in asking the rich for money, and an upbeat and likeable manner that will serve both my successor and MicroGrants well.

7) I like the subtitle of this book, "It's Working." The program is working, and it's *about* working.

8) The immeasurable qualitative virtue of *hope* is an indispensable ingredient on the part of the recipient.

9) It is important for grantees to be able to visualize a series of reachable plateaus.

10) The $1,000 amount is big enough to make a differnce, but small enough not to deter the rich from giving.

11) We should be realistic in assessing the plateaus targeted by the grantees. Politically incorrect realities such as IQ (intelligence quotient), EQ (emotional quotient), background, genes age, environment, and habits should be factored in.

12) Both quantitative measurements and qualitative virtues are important. Peter Drucker, the management guru, said, "If you can't measure it, forget it. But Albert Einstein said, "It's the things you can't count that really count"—things like industriousness, determination, and attitude.

People often ask me, "What motivates you?" In the early days I was motivated by aspiring to "a higher place in heaven." Later it was the "psychic income" or "feel good" quality that the work gave me. Recently I picked-up a concept from a movie my 13-year-old granddaughter Christine told me about. The a recipient of help asked the giver, "Why are you helping me?" The reply was, "because you deserve a chance, and I have the ability to give it to you." The MicroGrant recipients deserve a chance, and I (and generous donors—both the well-off and those who can afford just a little) have the ability to give it to them.

Those are the essentials of the program. Before you begin reading the grantees stories, please take a moment to note the wonderful contributors to this book (95 percent of whom volunteered their time) by reading the following Acknowledgments.

*May, 2009*

*Joe Selvaggio is the Executive Director of MicroGrants. He has spent more than 40 years working with the poor.*

## Acknowledgments

My gratitude to the scores of wonderful "book volunteers," listed here, is overwhelming. My sorrow to the scores of volunteers whom I forgot is also overwhelming. Please forgive me.

Great thanks and kudos to:

**Kitty Aal** for photography
**Crystal Adams** for administrative-assistant work
**Greg Anderson** for photography
**African Development Corporation**, Partner agency
**Ann Ayrault** for copy editing and general support
**Rick Blackmon** for facilitating photography
**Doug Benson** for more editing
**Tony Bouza** for organizing, editing, and introduction
**Betsy Buckley** for an entrepreneurial commentary
**Brett Burns** for interning as a full-time volunteer for 3 months
**Ted Cadwell**, Dorsey and Whitney, for legal work
**Andrea Cole** for photography
**Ron** and **Joan Cornwell** for a special grant for book related expenses
**Daily Works**, Partner agency
**Natasha Dikariva** for the logo
**LaVonne Easter** for writing the checks every Sunday
**Victor Easter** for assisting Lavonne Easter
**Rose Escañan** for marital support
**Tom Fiutak** for a liberal commentary
**John Grieman** for stretegic planning
**Nicole Harrison** for being the fundraiser
**Daniela Hofer-Johnson** for keeping the financials
**Jeremiah Program**, Partner agency
**Jim Klobuchar** for editing and preface
**Jim Lotter** for design
**Tom Lowe** for being the board treasurer

**Lee Lynch** for acting as the devil's advocate

**John Mauriel,PhD** for his focus and chapter on measureable results

**Bill Messinger** and **Malcolm McDonald** for Yale intern program

**Midtown Global Market**, Partner agency

**Nicholas Nhep** for write-ups of more stories

**Obermeier & Associates** for accounting services

**Mitch Pearlstein** for a conservative commentary

**Ted Pouliot**, mentor

**Prism**, Partner agency

**Project for Pride in Living (PPL)**, Partner agency, for use of its service center

**Sam Selvaggio** for being the board vice-president

**Dr. Rajni Shah,** for measuring results

**Dave Sommers** for talking through problems

**Latoya Spenser** for clerical work

**Carmen Slepek** for clerical work

**Summit Academy OIC**, Partner agency

**Terry Thompson** for general consultation

**Twin Cities Rise!**, Partner agency

**Dick Wilson** for conceptual help and for wordsmithing phrases like, "It's Working"

**Laura Waterman Wittstock** for a women-of-color commentary

**Dawn White** for being a reader

**WomenVenture**, Partner agency

**Yale interns**—Andrew Dayton, Dan Geoffrion, Catherine Bader, Jamie Kallestad, Sarah Hill, Winnie Tong, Berit Johnson, Greg Korb, and Steve McLachlan—for writing the stories

**Reid Zimmermann** for the Einstein quote, "It's the things you can't count that really count."

Special thanks also to:

**All of the financial contributors** to MicroGrants,

**All of the grant recipients** who opened their life stories to the world.

Joe Selvaggio

# 1

# The Entrepreneurs

### Heroes You Have Never Met

ON THE FOLLOWING PAGES we meet some of capitalism's most energetic new heroes, people of harshly limited means, struggling to reach a goal. Their drive, creativity, and faith, in response to a hand-up from the community, are the most persuasive endorsement of the often-abused economic path we call capitalism.

The need to control their own destiny is at the heart of their decisions to search for a new identity and fulfillment. Their methods vary. The constants are nerve, imagination and belief in their own talents and instincts.

Here we will meet whites, blacks, single mothers, immigrants, altruists and dreamers, who became the providers of a whole range of services and goods that have benefited thousands. It's a remarkable array of seekers and doers bound by one irreplaceable quality. Most of us call it spunk, a willingness to take a chance, to come back if it doesn't work the first time, to keep going, to try, work and believe.

Did most of them make it? Yes, and how they have made it! The pages ahead attest to the resilience and commitment of the human spirit when it is allowed to breathe.

Sue Webber

# Nurturing the Buds of Hope

"This is, like, the worst day ever," Sue Webber muttered to herself. Surrounded by flowers in full bloom and radiant greenery beneath the midday sun, the atmosphere of Harmony Nursery and Garden Center seemed to suggest just the opposite. But it wasn't the plants that were making Sue Webber feel stressed that day. Since taking over the nursery two years ago, she'd been logging 17-hour days and expending all the energy she could muster to turn her ownership of Harmony Nursery into a profitable venture.

With "big box" retailers like Lowe's and Home Depot threatening Sue's business, and a lack of credit preventing her from getting access to important flora dealers, the first two years were a struggle just to meet expenses. However, business is looking stronger this year. Sue has already noticed that, with help from MicroGrants in the spring, the nursery is doing better than ever before.

Although owning a nursery was a new challenge for Sue, she's always had a green thumb. She remembers her first plant purchase much as others might describe a favorite childhood toy. It was a shrub-rose from JC Penny that she brought home in a little bag for her mother. It may have fueled Sue's future passion for gardening. She spent more than 15 years working for nurseries and greenhouses to earn a living. Asked if she enjoys her outdoor occupation she explains, "You have to like it because you don't make a lot of money." But she persisted.

The real consequences of her low-income lifestyle hit hard for her and her two sons after Sue's divorce. Because she couldn't possibly raise two children with the unpredictable wages of nursery and garden work, she was forced to look for a more profitable option. She landed a job at Cargill as a computer network administrator and made enough money on her own to support herself and her two boys. Although she had never liked the idea of sitting in a cubicle in front of a computer screen where she "never saw the light of day," she found that administrative work was a necessary sacrifice to support a family on her own.

Sue tolerated the desk job for eight years before she was laid off, which forced her to drastically change her lifestyle. In spite of the fact that by then her boys were supporting themselves and working their way through college, Sue had to sell her house. Without a home or health insurance, she moved in with a friend and returned to greenhouse and landscaping work.

She remained determined to earn a living doing the work she loved. After she had worked a few years in nurseries and greenhouses, the owner of Harmony suggested that Sue take over the nursery when he moved to a new location. Since accepting ownership, Sue has been single-mindedly devoted to the enterprise. Working virtually without a day off for two years, and despite strenuous efforts, she has yet to turn a profit.

Then she wrote to MicroGrants. Purchasing garden inventory in the spring is always difficult for a small operator. Sue's young business attracted very little credit from the floral dealers. But when Sue's MicroGrant clicked in, it eased the transition to a new selling season.

Sue believes that her nursery provides a better service and product than the chain retailers, and she is committed to maintaining that competitive edge through services like home delivery and hand watering to ensure quality and added value.

Sue now displays a radiant hope for the future of her business. She predicts that the nursery is only two years away from turning a profit, and she is encouraged by the success of her business this year. Without the help from MicroGrants this spring, it's not likely she would be in the same position today. Although Sue claims that her only long-term goal is to get through tomorrow, there is clearly a much longer and more promising future in store for her and Harmony Nursery.

*Reported by Jamie Kallestad*
*June 11, 2007*

Jean Mary Lindquist:

# Massage Therapy as a Way Up

Jean Mary Lindquist is a 42-year-old single woman who lives in North Minneapolis. Jean studied biology at the College of St. Catherine in 1994. But she fell in love with alternative treatment methods after receiving her first massage, and she decided to become a professional massage therapist.

After attending the Northern Lights School of Massage Therapy from 1997 to 1998, Jean became a professional massage therapist in 2000. She has been in the business for eight years and is self-employed, working from both her home and her office in suburban Lake Elmo.

She has expanded her services to include a detoxifying therapy, which utilizes an expensive $2,900 machine that releases ions into a footbath and "pulls the toxins down the body and out through the feet." Since doing more than two or three massages a day is strenuous, Jean wants to do more footbaths and fewer massages.

She is also looking into Integrative Manual Therapy, which treats all areas of the body. Jean has been studying at the Connecticut School of Integrative Manual Therapy since 2004 and will complete her training in one year. She believes that after she is certified, she will be able to increase her income, which is now approximately $27,000.

Jean has several loyal clients, including whole families, who have stayed with her since the beginning. New clients usually hear about Jean through word of mouth. To increase her client base, Jean wanted to create promotional materials such as flyers, business cards and brochures. But she was under financial stress and could not spare the money.

She and her partner had bought a house together in January 2006, but they separated in the spring of 2007. Jean could not qualify for the mortgage with her income alone. She was caught in a bad position: she was struggling to increase her income in order to keep the house, and at the same time trying to get her partner's name off the mortgage.

Jean applied for a MicroGrant in January 2008 and received a check for $1,000 shortly after that. "The timing of the MicroGrant couldn't have been better," she said. She used $550 to create brochures and business cards, place an advertisement in Stillwater Magazine, pay for a website design class offered by WomenVenture and to help pay for the footbath machine. Jean used the grant carefully and still has $450 left to use for more advertising.

Jean said that MicroGrants took "some of the financial stress off." Although her new ad has not attracted many customers, Jean is optimistic. She can now use her computer to design a website for the business. It is likely to be seen by more people than the advertisement in Stillwater Magazine. Jean has other ideas for expansion. She plans to approach hospitals in the Twin Cities, hoping to be allowed to offer manual therapy to patients. She is also continuing her education in Integrative Manual Therapy so that she can offer more services to her clients.

In a year, Jean would like to make $5,000 a month, an increase from her current $2,500 to $3,100. In five years, practicing more manual therapy, she believes she will be able to expand her business even more. In the meantime, Jean keeps a spreadsheet of expenses. She also created a table that shows her monthly goals for earning and saving, which, with perseverance, she should be able to reach.

Jean credits MicroGrants with giving her the opportunity to better herself. With the money left from the grant, she will be able improve her business in the future. Jean has already overcome several financial obstacles and has many opportunities for growth. In Jean's words, "MicroGrants saved me and helped to augment my income."

*Reported by Winnie Tong*
*July 15, 2008*

Gary Paulson

# Altruism Can Pay

G ary Paulson is a 55-year-old, single Latino man with a busy life. He
holds down three jobs: He is a poker dealer at Running Aces Park, a
waiter at Levy's Restaurant in the Mall of America, and, most importantly,
the owner of his own business: holding free poker tournaments in the Twin
Cities area.

Combining interests and experience, Gary has been organizing the
tournaments, called Royal Flush Games, for three years. Gary explained
that these enjoyable games "keep people off the streets at night" and make
the community safer. About 50 to 60 people come every week. Gary said
that this group of poker players is surprisingly loyal, and they attend most
of his tournaments.

Gary's profit comes from the owners of venues where the games are
held. They pay him to set up the tournaments and are his main source of
income.

He makes about $30,000 a year and generously donates part of his
profits to an emergency food shelf where he volunteers. A saver, Gary manages to put something away every month. He may soon be increasing his
income by taking a part-time job at the food shelf.

Gary wanted to create a website to promote his poker tournaments,
but he didn't know how. In February 2008 he heard about MicroGrants
from one of his players. He applied and received a MicroGrant shortly thereafter. Part of it paid for a basic, low-cost website that a friend
helped set up. The remaining $800 was used for new equipment, facilita-
tor training, and an attendance reward program that encourages poker
players to return.

The new website provides a reference point for players. It includes the
rules of the game, and a forum for players to discuss poker. People from all
over the world can access the site, and Gary receives feedback from players

online. This is important because it allows him to tweak his program specifically towards the players and constantly improve it. Also, as a result of the website, more venues have invited Gary to organize tournaments.

Gary thanks MicroGrants "for the help that they've given me." At the website that MicroGrants helped pay for, people all over the world can read about Gary's program. Some may even use his ideas to help another community.

*Reported by Winnie Tong*
*July 11, 2008*

## Mary Johnson

# Undaunted

Mary Johnson, 61 and divorced, owns Grand Italian Ice, an Italian ice and frozen custard shop. It is located in Minneapolis' Midtown Global Market, an urban, indoor marketplace with fresh produce vendors, restaurants, and arts and crafts from around the world.

Italian ice is a dessert that consists of a combination of crushed ice and fruit-flavored syrup or fruit purees, similar to sorbet. In Minnesota, of course, sales are best during the summer months.

In November 2007, an inspector ruled that Mary would have to replace two cabinet doors to meet health requirements and keep her shop open. The $800 worth of repairs was a serious financial setback for her. Business being sluggish during the winter months, Mary lacked the money for these repairs.

Threatened with the possibility of losing her business, Mary applied for a MicroGrant in February of 2008. When she received the $1,000, she spent $800 to repair the two cabinet doors, and $200 for more product for the shop.

Five months after receiving the grant, Grand Italian Ice is still open and doing well. Mary credits the MicroGrants program with the survival of her little company. "Without the grant," she said, "I wouldn't have been able to continue my business because I didn't have $800 at the time."

While Grand Italian Ice does not turn a big profit, it is a moderately successful company with several notable assets. Mary owns her own equipment, with the sole exception of the batch freezer, a $16,000 item that she rents. She has hired an accountant who specializes in small businesses to prepare the company's sales tax and financial reports. Mary's education and experience come in handy, too. She has a B.S. degree in fashion merchandizing from the University of Wisconsin-Stout, and has worked in the retail business all her life. Mary has learned to be very organized and has strong people skills.

Even so, Grand Italian Ice faces several threats to its survival. Although Mary enjoys the atmosphere at the Midtown Global Market, she recognizes that its slow development confines her business. Nevertheless, the neighborhood has recently been cleaned up through massive community efforts, and the Market has become a bright, attractive, and safe place to eat and shop. She'd like to make her current location work, but recognizes that "being a business person, you have to treat it as business and keep emotions out of it." If the circumstances require her to move, she will.

Her operation also suffers from the fact that Italian ice does not have a large customer base in Minneapolis; many have never heard of it. Those who have find it a delicious, healthy, vegan treat, and ideal for lactose-intolerant people. Mary knows that she needs to devote more time and effort to marketing so that people become more familiar with the product.

The future of Grand Italian Ice holds both risks and opportunities. Until recently, Mary shared space with Golden Thyme, a coffee shop that closed at the end of June 2008. Mary will probably have to find a new location in the market because her current spot is too large without Golden Thyme. Mary will also need to hire some help.

On the other hand, Golden Thyme's closure opens new doors. Before, Mary was limited in what she could serve because she did not want to compete with her neighbor's menu. Now, she can add beverages such as floats and Italian sodas, which Golden Thyme used to sell.

Mary also sees a potential to expand into catering for weddings and parties. This would allow the business to increase its revenue and enable Mary to increase her $12,000 annual income while maintaining a profitable business.

At the same time, Mary is worried because the managers of the Midtown Global Market are considering granting a lease to a new malt and ice cream shop. She believes this will be a recipe for failure for both of the frozen treat businesses. She is prepared to leave the market if the ice cream shop does move in; she has already investigated the costs associated with moving her equipment.

Although Grand Italian Ice's fate is uncertain, Mary is pleased with how business is doing right now. She appreciates the grant she received, because it helped her to keep the company open through a financially precarious time. MicroGrants enabled Mary to avoid one obstacle, and being extraordinarily resilient, is determined to overcome whatever challenges lie ahead.

*Reported by Berit Johnson*
*July 3, 2008*

**The table below is typical of those created from the data collected for each MicroGrants recipient.**

| | |
|---|---|
| Age | 42 |
| Home zip code | 55411 |
| Marital Status | Single |
| Dependents | None |
| Yearly Income | $27,000 (varies) |
| Change in income since receiving grant? | No |
| Education | Some college, massage therapy certification |
| Race/Ethnicity | Caucasian |
| Obstacles to Employment | Fatigue after doing too many massages |
| Health Insurance | No |
| Government Assistance | No |
| Employer/Position | Self-employed/massage therapist |

Chingwell Mutombu

# Many Ways to Help

Chingwell Mutombu was born in the United States. Yet her life is closely intertwined with the Democratic Republic of Congo, where she grew up and where most of her family still lives. At the age of 32, she is married and living in Golden Valley, a suburb of Minneapolis. For the past three years she has run her own consulting business which is targeted towards non-profit organizations. However, the income it provides is insufficient to support her while giving her the ability to work towards a greater passion, developing a microfinance organization she started for women in the Congo. MicroGrants came into her life just months after she began her own consulting business.

Chingwell began her microfinance organization with approximately $3,000 of her own money to provide support for poor people in need of a "hand up," a concept strikingly similar to MicroGrants. The loans, which range from $50 to $150, have been granted to 100 individuals so far. Between her consulting business and the loan program, Chingwell has learned a great deal about social service and mentoring. Her goal is to expand the loan program to help 11,000 Congolese people. However to be able to provide for her family and work towards her goals in the Congo, Chingwell needed her own "hand up."

Chingwell applied for a MicroGrant in order to maintain her income while taking time off from her regular work to gain knowledge and skills that will improve her consulting ability and the loan program. Without the grant money, she could not afford to pursue these studies. With the $1,000 MicroGrant, Chingwell could afford to take time off from her consulting business to learn how to work more effectively. In an important way, MicroGrants is helping to further the cause of microlending. Chingwell also spent six months months job shadowing, networking and learning from Joe himself to strengthen her leadership and organizational skills.

Since her experience with MicroGrants, Chingwell has secured four major consulting contracts which brought in $40,000 for a single year, giving her the ability to sustain herself, her family and her project, First Step Initative. Reflecting on her own experience with MicroGrants, Chingwell believers the impact of small grants is limitless because the ripple affect can be felt across the ocean. The fact that she has been using the skills she learned during the grant period to raise the funds to support our efforts in the Congo, is in fact another indirect impact of MicroGrant. In her words, "We need an organization such as MicroGrants that believes in the human potential and the ability of people to create their own destiny. I am certainly a witness to the fact that a small grant can make a big difference."

*Reported by Brett Burns*
*June, 2008*

## Mari Harris

# A Personal Account:
# An applicant explains herself

(What follows is Mari Harris's own description of her experience with MicroGrants.)

I said in my grant application that I've got a plan: My goal is to focus my time and attention on booking myself from two to six to twelve months out—which would move my focus from short-term survival to the components that build a strong business and expand my potential to succeed. A grant would give me the opportunity—buy me the time—to spend two months away from the day-to-day grind and to initiate and implement my plan and strengthen my self-sufficiency. The long-term result will be the successful fulfillment of the objectives of the "Mari Harris Appreciation and Recognition Program."

The grant came. For two months I didn't have to worry about generating the money for my rent, so I could focus on other things.

The grant helped me to receive something I've always wanted and knew existed: financial assistance for an artist with something to give. It was empowering and rewarding. I'll always be grateful for it.

I had a lot of old debt. I am a multi-tasker, and I've struggled for many years without knowing where to put my time and attention. I didn't focus on my Appreciation and Recognition Program as much as I had thought I would in those two months.

But here's what's happened within the past year (2007): I have embraced my diverse interests and talents, and I've realized my marketability. In the past I've earned money in a variety of ways: singing, acting, leading training programs, and coaching. Sometimes I would feel like I was being "flighty," not a very empowering way to feel. But recently I made a list of all of the ways I have of earning money. I then organized information—my leads, ideas, resources, etc.—for each of my skills. I'm now clear about what to charge for each product and service, and am now moving forward in doing my marketing and sales. This, for me, is a huge accomplishment.

My Appreciation and Recognition Program, which I presented many times last year, and which shows up as the core of my performances, has evolved and spun off a second program—a five-session artist residency titled Giving Voice to Your Vision. Lynne Hoft, PhD, a respected educator and author who works with me as an advisor, suggested that I market this program to charter schools. I've begun the research, and I'll soon be making sales calls to them.

Tasika Sykes, who worked in management for Northwest Airlines, is also assisting my efforts. She hired me to do my Appreciation and Recognition Program for her staff, and was impressed by the power of my presentation. She is helping me get ready to present a new program to a man who works with a youth group, matching programs with funding sources.

So, where I am now is in a place of discovering my worth, creating partnerships, asking for and allowing others to provide help, working smarter, and enjoying the challenge of moving my plans forward. I expect that within the next five years, I will be earning good money as I promote wellness, self-sufficiency and community throughout the world.

The relationship with my customers and suppliers is solid: they can count on me to deliver what I contract for and beyond, and I can count on them to take care of me by providing what they've agreed to, to respect me, and to pay me. They love me and I love them. They refer me to others and they become loyal fans.

I pay rent and my portion of our household bills to my roommate, who owns the lovely home in which we live. Recently, I've begun paying the late penalty that he charges other tenants. That is a step up in my taking responsibility for my financial actions.

The relationship with my roommate is vital. We live, work, eat, dance, party, attend artistic events, travel, sail, dream and create together! It's a relationship that empowers us both. And yes, we get on each other's nerves sometimes. But we can resolve anything that comes up between us through communication and care. He truly contributes.

My strengths: I am effective at presenting ideas and creating partnerships to accomplish tasks; I utilize communication skills; I am well-developed as a coach and facilitator, experienced at working with diverse populations, and I am skilled at strategic planning. My weaknesses: forgetting my strengths and not using them.

I have a major opportunity coming up: I will be touring Europe, performing in London, Paris and Amsterdam. I am committed to celebrating the gift of the human spirit and welcome the opportunity to do it internationally!

My programs are designed to help people recognize their worth, feel good about themselves and build and expand from there. In good economic times or bad, there will always be a market for my services and products.

Do I have enough capital to maintain and grow my business venture? Not really. Currently I pay for things as I go along, and this is one of the main things that I will alter and transform as I earn the income that I am anticipating! And I will reinvest some of my profits to make my business work.

Completing this evaluation has been invaluable to me. It is a perfect complement to and a vital part of the grant—the completion of receiving this gift! The process of considering and answering these questions has made me be introspective. Writing about where I was, where I am, and what I project for the future has been a great exercise. I am conscious now both of what I've accomplished *and* of what's missing that I can now add to make the biggest difference in my businesses. Lastly, I thank you. I was empowered by receiving this grant, and I must say I feel even *more* empowered by completing this evaluation, and I give my sincere thanks for this program.

*Mari Harris*
*July, 2007*

Willetta DeYoung

## The Trials of a Trail Blazer

Willetta DeYoung is highly educated and deeply motivated. Due to her diligence and determination, this 40-year-old entrepreneur has her own digital textile printing business, called EDP Textiles.

Willetta's clients send photos, logos, or images via e-mail, and she prints them, at a very high resolution, onto whatever kind, color, or size of fabric that they choose. The advanced technology allows her to cater to a wide range of clients. They hire her to create many kinds of textiles, from fabric for wedding venues, to baby blankets, to banners for a business in France. No challenge is too great. Her skill and creativity are evident from studio displays, plaques listing her accomplishments, and samples of her beautiful textile printing.

Willetta grew up on a farm in northern Minnesota. She wanted to be a fashion designer, but was told that she could not make her living that way. She went to Concordia College in St. Paul and became the first student to major in Communications. Her plan was to become a news anchor, but her heart was not in it.

After graduating, she took classes in pattern making and product development at Minneapolis Community and Technical College. She also completed a graduate degree at the University of Wisconsin-Stout in textile design and retail marketing. She finished the three-year program in one and a half years with a 4.0 grade point average, while commuting from South Minneapolis (70 miles away).

After that, she worked at Fingerhut in quality assurance, Gordon & Ferguson in product design, and Dayton's in field care, before she was recruited by Target. She worked in textile research and development and traveled all over the world. After six years, Target began to reorganize and restructure. Willetta negotiated a severance package.

She decided to become a graphic artist, and worked as a graphic designer at Grace Church in Eden Prairie, MN. She found the work enjoyable and interesting, although it was difficult for her to spend so much time in front of a computer. Through her job at Grace, she learned about an organization called "Sewing the Seed," which works in South Africa teaching community groups how to sew textile products and how to run small businesses. She signed up to travel to South Africa to be a mentor.

Willetta's experience on that trip changed her life. She remembers coming home and thinking, "Wow, I have a good education, I have skills and talents. I want to start a business!" She began to consider what areas interested her, and began to draft a business plan.

Willetta knew that digital textile was an up-and-coming technology. During the time she was working as a graphic artist, she discovered through a Google search an article about a digital textile printer. Her initial reaction was, "I have to get that thing!" She sent Dupont an e-mail inquiry and they returned the information she was looking for. After spending a year completing her business plan, she had the printer installed in her office. As of September 2007, she had been in business for three years.

Willetta's printer is the fifteenth of its kind sold in the US, and the hundredth in the world. She bought it and a second piece of equipment she needed with the help of a loan from the Small Business Administration. At the time, she had good credit.

She also had the professional background and experience to support her new business. However, entering the world of digital textile printing in its early stages proved a challenge. Her first few years were spent educating potential clients about the benefits of the new technology. During her first year in business Willetta focused on custom-printed textiles for the residential interiors market. All of her research pointed to this area as the most promising for the technology.

The interior market was not receptive. Willetta described her method of creating a new design as "experiencing the world, reading, traveling, taking it all in, absorbing it, and coming out with something new and cool that nobody's even seen before—and that's a wow! shazam! of a design." The interior designers wanted to see her line of fabric and were frustrated when she told them she makes custom designs and prints. Even after she assembled a swatch book, the interior designers resisted.

The new business was struggling. Willetta heard about MicroGrants through WomenVenture, applied for a grant, and received $1,000. She used the money to pay for her living expenses and rent. She had hit rock bottom and needed to make big changes. The MicroGrant motivated Willetta to keep working hard.

She rewrote her business plan and restructured the company. Her new market focuses are branded textiles (items featuring corporate logos), high-level events, commercial interior decorating, and mass customized materials, such as blankets or banners.

Currently, Willetta is focusing on getting into commercial areas. She can offer small, specialized orders, allowing the clients to choose whatever color, photo, or logo they want. Her machine can also print at an extremely high level of quality, attracting many potential customers. She was close to landing a contract with Best Buy, but her company was deemed too small. Willetta was frustrated because she was confident that she could have completed the job.

Willetta's highest-paying project was designing fabric for a wedding for a wealthy family from Chicago. The family found her on the Internet and originally ordered 500 yards of printed fabric. After the family flew to Minneapolis to meet her, they increased the order to 2,000 yards of cotton-linen cloth for decorating tables and making cushions, 200 yards of awning fabric for tents and cabanas, 50 yards of polyester satin for family photos, 15 custom designed linen outfits for hostess girls, and 75 neckties for busboys. In 2006 she earned over half her income from that one job, and won an international award for the design.

Interns from local universities come to work with Wiletta, but she has no permanent employees. She needs a printer operator—someone not only capable of running the printer, but designing as well. She has worked with temporary agencies that specialize in printing, but after seven operators, she has not found the right person. It is difficult to find an employee with the skill and dedication to learn how to work the printer properly.

Willetta has faced the difficulties of a pioneer in her field. "The biggest obstacle I find," she said, "is trying to sell my product to potential customers who fear change. They just don't want to change." Willetta knows what she can do. The younger generation understands that the world is changing, but the people of her generation or older sometimes do not. And the elders are generally in the decision-making roles of companies that she woos.

Finding a customer base is a struggle. She said, "A lot of people who come upon me while researching the process or who find me on the Internet, are developing a brand new product." She has been getting customers who are not in established markets. If her customers themselves do not have a regular client base, it is more difficult for Willetta to establish repeat customers as well.

Willetta lives for a challenge. It is her chief motivation to push on. She is obsessed with fabric and likes being her own boss. Her talent, resourcefulness, and innovative ability to compete in the digital textile world should make her a success.

MicroGrants played a small but important role in helping Willetta keep her head above water at a difficult time. Without the grant she would have been unable to pay for her personal living expenses and may have had to take money out of her business, causing further setbacks and problems. She is financially on track for an average small business, and hopes to be profitable in two years. Willetta's high standards for herself, combined with her resolve to succeed will ensure business growth in the years to come.

*Reported by Cathy Bader*
*July 12, 2007*

## Shegitu Kebede

# Dynamo

Those who know Shegitu Kebede often refer to her as a one-woman nonprofit organization. She is the sole creator of several community-based programs in Minneapolis and has single-handedly employed 38 women in her own cleaning business. Her "office" is a converted apartment, literally stacked to the ceiling with sewing fabric and school supplies donated in support of her community work.

On most afternoons, this space is filled with the children of immigrant or low-income families, who come to Shegitu for help with homework, computer skills, and learning English. At other times, the soft whir of sewing machines fills the room as women from many backgrounds gather for sewing classes, tea, and fellowship. With a tiny budget of $5,000 a month, Shegitu stretches every dollar to provide services to her community, while taking just enough to support herself and her two children. As an immigrant herself, Shegitu is thankful for those who have helped her achieve self-sufficiency in America, and she now feels responsible to help others working toward the same goal.

Shegitu spent most of her childhood in an orphanage. "The person I call 'Mom' is from Norway," she explains, recalling the missionary who adopted her. Although the orphanage provided a safe environment for many years, continuing instability in Ethiopia forced Shegitu to flee to a refugee camp when she was 16 years old. While living as a refugee in Kenya, Shegitu had her first son and struggled to live on her own. After four years living in exile, Shegitu was granted sponsorship in the U.S. and readily accepted the opportunity to immigrate to America and seek a better life.

After she arrived in Minneapolis in 1990, Shegitu began what she now describes as "the loneliest year of my life." With no family, no knowledge of the area, and only limited English, she faced the same challenges that most immigrants still face. However, she was determined to overcome the cultural barriers—even if it meant learning English by watching Sesame Street with her three-year-old son. Through her sponsor, Shegitu got a factory job when she arrived, but soon aspired to find something more meaningful.

Recognizing the needs of single, immigrant mothers, Shegitu devoted herself to helping these women make the transition into the American workforce. For several years she worked through non-profit organizations helping the women apply for jobs. She found this work fulfilling, but noticed a fundamental flaw in the system. Most women who came to her for help lacked basic skills, and were not qualified for the work they were applying to do. "Some of them didn't even know how to use a broom!" Shegitu recalls. Confident that she could help these women on her own, Shegitu opened her own cleaning business in 2003.

From the beginning Shegitu was well-equipped with enough motivation, patience, and devotion to make it work, but she lacked funding. "The funny thing is I didn't have money. I didn't have anything," Shegitu remembers. "I just started." She applied for a MicroGrant to help pay for vacuum cleaners, mops and cleaning supplies. Because her business was an investment in the entire community, it was easy for MicroGrants to offer Shegitu $1,000 to help her get started. Now able to buy the equipment she needed, Shegitu found more clients and hired more employees.

Through her business, Shegitu helps immigrant women gain valuable job skills. After a period of training, and when the women have demonstrated their ability and commitment to work, she helps them find jobs in larger institutions. Since starting the business, Shegitu has employed 38 women and has earned valuable partnerships with Augsburg College, Fairview Medical Centers, and the University of Minnesota.

Building upon the success of her cleaning business, Shegitu started an after-school program for the children of the single mothers she employs. With the help of college interns and volunteer support, the program serves over 50 students and runs a school-supplies drive each fall. Her latest project, a sewing class for immigrant women, has become a support network that allows women to help one another solve issues of parenting, employment, and even domestic abuse.

With such an impressive record of community service, it's no surprise that Shegitu has earned the "non-profit" label. However, the tag is nothing more than a nickname. Shegitu still funds all of these community programs from her own checkbook. In recognition of this fact, MicroGrants supported Shegitu with a second MicroGrant in 2006. This allowed her to order business cards and increase the visibility of her work in the community.

"All these programs are possible because someone was there for me when I needed some help," Shegitu explains. "Now it is time for me to return the favor." Rather than affecting just one family, the benefits of this small "hand-up" have been extended to an entire community because MicroGrants chose to invest in one of the area's most valuable resources— Shegitu Kebede.

*Reported by Jamie Kallestad*
*July 19, 2007*

ASHLEY COLEMAN

# Notes From the Underground

I am a 21-year-old African American woman and this is my story. I was brought up on the south side of Minneapolis. My immediate family consists of my mother, father and younger brother. My mother was the enforcer of rules and instiller of values.

Mom taught me how to be a lady, and how to have self-value, faith, and self-respect. Through her I came to appreciate the importance of a college education, and a belief in the power of God. Incorporating these values into my life on a daily basis keeps me grounded. Some days are better than others. I've found that the best way to deal with any kind of day is to extract a lesson out of every situation, whether good or bad.

I see problems in our community that are being swept under the rug. Drugs, sex, teen pregnancy, and violent behavior are major dilemmas, but I see no improvement. These problems are rooted in poverty. Lost souls need to be guided, educated, supported, and shown that there is a way to break the cycle of defeat. We need trustworthy people who won't pass judgment on those who are failing. I like to help people, because there's more to life than just focusing on myself.

I went to Minneapolis public schools: Hale Elementary, then Field School, Anthony Junior High, and I graduated from the Inter-District Downtown School. After high school, I attended Augsburg College, a private school, for a short time and then transferred to Minneapolis Community & Technical College. After next semester, I plan to attend Metropolitan State University, where I'll focus on a degree in marketing and advertising. Throughout my educational career, I've always taken pride in my work. Receiving good grades is important, because it validates the results of being academically dedicated.

Along with pursuing an education, I focus on my small business called *Diva Rags and Suave Clothing*. I started the business with the support of my mother, Lynn Coleman, when I was fifteen years old. My mother is my "Momager" (Mom and manager).

*Diva Rags* are scarves and shawls embellished with glitter and rhinestones. The glitter will not shed, can be washed, and each scarf has its own distinctive design. Suave Clothing is my line of customized clothing and shoes. I enjoy designing, because it is an outlet for artistic expression. Designing clothes is like basketball: everybody claims they can play, but people who have a passion for the game stand apart from the rest. I want excellence, and in order to achieve high standards I must continue to stay focused, dedicated, humble, and open to constructive criticism.

Financially, *Diva Rags* and Suave Clothing is in good shape. The business isn't in debt. I appreciate Joe Selvaggio for providing a $1,000 Micro-Grant. Before I got the $1,000 I was starting to get discouraged that my business was developing so slowly. The grant showed that others believed in me, which encouraged me to work even harder toward becoming a successful businesswoman.

The grant allowed me to buy quality fabric and business cards, and it covered the costs of selling products at Midtown Global Market, the Farmer's Market, and on www.divarags.com. This increased my business by 15% and gave me a path to get more business as I can handle it. It also made me think about the proper use of money. I understood that I had an extra $1,000 of "equity." It was my own money and I didn't want to waste it by spending on things that wouldn't support and/or enhance the business. I still have $1,000 showing on my balance sheet, and I'm going to make it grow.

Within five years I want to have a store and earn a Master's Degree. I also want to implement a program to help young people capitalize on their talents, focusing on ending mental slavery—destructive thoughts that can limit one's potential.

In ten years I want to be an investor in the MicroGrants organization. I would like to invest in the lives of those who need financial support. The torch of support must be passed on from one person to the next so that we can reach a level of collective strength, maintaining an economically strong and viable nation. Ultimately, God has a plan for me, and I'll continue to represent the strong values I believe in and stay focused throughout my journey.

*Ashley Coleman*
*July 25, 2007*

Stefanie Blommer

# Integrating Beauty

Stephanie Blommer, a 29-year-old, white, single mother of two, bought a salon in St. Cloud in November 2007. She quickly noticed that many ethnic people in the area were driving as much as an hour and a half to the Twin Cities to get their hair done. She realized that if she were able to offer services for ethnic hair, she could attract more customers. She hired an African American stylist who was trained in styling ethnic hair to help boost sales, provide services to an untapped market, and create a multicultural salon.

Despite the new services, her business was going into debt. Although the salon had been around for some time when Stephanie bought it, she found that it was difficult to alert the community that it was still open for business, that it had a new name (Hair Concepts Studio) and new services. Because many people were not familiar with the shop, few customers were coming in.

Stephanie's family was struggling because of the salon's financial difficulties. It was difficult for her to take care of her two children, Dillion, 10, and Autumn, 2, while operating the salon. At the time, she was also going through a divorce, which was not only stressful, but time-consuming.

To combat her salon's financial strain, Stephanie tried to keep expenses low. She used energy-efficient lighting and kept the front door open on hot days in order to use the air conditioner less often. However, cutting costs could only do so much when business was nearly nonexistent. It was obvious that a demand existed for a multicultural salon in St. Cloud; the consumers simply needed to know that one existed.

In December 2007, Stephanie applied for a MicroGrant. She used the $1000 to pay for a new sign in front, for mailing advertisements, and for an article in the local newspaper. After this advertisement, business improved, and Stephanie was able to get more clients. She was even able to hire a new stylist and add a nail station, transforming the salon into a salon/spa. Although she is still not making a large profit, Stephanie's business is no longer going into debt as it operates.

Stephanie has big goals. In one year, she wants the salon to be successful and turn a larger profit. In five years, she would like to expand her business into several salons. She also hopes to open a salon closer to the Twin Cities, where there are more people.

*Reported by Sarah Hill*
*July 11, 2008*

Kanika Baker

# Capitalism's Beauty

So you want to lead a band? Try starting your own salon while having four little kids around. Kanika Baker, a 33-year-old African-American, is a single mother of four, including three-year-old twins.

Kanika began her career as a hair braider when she was 16 years old. She later attended the Scot Lewis School of Cosmetology in Minneapolis. After graduating, she worked in franchised salons under the tutelage of industry veterans. However, because she wanted to offer "personalized service in a cozy atmosphere," she decided to stop working in these places and open her own studio.

In October 2007, the dream jelled when she opened Realistic Manes Salon Concepts in Minneapolis. Kanika was driven. Her philosophy: A person is not a number; people should be respected for who they are, not for what they have.

She exhausted both her time and money in salon equipment and decoration, leaving only a pittance for advertising. "Word of mouth is great advertising, but there are so many other avenues I can pursue," she said. Kanika used the $1,000 she received from MicroGrants to make business cards, create a flyer, make a brochure, put numbers on her business door, buy a sign for her business, and develop a website. The literature and website, added to word of mouth recommendations, helped people learn about the salon quickly, and accurately. In addition, the numbers on her door and the large sign over her salon made the business more visible to newcomers and walk-ins.

Now Realistic Manes has seen a steady increase in the number of clients who come to this multicultural salon. Only eight months after receiving the grant, Kanika has seen an $8,000 monthly increase in the salon's revenue. The increase in clients has allowed Kanika to go from being the sole stylist to having five stylists and a barber at Realistic Manes.

This entrepreneur has many aspirations for Realistic Manes and for herself. She intends to remodel her small salon within the next year. She plans to move her family from an apartment complex to a rental house. The boost MicroGrants has given Kanika and her family is significant. As she explains, "It was a blessing just to have some help."

Kanika started with a small space in Minneapolis and now has a seven-station salon, including two barber stations, as well as two nail tech areas with pedicure equipment. The stations are bright, shiny and the salon is very high-tech.

Her salon will soon carry an exclusive line of products from her suppliers, allowing it to make more revenue from sales. The small grant has opened many doors that would have been difficult for Kanika to open alone. As Kanika said, "When I needed the grant, it came."

*Reported by Sarah Hill*
*June 3, 2008*

LAVON JORDAN

# Progress Without Self-Pity

Lavon Jordan smiled enthusiastically as he sat down at Dunn Brothers coffee shop. Talkative and open, his personality helps him connect with others. Lavon is a 23-year-old African American. He is married with two young children, one newborn, and one 4-year-old. He holds two jobs: primarily, he works as a recruiter for Twin Cities RISE! (TCR!) [An organization that trains people to move out of poverty into well-paying jobs.—ed.] But he also founded his own business, Minnesota's Underground Music Business Group (UMBG).

Lavon matches TCR! graduates with job offers from local companies. Networking is an important aspect of both his jobs, and he also feels that TCR! whose mission is to "deliver the best candidates to our clients." is a great support group." To become more qualified for his career, Lavon saw the need for a college education. He used the $1,000 MicroGrant to pay for part of his tuition towards earning a Business and Management degree.

Lavon bought a used Dell laptop from Craigslist and takes classes on-line through the University of Phoenix. He uses the computer at home and when he is on the go to do homework and research. His virtual classroom uses "online threading," which enables students to do homework and respond to class assignments at any time, from wherever they are. He is saving money for his next set of credits and will finish the program in a year.

There have been setbacks. At the age of 18, Lavon was arrested for gun possession when his ex-girlfriend called the police. He was also briefly involved in gang activity. Lavon says that the most important thing he learned was that "decisions you make can and will affect you later, positive or negative." He demonstrates the insights gained by saying, "being a man doesn't consist of holding a gun. Being a man consists of the actions you take."

Lavon now supports his family on $31,000 a year without government financial assistance. He believes his two jobs do not create undue stress on his family and describes himself as a "stickler for budgeting." Despite that, he doesn't have much capital to invest in his burgeoning business, UMBG. But he avoids self-pity.

Lavon always dreamed of starting his own music company geared towards local artists and businesses. He recently started UMBG with a friend and has plans for expansion. He has a web page, but mostly promotes on the street. He and his associates "blitz a highly populated area with flyers and ticket sales" for their next concert or show. His current project involves local artists playing at Epic, a Minneapolis nightclub.

Lavon has ambitious career goals, aiming to be the Director of TCR! within five years. According to his mentor at TCR!, "Lavon has specific plans and is thoughtful about what this will involve—how he will have to apply himself, pursue courses and be realistic about the difficulty start-up businesses can encounter."

*Reported by Winnie Tong*
*June 2, 2008*

TERESA ROGERS

# A Chance to Show Off

Teresa Rogers met me at a coffee shop on June 10, 2008, prepared to prove that she was progressing towards the goal of establishing her own successful wedding and event planning business. She opened a full but well-organized folder, pulling out sheets describing her company's services and billing procedures, as well as a resume with several professional wedding planners listed as references.

Although Teresa's business, Show Off Events, currently is not turning much profit, it is clear that Teresa is determined to succeed in her endeavor. When asked how she would know if her plan was failing and needed to be altered, she replied, "my plan won't change." Whatever it takes, Teresa Rogers is going to keep her dream alive.

The $1,000 that Teresa received from MicroGrants in December of 2007 has helped her begin the process of turning her company into a profitable business. She used the grant to buy stationery and office supplies, as well as to print and circulate information about Show Off Events and the services she provides. The promotional material includes Teresa's contact information and six reasons why a potential customer should choose her as an event planner.

Increasing the public's awareness about Show Off Events is extremely important for Teresa's future success. She needs to widen her customer base in order to make enough money to succeed. Currently Teresa does a lot of work for friends and family, but she finds that she can't charge what she needs to without making them mad. Although supportive of Teresa's talent and vision, they often expect her to work for them at a discounted rate because of their close relationship. These low-paying jobs do not allow Teresa to make a profit. She needs to find new clients and charge prices high enough to get Show Off Events off the ground. Increased advertising is essential.

In addition to trying to spread the word about her company, Teresa is currently taking classes in Interior Design at Century College. She hopes to combine her event planning business with interior design services in order to expand the company and increase revenue. She also intends to apply for an event planning license after completing school in the spring of 2009. As Teresa explained, "I'm charging less than I'm worth because I don't have a license." With the credibility that this credential would give her, Teresa would be able to raise her prices to a level she believes would more accurately reflect the work she does.

Although Teresa has a long way to go before she has enough jobs to make Show Off Events profitable, she has the passion for her work that an entrepreneur needs to succeed. Teresa has been interested in design since she was a little girl. As a child, she would "redecorate" the family house, only to be scolded by her mother, who did not like to come home to find the furniture rearranged every day. Teresa's natural talent for interior design has only grown since then. She has been planning events and decorating for six years. "I have a creativity in my head that will never stop," she insists.

While Teresa has a natural aptitude for interior design and event planning, she'll have to overcome several obstacles if she's to make her dream of a successful business a reality. In addition to finding ways to attract new customers, Teresa also needs to figure out how to overcome such personal challenges as her severe asthma.

Only time will tell whether Teresa will be able to pull through and make Show Off Events a profitable company. But her passion for the work, and the money from MicroGrants that she used for advertising, have enabled her to start moving in the right direction.

*Reported by Berit Johnson*
*June 10, 2008*

SHEA HALSTEAD

# Working, Planning, Expanding

Shea Halstead, a single, 35-year-old, African American woman, is currently working as a guest relationship representative for Target Financial Services. She also owns and operates her own cleaning business.

When Shea applied for a MicroGrant during the winter of 2007-2008, she was struggling. She had recently gone through a divorce and was adjusting to living on a single income. Her home was also in foreclosure. In addition, her computer broke down, making it difficult for her to solidify her business "in a professional manner."

When Shea received her grant, she said that "it really helped out when I needed it." She used most of the grant to buy a new computer, and the remainder to pay for an eight-course business program called "Planning to Succeed." She took the classes through WomenVenture, which provides the technical tools and emotional support for women to start and grow their own businesses, find a job, or develop a new career path.

With her class work almost over, she has been thinking about her business plan and the future. She currently has nine regular cleaning clients, many of whom she has had for years. She is working for Target Financial to provide a stable financial base and also to receive benefits such as health insurance. However, she would like to expand enough to cut back her hours at Target and sustain herself solely through the cleaning business. Advertising looks promising, but at the moment, it may be out of reach.

Shea has set several specific goals for her future. In one year, she hopes to stop working at Target Financial and to support herself entirely through her cleaning business. She aims to have fifty regular clients with six people working for her. She would also like to make her business more energy-efficient by using environmentally friendly cleaning products, and by buying a high quality front-loading washing machine, which uses 50 percent less water, less soap, and less energy than a traditional top-loader.

In five years, Shea envisions having a successful, self-sustaining business and happy employees. Eventually she hopes to expand her business by offering shoveling, handyman home services, and corporate cleaning. She would also like to offer daycare and babysitting, services needed by women.

Things are beginning to fall into place for Shea. Her home is no longer in foreclosure but rather in forbearance, a postponement of foreclosure which gives her the opportunity to make up the overdue payments. She also believes that she is one-third of the way towards being where she would like to be. Creating a business plan through WomenVenture will help her to achieve her goals. "I've been running the business out of sheer will and determination," she said. "If I can do it that way for nine years, it will work when I have a business plan." Without MicroGrants, Shea may not have had the opportunity to take business courses through WomenVenture and improve her business model.

*Reported by Sarah Hill*
*July 11, 2008*

Renisha Gray

# A Capitalist's Struggles

At the age of 27, Renisha Gray has already accomplished more than others might in a lifetime. She graduated from the University of Minnesota as a Global Studies major and later took classes to become a certified Global Career Development Facilitator (GCDF). Although she does not work as a GCDF, the classes have provided her with an attractive career alternative and opportunities for further education in the global studies field. Renisha, an African American, is married and has two sons, 2-year-old Ijahrod and 3-year-old Ijahvonn. In 2006 Renisha opened her own shop, Change of Style, in Minneapolis' Midtown Global Market.

Change of Style sells clothes, shoes, body products, and other accessories. Since Renisha wants to avoid buying products from sweatshops, all of the merchandise is fair trade. She applied for a MicroGrant in July of 2007 to provide the company with the capital it needed to continue to grow. Renisha used most of the $1,000 to cover overhead costs and to expand her inventory by purchasing more body products, including spices and body oils. She used the remainder of the grant to help pay her employees' wages.

Renisha credits MicroGrants for playing a major role in providing her store with the resources needed to thrive and increase its net earnings. She explained: "without the grant, we would not have been able to purchase the products to keep the business afloat." Renisha's business is still profitable today, making $2,000 to $2,500 per month. Renisha has also increased her own personal income by $200 per month since receiving the grant.

Like many small businesses, Renisha's store is still facing threats to its survival. The main problem is how to finance it at a level that will keep it developing. In the past, she has had trouble providing funds for Change of Style because a small business's credit is often based on the owner's personal credit. Renisha has been hesitant to take financial risks. However, she recently heard of a company that focuses exclusively on a business's credit, without creating repercussions for the owner's personal credit. Renisha is excited to look into this potential solution for financing Change of Style. Se knows, however, that such promising alternatives have sometimes been clever traps for the unwary.

Renisha has several ideas to expand the business once she finds the funding. She plans to set up online purchasing for her store soon. She also wants to increase her wholesale business. Within the next several years, Renisha would like to set up two entities under her company to provide what she terms "holistic care." The first would be a daycare center, and the second, a personal care assistance (PCA) company. These would allow Renisha to serve people's needs in a way that goes beyond providing the material products that Change of Style sells.

Despite the economic recession, Renisha remains optimistic about her company's future. She recognizes that the market will have its ups and downs, yet she believes that Change of Style still has a lot of room to develop. "Right now," she says, "I'm still in the growth stage. All I think about is growth." She has a realistic goal of increasing the business's income to $5,000 per month in the near future.

Renisha has set the bar high. She has ambitious career objectives and a positive attitude about her ability to achieve them. Renisha also recognizes the integral role MicroGrants played in getting her company to where it is now. She appreciates the grant because it helped her stay on track with her business through a time when she questioned whether Change of Style would be able to survive. What she likes about the MicroGrants program is "that people at MicroGrants give you the opportunity to succeed." Having been given this opportunity, Renisha plans to take full advantage of it.

*Reported by Berit Johnson*
*July 24, 2008*

James Byron

# Working, Scrimping, Planning

Six months after James Byron received a MicroGrant, he still owned a stall at the Midtown Global Market, where he sells women's purses and other accessories. A handful of his customers have been with him from the very beginning, and he likes "the satisfaction of seeing a happy customer."

James also sells his products online. When his old computer broke down at a critical time, he was in trouble. He could not go online, even to check e-mail. He used the $1,000 MicroGrant to buy a computer, printer and scanner for his company.

He is determined to succeed and plans to have his own storefront in a year. The Midtown Global Market is ethnically oriented, and he wants to break out of that limiting label to make his shop a more broad-based women's accessories shop.

James has to work hard to make ends meet, even with his wife working. He has already "cut corners really sharp," by selling his car and riding the bus to save gas money and car insurance. When the landlord increased their rent, his family returned to a less expensive place where they had lived before.

James's 17-year-old son will be starting college soon, so he is saving as much as he can for educational expenses. James appreciates Micro-Grants for coming "at a time that I really needed something, and for giving me a boost."

*Reported by Winnie Tong*
*July, 2008*

# 2
# First Jobs

THE FIRST JOB—a really virginal experience. Who among us can forget its impact—for better or for worse? That entry point becomes the moment when hopes, dreams, or expectations meet the sobering reality of the everyday demands of the job.

Initiations and the rites of passage are unforgettable markers on our life's trek. The first day of school and the launching into the world of earners. Graduations, marriages, retirements and that first date. Emblazoned in our memories forever. The mileposts that mark our lives.

Ahead we meet some of the folks who faced their introductions into the world of work.

Foster Asomani

# An Innocent Abroad

Foster Asomani was enthusiastic. The 47-year-old father of two had been trying to contact MicroGrants to say thank you for the help. When we arrived at his house, he came outside excitedly to welcome us into his home.

Foster's living room was bustling. His wife runs a daycare with as many as ten children. The Asomani living room was filled with toys and large, plush, stuffed animals. The walls were painted brightly and the living room was spotlessly clean. The children sitting on the sofa had one eye on the Disney Channel and the other on the three strangers talking to Foster.

Foster was born in West Ghana, Africa in 1960. He grew up there, but moved to Israel in 1989. He lived with a number of families and found work doing odd jobs. In 2001 he and his then-pregnant wife decided to move to the United States. Foster did not speak English and had to learn after he arrived. He also did not have much education because he grew up in a small village where schooling was not available. Foster brought letters of referral from the families he had stayed with in Israel, hoping to find work in the United States. Foster and his wife had heard good things about Minnesota, and they settled in Minneapolis.

The adjustment to living in America has been a challenge. Foster arrived with almost no money and has been struggling to make his way ever since. His first job, at Walmart, he said helped him tremendously by teaching him how to fit into society. He worked part time—only four hours a day. At a rate of $8 an hour, he wasn't earning nearly enough to support a family.

Foster has a big heart and wants to help people in need, although he can't afford to be as generous as he would like to be. While he was working at Walmart, he had quite a bit of free time at home. To fill the hours, he watched television, where he saw an advertisement for a project called Feed My Starving Children. Foster was so moved by the images of the emaciated children that he sent a letter promising to contribute money if he got a better job. He did send some money to the organization, but eventually he realized that he could not afford to continue. Family had to come first.

He had, and to some extent still has, a rosy vision of America—although some of his experiences in this country have come as shocks. Television exerted a strong influence on him. He saw a pitch that promised that he could make money working from home. Excited about this opportunity, he sent a check for the specified fee. The company took his money, but he got no job. He began to feel disillusioned when he discovered that many advertisements on television were not trustworthy.

One evening Foster saw Joe Selvaggio on a television program and learned that Joe had helped someone from Somalia. At first he was afraid that this could be yet another scam. But he cautiously began to believe that an organization called MicroGrants could really help poor people. He applied for a MicroGrant and received $1,000.

Foster spent his MicroGrant on supplies for his business, which he called Discount Carpet Cleaning. He bought a sprayer, chemicals, and insurance so he could start a company, and he took out a loan to finance a van. Foster's MicroGrant also helped him to advertise. Before Foster received the MicroGrant, he had been spending most of his money on advertising with almost no success. His lack of experience in business cost him between $6,000 and $7,000. Foster plans to hire an answering service to take business calls, because it is hard for potential customers to understand him on the phone with his heavy accent.

Before Foster received the MicroGrant, he had not been getting very many jobs. He was behind on his credit payments and he needed additional equipment in order to be hired. He went to MicroGrants for the money he needed to buy the equipment.

The carpet cleaning business tends to be somewhat seasonal, with demand increasing in the spring and summer months, and Foster hopes that his orders will increase this summer. But most importantly, he believes that his company will succeed and provide a living for him and his family. He has an optimistic attitude and is still grateful to be living in America.

Foster's MicroGrant woke him up. He was losing hope, and the grant helped him regain his positive outlook. He believes there is opportunity in America. (At the same time, he is learning about the limits of trust.) Foster says that MicroGrants has shown him that good things can happen in America when you open your heart and listen carefully.

Through all the struggles and setbacks, Foster has remained hopeful and upbeat. His wife's steady income from her daycare business helps to support the family. Foster is strongly grounded in his belief that helping others is important. Although Foster himself may not be in the position to do this quite yet, it is refreshing to encounter an individual who has such a generous spirit.

*Reported by Catherine Bader*
*June 8, 2007*

DANYALE TURPIN

# Family as Crucible

It was a perfect opportunity. After a year of intensive job searching, Danyale Turpin, an African American of 22, had finally found stable employment as a direct support professional at a nursing facility: Olu's Home, Inc. Having recently obtained certification as a nursing assistant, this single mother was excited by the new position and more than ready to move out of her mother's house into her own home. For the first time in her life, Danyale could be self-sufficient.

As she trained for the new position, she learned that she would be expected to transport patients and quickly realized that she would lose the job if she didn't have a valid driver's license. Although she quickly took and passed the driver's test, $600 in unpaid traffic tickets stood in the way of her getting a license—and keeping her job. MicroGrants stepped in because Danyale had demonstrated her potential by finding a stable job. Since receiving the grant, Danyale has moved into her own home and continues to grow in her career.

With a daughter on the way, and her hands already full with an energetic three-year-old son, it seemed that Danyale had more than enough commitments to keep her busy outside of work. Yet with quiet confidence, she cited her children as her primary motivation for pursuing a career and improving herself through education. "I want to better myself so that my kids can live better and have stuff that I didn't have," she said.

Danyale has worked hard to ensure that her children never experience the family trauma that cast a shadow over her own childhood. She grew up in a family of eight. Her parents' relationship was unstable, marked by domestic violence and drug abuse. The family moved frequently, and eventually began to split up in Minneapolis after Danyale's father was sent to prison. Although Danyale faced terrible challenges, she chose to learn from her experiences rather than be defeated by them. "It affected me," she confided, "but I still had to grow up and be a woman. It made me responsible."

After moving to Minneapolis, Danyale had worked at several "odds and ends" jobs, but she struggled to find a stable career path. After having her first child in 2004, Danyale began receiving public assistance from the Minnesota Family Investment Program (MFIP). The financial help enabled her to provide for her son, but she was in a constant state of upheaval as she moved between temporary homes and temporary jobs. "I didn't want to be a telemarketer forever," she said.

She enrolled in a nursing program in hopes of earning a better living and supporting her family without public assistance. Today, Danyale has her Nursing Assistant certification and has added the credential of Medical Administrative Specialist. The position with Olu's Home seemed like the perfect place for her to develop in her career. But without MicroGrants, the unique opportunity might have been lost.

In July of 2006, Danyale applied for a MicroGrant to pay off the driving violations so that she could get her license. Without the timely direct assistance from MicroGrants, she would have been forced to give up the position with Olu's Home and find a job without driving requirements. Because transporting patients is often a component of a nursing assistant's responsibilities, it would have been difficult for Danyale to find another position in her field.

When she applied to MicroGrants, Danyale was still living with her mother and relying on public assistance to raise her son. Since receiving a grant, she has moved out of her mother's house and now lives with the father of her children. He repairs cars for friends and relatives, which makes his income unpredictable.

Although Danyale still receives government support to pay for food, she hopes to be entirely self-sufficient soon. Her position at Olu's Home offers opportunities for advancement. Her current goal is to move up to lead staff. Danyale explains, "I would be making more money and would be less dependent on other people." To help reach her goal, Danyale has registered for the Licensed Practical Nursing program at Anoka Technical College, the next step in a promising career.

Danyale is extremely grateful for the opportunities that two Micro-Grants have made possible. She received a second grant of $200 in 2007 to help with a down payment on daycare service. This will give her the flexibility to both work and go to school.

She is excited about having her second child and hopes to provide both of her children with possibilities that she never had while growing up. "MicroGrants gives people the opportunity to do more and work for themselves. I'm happy that there is a program like this to help people better themselves and actually help them grow," she said. Today, Danyale looks forward to continued personal growth through education, work experience, and independence.

*Reported by Jamie Kallestad*
*June 25, 2007*

Nancy Ateka

# Lonely Struggle: Incremental Progress

Nancy Ateka is a 23-year-old immigrant from Kenya. Although she does not speak English very well, she has found a way to live in America while working full-time to support four family members in Kenya. She is a virtual Energizer Bunny of motivation.

Nancy moved to Minnesota in January 2006 with the help of an uncle, her only relative in the United States. Her first job was at Project for Pride in Living (PPL). A friend, Lydia Ogero, also from Kenya, referred her to MicroGrants when transportation became a problem.

Nancy borrowed her uncle's car to drive to school and work, as she saved a little at a time. Unfortunately, two unrelated events changed her situation: Her uncle needed his car back, and, at the same time, violence broke out in Kenya in an election dispute, during which several people were killed. The rioting that followed prevented the rest of Nancy's family, who live in Kenya, from going to school or work. Nancy had saved for a car, but decided to send the money home instead.

Nancy applied for a $1,000 MicroGrant to make a downpayment on a car and to help pay for tuition. It was approved and she enrolled at North Hennepin Community College in the Registered Nursing program.

In addition to attending school, Nancy also works as a home health aide at Whispering Pines, an assisted living facility. She works 8 hours a day when school is in session, 16 hours when it is not. Nancy is single and shares an apartment with a roommate. She keeps a close eye on her expenses: she spends about $500 a month on rent and utilities, $300 on car payments, $60 on the phone bill, and some more for food. Nancy has a support group of friends also from Kenya, but feels that "they cannot help much because they have their own things to do."

Despite being frugal, Nancy finds it hard to make ends meet. She earns around $24,000 a year and is the sole supporter of her family—her father, two younger brothers, and a younger sister. Obtaining a college degree is crucial to finding jobs in Kenya. Her siblings will need her support until they graduate. Fortunately, the older of the two brothers will graduate in a year, which will take some of the pressure off of her. Nevertheless, the rest of the family still needs help. Her sister is in middle school. Her father, who used to have a high-paying job in England, is unemployed. He moved back to Kenya after Nancy's mother died.

Nancy cried as she reminisced about her family; she misses them dearly, but at the same time, they are a huge responsibility on her shoulders. Still, she has high hopes for the future and is determined to keep going. She wants to be a registered nurse because she finds helping others meaningful. She also would like to start a program like MicroGrants in Kenya. "It's good and it helps people," she says.

*Reported by Winnie Tong*
*May 29, 2008*

## Freddie Chappell

# Sobriety's Promise

Freddie Chappell met his guest at the threshold of his transitional home in North Minneapolis. Freddie emerged into the sunlight with an easy smile and seemingly unprompted laughter. Gospel music drifted down the hallway from a back room. The entire building exuded an aura of spiritual ease, of which Freddie himself was the embodiment. Sitting comfortably in the living room next to his wife of two years, he clearly relished explaining his work, his faith, and his goals for the future.

Yet as Freddie spoke of the circumstances that led him to this all-male group home, it became obvious that he had spent most of his life without the very things that make his life so fulfilling today. Freddie is an African

American, born on a farm in Arkansas 45 years ago. His family moved to Mississippi when he was 3. Despite his rural upbringing and supportive family, Freddie lapsed into drug use soon after entering the Mississippi school system.

As he explained it, "I came to that fork in the road and I chose the wrong path. I started doing a lot of selfish things." He has borne the consequences: he lost touch with his faith, alienated himself from his family, and could not hold a steady job despite seven semesters of college. He moved several times between Mississippi and Milwaukee, but found it difficult to support himself in either place. As drug abuse and unemployment continued to erode his self-esteem, he considered suicide.

Getting married in 2005 was a positive life change for Freddie. But his wife, too, was addicted to drugs. Needing a new environment and a fresh start, they decided to leave Milwaukee and move to Minneapolis. They had only enough money to pay for one bus fare, but thanks to the kindness of several strangers and one compassionate bus driver, the couple managed to make it.

When Freddie and his wife arrived in Minneapolis in April 2006, they were homeless, jobless, hungry and broke. They lived in a Salvation Army shelter for one month. Although their situation was grim, Freddie and his wife were determined to make a fresh start. "We decided not to wallow in our losses, but to try to get some stability and structure in our lives," Freddie said.

Because he and his wife realized that the first step towards stability was accepting and dealing with their drug addictions, they enrolled in separate in-patient drug treatment programs. Both graduated successfully in 96 days.

After completing the program at Turning Point, Freddie changed the direction of his life. He moved into drug-free transitional housing, renewed his faith, and began looking for stable employment. With the help of PPL and the North Side Jobs program, Freddie learned how to present himself in an interview. After almost a year of drug treatment, job training, and spiritual renewal, only one minor obstacle prevented Freddie from obtaining employment—he needed new clothes.

There are free clothing stores, of course, but Freddie is a larger man and needed to buy clothes. In order to overcome this last remaining hurdle,

Freddie applied for a MicroGrant. When he received the check in December of 2006, he immediately went to buy clothes. He used his $1,000 grant carefully to pay for the relatively expensive "Big and Tall" business attire he needed to be prepared for interviews. "Having nice clothes helps with your self-esteem; it makes you walk with your head up," he commented.

Thanks to his newly refined appearance, Freddie felt more confident and better prepared to enter the workplace. He described the conclusion of his job interview at Caterpillar: when the interviewer asked him if he had any final questions, Freddie's response was, "when do I start?" He was hired two days later.

Freddie has been with Caterpillar for almost six months and has not missed a day of work. A mechanic by trade, Freddie loves going to work and is thankful for the opportunity to use his skills again. "MicroGrants gave me an opportunity and I'm taking it and I'm running with it," he said proudly.

Today, Freddie and his wife have been sober for more than a year. Although they live apart in transitional housing, Freddie is saving money and looks forward to the day they will move into their own home. "I'm not where I want to be, but I'm sure not where I used to be," Freddie says, looking back on his struggles.

With the help of his support networks—including MicroGrants—Freddie has grown personally and is leading a much more rewarding life. Happily married, working full time, and reinvested in faith, Freddie is confident that he is headed in the right direction. When he arrived in Minneapolis, he was at a low point, but determined to start a new life. He has emerged from a dark past and is re-integrating himself into the working world.

*Reported by Jamie Kallestad*
*July 3, 2007*

CRAIG EBERT

# Finally Clean and Climbing

It took Craig Ebert more than 30 years to get clean. As he sits calmly outside a Minneapolis coffee shop, in the shadow of the apartment building where he grew up, his attitude reveals no hint of the pain and personal dissatisfaction he endured for many years. Alcohol and drug abuse have haunted his life since childhood. When he was 13, Craig's father died of alcoholism. Soon after, Craig began experimenting with drugs.

Because Craig became a "functional addict," he was able to maintain temporary employment and support himself for many years—but this only masked his drug problem. Without a college degree he was limited to jobs that left him unfulfilled. He occasionally lost solid employment due to drugs. As his living conditions and family ties deteriorated, Craig entered several rehabilitation programs, but always returned to his old habits once they were over and he went home.

In 2002 Craig came to a conclusion: "This has just got to end." He made the crucial decision that year to move out of his old apartment in South Minneapolis in order to escape the familiar environment of drug abuse. Since that move, Craig has turned his life around.

After leaving the apartment, he spent 3 years at the Park Avenue Center in Minneapolis. Although he initially went to the center for the substance-abuse treatment program, he stayed on as a house manager. He was offered the position soon after he finished his rehabilitation program. Craig's time at the Park Avenue Center allowed him to build his self-confidence and think about his personal goals.

"After I got clean I started to get motivated," Craig explained. "Once you get your head on straight you get your life back." While living at the Park Avenue Center, Craig found stable employment with a lumber company and immediately began saving. Soon he had earned enough money for the down payment on a house in Brooklyn Center, and he went back to school for the first time in over twenty years.

Craig is 48 and single. Clean for five years, he is now living in his own home and is working towards an associate degree at Minneapolis Community and Technical College (MCTC). In addition to his employment with the lumber company, Craig works part-time at a halfway house for men. Craig says of his busy schedule, "I basically work and go to school and do homework…and work on my house. My life is full now."

Craig has been eager to share his personal insights and help others to learn from his experiences. After he graduates from the Criminal Justice program at MCTC, Craig plans to work with at-risk youth as a juvenile probation officer or a guardian ad litem. He said, "I feel I've got a lot of personal experience and knowledge. I can empathize with the troubles people go through."

Unfortunately, earning a "two-year" associate degree was taking Craig much longer than the title implies. He couldn't afford to sacrifice work hours for classroom time, so he spent five years attending school part-time. At his age, Craig wants to finish his degree as soon as possible.

He applied for a MicroGrant in order to accelerate his education by taking time off work. When he received the grant in July 2007, Craig was shocked. "I thought there was no way I'd get it because I work so much," he commented. Although Craig was earning a stable income at the time, his house payments, bills, and food consumed nearly his entire paycheck, leaving very little money to pay for his classes.

Craig used all of his MicroGrant for tuition. This gave him the flexibility to take time off work and register for a fuller course load. Before getting the grant, Craig could earn only six credits per semester. But after he got it, he started taking nine. He now expects to graduate soon. Craig has taken coursework in psychology, criminal justice and constitutional law and has been a proud, straight-A student since enrolling in MCTC.

By earning an Associate Degree in Criminal Justice, Craig will be one step closer to realizing his ultimate goal of helping at-risk youth. He believes that by working as a probation officer or guardian ad litum, he can help young people to avoid the mistakes that led him into a cycle of drug abuse. "I'm kind of a success story," he will tell you, looking back on the difficulties he has overcome.

Craig is intelligent, motivated, and confident. Even without the help of MicroGrants, he would probably still complete his degree, but it would take him much longer. He is grateful for the help from MicroGrants. Eager to make up for lost time, Craig is excited that he will soon be able to share his experience and make a difference in the lives of others.

*Reported by Jamie Kallestad*
*June 28, 2007*

The table below is typical of those created from the data collected for each MicroGrants recipient.

| | |
|---|---|
| Age | 45 |
| Home zip code | 55411 |
| Work zip code | 55411 |
| Marital Status | Married |
| Dependents | 1 |
| Yearly Income | $33,000 |
| Education | High school, 3 1/2 years of college |
| Race/Ethnicity | African American |
| Obstacles to Employment | Transportation |
| Health Insurance | No |
| Government Assistance | No |
| Employer/Position | Caterpillar Inc/ Cooling installer |

Sean Allen

# A Battle To Escape

Sean Allen is beginning to succeed in Minneapolis, but it has been hard. He moved to the Twin Cities in July 2006 at the age of 36. Before that, he had lived for 33 years in Milwaukee, where he had not only felt trapped, but was continually in trouble with the law. He was surrounded by people he had known throughout his life, but they seemed to hold him back from trying to achieve a stable and productive existence. He escaped to Minneapolis and is building a foundation that will enable him to become self-sufficient.

Milwaukee was a tough place for him to live. He had no employment connections, and consequently it was very difficult to find a job. According to Sean, Milwaukee has no social services network like the one in the Minneapolis area. To complicate matters further, he had been involved with a tough crowd when he was younger. He spent time in prison as a young man. After he was released, he continued to get into trouble and ended up behind bars again for more than four years.

One good thing did come from his jail time: he was able to earn his high school equivalency diploma. Between jailings, he had completed six semesters at Milwaukee Area Technical College toward a degree in business management and sales. He wanted to finish and graduate, but because he had been arrested at school, he was too ashamed to return after his release.

Sean tried to help himself, but found it very difficult to make progress. The first obstacle was that he was surrounded by the same people who had been a bad influence in the past. Today, fifteen years after his last arrest, he says that a fourth of them are dead, and most of the others are "strung out" on drugs. In fact, of that group, only two people other than Sean were able to escape their former self-destructive lifestyle.

The second obstacle was his criminal record. Because of it, businesses did not want to hire Sean and he could not find work. He was employed only sporadically during the fifteen years after he was released. Finally, through a friend of a friend, he was able to get a job at a laundromat. By saving as much as he could, and with some help from his employer, he was able to leave Milwaukee and move to Minneapolis.

Minnesota felt like a breath of fresh air. Sean enrolled in Project for Pride in Living's Train To Work Program. He learned how to write a resume and how to interview for a job. In addition, he regained the confidence that he had lost during the long periods of unemployment. Unbeknownst to him, his criminal record had been erased, so he had a clean slate when he came to Minnesota.

His supervisor at the Train To Work program told Sean, "You are going to succeed because you just don't sit around and wait for something. You go get it." He replied, "I have to. I'm getting too old. I'm 37." Knowing he had to be proactive to be successful, he searched the online employment database at PPL every day and followed each lead that he found. Initially he had no luck. But one woman he spoke to was so impressed by his determination that she referred him to a temporary employment agency. Through the agency, Sean got a six-month job at Macy's.

As soon as the job came to an end, Sean returned to his search. Ironically, while he was working hard to find another position, an employer found him. Hennepin County Medical Center needed a temporary worker, and Sean's temporary agency recommended him for the job. He was hired and was placed in the food department, where he still works.

He logs around 40 hours per week and has worked 320 hours since he began in April 2007. If he completes 200 more hours, he will be eligible to become a full-time employee. His pay will increase from $9 per hour to $10.50 per hour. As a full-time employee, he will be able to join a union and receive benefits like health insurance.

In January 2007, Sean ran into financial trouble. He was trying to support two daughters living with two different mothers, and he was still paying the hospital bills for the births of both children, who were born in 1997 and 2000.

It was essential for him to stay in the small apartment he rented because it was near a bus line. He didn't have a car—or a driver's license—and needed to take public transportation to get to work. Weighed down by his bills, he fell behind on his rent and was almost evicted.

Sean heard about MicroGrants from an advisor at PPL. He immediately applied and was accepted. As soon as the check came in the mail, he gave it all to the landlord. He paid all of his past due rent and prepaid through the following month.

Sean hopes to become a full-time employee by the end of the summer. He is not sure of his long-term plans because he wants to solidify his work record first. He is considering enrolling at Minneapolis Community and Technical College.

Sean is also in the process of getting a driver's license. When he was a boy, he was a passenger in a car that hit a little girl. The experience was so traumatic that he thought that he never wanted to drive a car. But now he realizes that being able to drive would give him more independence and more employment options. He has started taking driving lessons.

The MicroGrant came at a time of despair. When asked what would have happened if he had not received it, he says, "Honestly, I don't really know. I think I would have moved back to Milwaukee." MicroGrants provided the safety net that enabled Sean to keep moving toward a stable future. It allowed him to keep his apartment, which, in turn, made it possible to commute to his job. And he was spared a return to his old, troubled life.

*Reported by Daniel E. Geoffrion*
*July 10, 2007*

Teresa (Last name withheld by request)

# Finding Her Way

Two years ago Teresa was serving the final months of a 13-year prison term. She was emotionally unstable and was physically and psychologically separated from her three children. Today, Teresa is an involved and supportive mother and a dedicated employee who has worked hard to rebuild her own life, as well as those of her children. With the help of a $1,000 MicroGrant, Teresa has been given a chance to accomplish her goals.

On her release from prison, Teresa enrolled in at Project for Pride in Living's PPL SHOP, a nine-month program that provides on-the–job training for unemployed adults looking to gain work experience and life skills. With the guidance of dedicated PPL staff, she was able to learn the skills needed for success in the working world, and she distinguished herself as one of the hardest-working participants in the program.

Teresa's success at the PPL SHOP, along with the undergraduate degree that she completed during her time at the Illinois State Penitentiary, gave her the confidence and training she needed to enter the workforce. The mistakes of her past, however, severely limited the opportunities available to her. Furthermore, previous fines and fees, which grew during her years of incarceration, left Teresa in debt and without a driver's license. Thus she was unable to pursue even the employment prospects that were within her reach.

Teresa learned about MicroGrants through her mentor at PPL, and immediately applied for assistance to pay off the debts that were preventing her from moving on. Her request for a $1,000 grant was approved, and the funds were allocated to the PPL SHOP. The staff helped Teresa to set up a budget and payment plan so that she could responsibly fulfill her obligations and take the next step.

She has since become debt-free, and is in the process of getting a drivers license. When she is able to drive, she will have many more options for full and/or part-time work, and employment will allow her to make the final transition between a troubled past and a bright future.

Since becoming involved in PPL and MicroGrants, Teresa has come a long way, both professionally and personally. She has renewed her relationships with her three children—most notably her sixteen-year-old son, with whom she now lives, and who has stuck with her during her past failures and current successes. Teresa has also begun making daily entries in a personal journal, allowing her to track her emotional development, as well as her professional growth. She is eternally grateful to MicroGrants, she says, for giving her the ability to help herself, for the hope of a better life, and for the opportunity to become a better person. She hopes to one day become a MicroGrants donor so that she can give the same opportunity to another person in need.

*Reported by Andrew Dayton*
*January 19, 2007*

# 3
# Bootstrappism
# Through Learning

THE PEOPLE ON THESE next pages are too often portrayed as life's "losers": victims, welfare queens, teenaged mothers, addicts, thieves, scoundrels, and abusers. Among the lessons we learn from their stories is that these labels can be grossly unfair.

Here we find that gullible believers in advertising schemes waste precious assets pursuing dreams promoted on TV. Welfare cheats can be desperate mothers trying to keep their children from starvation. Unwise young women believe the flattery, and spend the rest of their lives trying to protect, feed and raise their charges—or the products of their folly. Immigrants immediately get it—education is the ladder.

By understanding their lives we can discover the universality of it all—the plight of those trapped in awful circumstances and their bravery in trying to survive.

Another constant—besides the need to control one's destiny—is the search for education. The middle class is well aware of its power, but the underclass comes to this knowledge slowly.

Credentials matter. A driver's license can make the difference between having a job (and a home) or living in a shelter. A degree is a union card to opportunity.

On the following pages we feel the tears and the will to make it behind the cold statistics.

Zeinab Alol

# Giving Back

Zeinab Alol is not a typical 27-year-old woman. She has lived in So-malia, Egypt, Australia, and Minnesota. Because of her immigrant status she is not eligible for financial aid through conventional sources. Yet she has dedicated herself to bring what relief she can to her native land of Somaliland, one of the most violent parts of the world.

Zeinab grew up in Somalia, but moved to Egypt for educational op-portunities before civil war broke out in her home country. (Somaliland separated from Somalia in 1991.) Zeinab graduated from high school in Egypt in 1998, went to Australia to work as a lab technician for two years, then immigrated to the United States in 2003, entering through Seattle. She picked up new insights from life experiences in each country where she lived. Zeinab was excited to come to the United States. "We all know that America is the land of opportunity. That's actually what people call it," she said.

She moved to Minneapolis because she had a cousin who lived in the Twin Cities. Zeinab began working as the Immigrant Services Coordinator at Project for Pride in Living (PPL) in March 2005. She found the job at PPL through her previous position in the St. Paul Public Schools, where she did outreach work in the Somali community. As of July 2007, she had been employed by PPL for over two years.

Zeinab is a student at the University of Minnesota. Due to her immi-gration status, she is not eligible for financial aid from the school. She ap-plied for a green card three years ago and is still waiting for it. To meet her expenses, she took out a bank loan, which is accumulating interest while she is in school. She has a background in biology, genetics, and chemistry, and she may get a bachelor's degree in medical technology. However, she would like to be a social worker.

Even with the loan, Zeinab could only afford to take one class per semester. This is where MicroGrants stepped in. Struggling to pay for college, Zeinab spoke to Joe Selvaggio about the high cost of tuition. He sympathized and encouraged her to apply for a $1,000 MicroGrant, which she has used to help her continue her education.

In addition to commitments as a student and her job at PPL, Zeinab spends what free time she has trying to help the people of Somaliland. Since declaring independence from Somalia, Somaliland has received little financial support from wealthier countries. It is so poor that it is unable to provide education for most of its children. In 1994, Zeinab returned to Somalia and Somaliland for two weeks. She described it as a disaster. She said it looked as though a tornado had blown though. There was no running water or electricity. There have been improvements in infrastructure since then, but there are still no public schools or libraries.

To help the people of her country, Zeinab and her friends established an organization called Educational Opportunities for Somaliland. "In my experience," she said, "I've seen a lot of problems from afar because of civil wars and lack of education." One of the biggest issues is the lack of books available to university students. "There are two or three textbooks for 100 students," she said. This is clearly not sufficient to sustain serious higher learning. Zeinab has partnered with an organization called Books for Africa, which will collect appropriate books for the project. But they have asked Zeinab and her group to raise $9,000 to cover the costs of shipping. They are currently working toward this goal.

Zeinab is trying to share the good fortune she has had in the United States with people struggling in Somaliland. "The busier you are, the more productive you are," she says, proud of the organization she founded. It was her father's spirit of generosity that motivated her to reach out to the people of her country. It all started when her father called her after she moved to the United States. He asked her to send $200 every month to former neighbors in Somaliland. The husband had died, leaving an uneducated wife and nine children. Zeinab was hesitant at first because she was facing her own financial difficulties, but decided to do it anyway. "The money I send every month to support this family means a lot to me," she said. Zeinab feels that if she helps even one child, she will feel like she has made a difference.

Zeinab's future goal is to finish her degree. And each day she strives "to help out the people who need help, and find them resources," which she does at PPL. She also hopes to return to Somaliland to see her family and neighbors, and also to observe how things have changed since her visit in 1994.

Zeinab faces many challenges, but she has the motivation to overcome them. There is no doubt that she will one day complete her degree program at the University of Minnesota and meet her fundraising goals to send books to Somaliland. Zeinab is grateful to the people who are supporting MicroGrants. "They are helping out a lot of people who really need help," she says. By investing in Zeinab, MicroGrants is encouraging, with a financial boost, a woman who is selflessly helping people in the Twin Cities, and in Africa.

*Reported by Cathy Bader*
*July 17, 2007*

The table below is typical of those created from the data
collected for each MicroGrants recipient.

| | |
|---|---|
| Age, Gender | 48, Female |
| Home zip code | 55113 |
| Marital Status | Married |
| Dependents | 5 |
| Yearly Income | $20,000 |
| Change in income since receiving grant? | No |
| Education | GED, nursing school, nursing certificate |
| Race/Ethnicity | African American |
| Obstacles to Employment | None |
| Health Insurance | Yes |
| Government Assistance | No |
| Employer/Position | Abbott Northwestern Hospital/ Nursing Assistant |

BOOTSTRAPPING THROUGH LEARNING

VENUS AGBAY

# Altruistic Little Powerhouse

Venus Agbay's apartment might be mistaken for a grammar school for girls: Rows of tiny shoes are arranged in perfect order next to the door, and stuffed animals are arrayed neatly on shelves. But the only occupant is a small, smiling twenty-two-year-old woman whose shirt reads, "Plant a Tree: Make Mom Proud." Yet even though Venus is a tiny woman, she has been able to carry her family towards a better life. She has become self-sufficient herself, while enabling her brothers and cousin to take steps toward independence as well. She used her MicroGrant to expand opportunities for herself and her family.

A few years ago, Venus's Filipina mother married an American man, and she wanted to bring Venus and her two brothers to America. Immigration laws make that hard for family members over 21. Because Venus's older brother was 23, he had to stay in the Philippines, but her 18-year-old brother was allowed to come. In March 2005, when her stepfather was allowed send for her, Venus was almost 21. Her application had not been finalized. Then, five days before her 21st birthday, it was approved and she was allowed to enter the US with legal immigrant status. Venus barely made it to America before the deadline.

Soon after she arrived, she started working at a restaurant, where she made only $7 per hour and could work only 30 hours per week. It was difficult for her to support herself on such low wages.

She applied for a MicroGrant and was accepted. Instead of using the money solely on herself, she spent some of it for shoes and clothes for her two brothers so that they could look presentable. She used what remained to pursue her passion, singing. She bought CD graphics, CDs, a CD-player, a portable amplifier, and the microphone she needs to perform. She also bought a dress to wear for singing jobs.

In February 2007, after receiving the grant, Venus got a job at the Ford Motor Company installing gas pedals and putting screws in the doors of Ford Rangers. The work is physically demanding and tiring, but she says it is worth it because of the paycheck. Her salary was $20 per hour and she worked about 50 hours per week.

Her take-home pay of $2,800 per month enabled her and her extended family to take important steps. She rented an apartment, where she lives with her younger brother. He is attending a high school for immigrants. Venus believes in the value of education and, she won't allow him to get a job (except during the summer) until he finishes his education.

Venus also sends money back to the Philippines to help her older brother. Her generosity is best illustrated in the way she is helping a young cousin, also in the Philippines. The cousin's mother died and the father deserted the family, so the girl had no one to look out for her. Venus offered a helping hand by paying for her college tuition—even though she doesn't have enough money for her own college education.

Venus is trying to save for her own college tuition. The Ford plant is scheduled to close, and Venus will lose her job. She hopes that by then she will have saved enough to finance her education. If she hasn't, she plans to take out loans to go to school to study accounting and banking. In the Philippines, she had useful experience in the insurance industry, which could help her in the future.

The past fifteen months have been a whirlwind. She came to America, struggled to survive, but now has found a job that enables her to thrive. She is too busy and exhausted to sing professionally on a regular basis with a group, but she has had solo performances at community events, such as a recent fundraiser for the Philippine community. Venus is not satisfied with just making her own life better. She generously helps others get on the road to success.

*Reported by Daniel E. Geoffrion*
*June 23, 2007*

MARIAN ADEN

# Struggling Toward the American Dream

Marian Aden is a 43-year-old Somali immigrant. She has been raising seven children single-handedly since her husband left her and went back to Africa. It was difficult for the MicroGrants intern to reach her because she was busy either working or taking care of her children. But she eventually found time to talk about her life.

Marian graduated from high school in Somalia and in 1993 moved to California, where she studied Child Development at San Diego Community College. She later moved to Minnesota with her husband and has lived here ever since. They separated several years ago, and her husband subsequently left the country because he did not want to pay child support.

Marian's seven children are doing remarkably well, especially considering that they are all supported by Marian's income of $24,000 a year. Marian works as a teacher's aide at the Twin Cities International Elementary School in St. Paul. Her three older children are in college—two at the University of Minnesota and one at the Minneapolis Community and Technical College. They pay for their tuition through scholarships and work-study programs.

Marian says that college is still costly because "textbooks are expensive." Her other four children are in school: one is a senior in high school, one is in 7th grade, one is in 4th grade, and the youngest is in kindergarten. The state provides day care for the youngest child while Marian works. Since she only works during the school year, Marian stays home with the children during the summer.

In the spring of 2007, Marian's car broke down. Without a car, it was difficult for her to commute from her home in North Minneapolis to her job in St. Paul. It was also hard for her to transport the children to school and to extracurricular activities. A friend picked her up and dropped her off at work, but the timing was hard to coordinate. This could not be a long-term solution, but Marian did not have enough money to fix her car.

She heard about MicroGrants from Tina Wombacher, director of employment training at Project for Pride in Living (PPL). In May 2007, Marian applied for and received a $1,000 grant. She used all of the money to repair her car. The final bill was actually more than $1,000, but Marian was able to make up the difference. The help that the MicroGrant provided enabled Marian to maintain her work and life balance.

Marian hopes to return to college for further study of child development. She will then have the credentials to earn a higher salary to better support her children. Currently she is still struggling financially. Marian tries to save a bit each month, but ends up using all of her paycheck for necessities.

Recently the rent for her house in St. Paul increased to $500 a month. She had signed a one-year lease as part of a Section 8 housing (partially government-subsidized) contract, and consequently cannot move out. When the lease expires, Marian wants to move back to another Minneapolis neighborhood where she has a more supportive community of friends.

Marian says that she "tries to be strong, keep her job, and be a good mom." She has undergone many hardships. Nevertheless, she is determined to keep going and is grateful to MicroGrants for giving her the help she needed at a difficult time. As she said, "MicroGrants helped me a lot and allowed me to sustain myself and my family."

*Reported by Winnie Tong*
*July 20, 2008*

SHANTEZ BENJAMIN

# Focused

Shantez Benjamin is a 27-year-old, single, African American woman. She spends most of her time working and studying accounting. She lives in an affordable apartment with her brother in Richfield, Minnesota.

After graduating from high school, she earned an associate in arts and sciences degree, and has been studying online through the University of Phoenix for three and a half years. In the fall, she plans to start taking classes at Metropolitan State University. With financial aid, she will be able to complete her B.A. in accounting in six months.

Shantez works part-time as an accountant at Beatrice, David & Associates, a small company that provides financial services for other businesses. She has been there since 2000. Since last year, her income increased from $20,000 to about $35,000 a year.

Although she has no dependents in the US, she has four sisters and four brothers who, like her mother, live in the Caribbean.

Shantez has several goals for the coming years. In a year, she hopes to gain more experience as an accountant and complete her B.A. degree. In five years, she hopes to complete a master's degree, pass the certified public accountant (CPA) exam, and be an auditor at her company.

Though Shantez has a good salary and financial aid, going to school is still expensive. She said that she learned to "cut out want from need." Gaia Richards, of Midtown Global Market, referred Shantez to MicroGrants in a time of need.

In January 2008, Shantez applied for and received a MicroGrant. She used $250 for a printer, so that she would not have to run to work to print out homework assignments; the remaining $750 helped pay for tuition. Shantez said that MicroGrants changed her perspective on money. She said that she has tried to manage her finances more effectively since receiving the grant, putting money aside every month.

She said that the MicroGrant will help her to "complete my goal and my dream of being an accountant." Now, Shantez wants to give back to the community because of the help she has received. She has done some accounting work for nonprofits in the past and plans to continue this work after she has finished her master's degree. Shantez is grateful to Micro-Grants. She said that it is "a wonderful program that helps people better their lives."

*Reported by Winnie Tong*
*July 7, 2008*

Meng (Mikayla) Che

# Pursuing the American Dream

Meng Che is a 25-year-old Chinese woman who was drawn to America by Cupid. She received a MicroGrant in 2006, and has since then begun to achieve many of her life's goals.

Meng graduated from high school and college in China. She completed her B.A. in law at Shandong University about five years ago. After she passed the law examination, she was able to work as a judicial assistant at the Shandong Supreme Court. This was a high-level position with a good salary, especially for a graduate student. If she had stayed in China, Meng could have become a judge after gaining a few more years of experience and passing a series of examinations.

In 2003, however, her life changed. She met and fell in love with David Schladt, an American who was in China as an exchange student for the summer. But David had to return to the University of Minnesota to complete his Ph.D. in plant biology. At the time, Meng was finishing her second year of law school at Shandong University. She graduated a year later and joined David in America. They married during her first week in the US.

Life in America proved more difficult than Meng had expected. She had earned a good income in China, whereas in America she and David were struggling just to get by. They lived in a tiny apartment and had no financial support from their parents. Meng could not get a work permit or a green card since she had just arrived, so the couple sustained themselves on David's meager financial aid of $1,000 a month.

In 2006, Meng met Joe Selvaggio. She said that after talking to him about her situation and her goals, Joe thought she "had great potential." Meng received a MicroGrant of $1,000 in August 2006. With this support, Meng bought books to prepare for the LSAT, paid the application fee for the University of Minnesota Law School, and bought a lot of groceries. In Meng's words, "though it was not a lot of money, it really helped out."

Shortly after she received that grant, Meng also received a work permit. For awhile she did odd jobs such as being a restaurant hostess. In her spare time, Meng volunteered at the Hennepin County Adult Probation Center. Later she was hired by the Foley & Mansfield law firm as a legal assistant. Now, she works as a legal assistant at the Valspar Corporation. She says she loves the job, although her pay is low because she is still a student.

In 2007, Meng was admitted to the Masters in Law for Foreign Attorneys program at the University of Minnesota. She maintained a 3.8 GPA and was the speaker at the graduation ceremony in May 2008.

More good news arrived recently: Meng was accepted into a two-year Juris Doctor program at the University of Minnesota Law School. After that, she plans to take the Minnesota Bar Exam to become certified as a lawyer.

Meng has worked hard to get to where she is today. She said that life was really difficult when she first arrived in America. Now, two years after receiving the MicroGrant, Meng has come a long way. Although money is still tight, the future looks promising. Meng is grateful to MicroGrants for the boost that got her through a tough time. Meng says that MicroGrants gave her "the first hope and helped her believe she really has the potential to reach her goals."

Meng and David clearly seem destined for lives of accomplishment, but a timely intervention gave them a needed boost.

*Reported by Winnie Tong*
*July 27, 2008*

ANNETTE HOLDEN

# Unexpected Talents

Annette Holden might easily have become a permanent fixture in the widely scorned culture of the "welfare queens" of the late 20th century, when well-intentioned programs of public assistance often turned into unsupervised grab bags.

Annette paid the price for her early association with welfare fraud: a felony conviction. But she learned from the experience, straightened out her life under enormous handicaps, and ultimately fought and won a battle to erase that felony stigma from her record.

She now earns $42,000 a year as a respected administrative assistant with the Medtronic Company today. Her five children have grown up and she has 16 grandchildren.

Far from becoming the face of the welfare fraud that forced radical reforms in the 1970s and 80s, today she is a poster child for thousands of women who have worked their way out of humiliation, rescued their families from poverty and crime, and who command admiration today as genuine winners and role models for their children and friends.

An African American, Annette grew up in a poor part of Chicago, where she began receiving welfare in 1977. It was difficult for her to provide a safe environment for herself and her five children. When her oldest son turned 12, the gangs in her Chicago neighborhood began to harass him. Fearing for his life, Annette moved to Minneapolis in 1985 because it offered a safer living environment. While in Minneapolis, Annette remained on welfare.

In 1988 Annette discovered Project for Pride in Living (PPL), an organization that assists low-income individuals and families to work toward self-sufficiency by providing housing, jobs and training. After working with PPL for a year, she completed a GED. "I always knew I could learn,"

Annette said, "I just didn't have the opportunity." While working with PPL, she discovered that she loves learning. She now considers her strongest skills to be her ability to grasp things quickly, to work with computers, and to adapt to changes. It was something she would never have imagined when she first moved to Minneapolis.

Nevertheless, Annette was still struggling to keep her family together in the late 80s and early 90s. At the time, she was in survival mode, single with five young children. In 1989, worried that she would not be able to provide for her family on her meager salary without welfare, she didn't inform the government that she had a job. As a result, she was convicted of welfare fraud in 1992. After being convicted of a felony, Annette said, "I was stuck for years because I got turned away from a lot of jobs." From 1992 until 1998, Annette and her family were on welfare when she was between jobs. She got her last welfare check in 1998.

To clear her name, Annette filed a lawsuit to expunge all records of her conviction. She succeeded, and her record was cleared in 2002, removing a major obstacle to finding employment opportunities. Eventually, Annette was able to get her life together. Over the years she landed jobs as a patient scheduler, administrative assistant, and executive assistant at several hospitals and clinics and at a treatment facility. In the spring of 2006, Annette completed her associate degree in business administration from National American University.

In March 2007, Annette began working as a human resources administrative assistant for Hennepin Faculty Associates, making around $30,000 annually. She wanted to do more, and sought advanced employment opportunities. Her goal was to become a human resources manager within four years. She decided to enroll in the Minnesota School of Business (MSB) to obtain a bachelor's degree in human resource management and business administration in July 2007.

Annette's precarious financial situation made it hard for her to begin classes at MSB. At the time, she was paying off past student loans and supporting her two grandchildren, Shaleece and Quintez, who were living with her. She did not have the money to buy books and pay for two of her classes. In June 2007, Annette received a MicroGrant. She used half of it to pay for books, and half of it to help pay for tuition.

Now, Annette's life is falling into place. In October 2007, she began working as an administrative assistant at Medtronic. Her annual salary increased by about $12,000. She also moved from an apartment to a town-home in April 2008. In addition, she intends to finish the three-year program at MSB in December 2010. Because Shaleece and Quintez moved back in with their mother in fall 2007, it is easier for Annette to pay for her tuition while working and focusing on her studies. In three to four years, Annette hopes to attain her dream of becoming a human resources manager. She is also considering opening up a small daycare in her home to improve her financial situation. Annette credits MicroGrant's help. She believes that the grant program is a "very wonderful program for short-term emergencies" and a hand up, not a handout.

*Reported by Sarah Hill*
*July 9, 2008*

## Mercy Ollor, interview with Godwin Ollor (husband)

# The Academic Bootstrap

A 48-year-old Nigerian woman, Mercy Ollor, received a grant in October of 2007 to help pay for her preparation for the Nursing Council Licensure Examination. At the time of her MicroGrants interview, she was studying for her examination.

So her husband, Godwin, came instead to tell about the family's tumultuous history and about their five children. They were refugees who immigrated to America in 1998 after being driven from their native Ogoni village during assaults on the Ogoni by the police arm of the Ethiopian military. Many people died. Fearing for their lives as Ogonis, the Ollors lived for two years in a refugee camp before being granted asylum and obtaining their green cards to live in the United States.

The American chapters in the family's saga began in Memphis, Tennessee, where they lived for three years while working to lift themselves into the American mainstream. These were people who did not come to America for sanctuary alone. They wanted to contribute, to enter the American community—they wanted to work and to achieve.

Godwin was accepted by the University of Mary in Bismarck, ND, where the family settled in 2001. He received his master's degree in 2004. Looking for wider opportunities than were available in Bismarck, he moved with his family to St. Paul. But the only jobs available to both Godwin and Mercy offering a living wage were $15-an-hour positions as nursing assistants. That might have been enough for two people, but there were five children to consider, the oldest of whom coveted a college education and had the drive and intellect to earn advanced degrees.

But working as a nursing assistant, Godwin Ollor told the Micro-Grants people, was not what he had envisioned when he undertook his graduate studies. There was no real opportunity to advance on the wage scale, he said, no jobs paying enough to raise five children with any hope of a future. It was difficult for the couple to pay for such basic needs as utilities and food.

A year ago Mercy decided to become a nurse to ease the financial stress. For this she would have to pass the Nursing Council's examination.

Godwin's presentation was persuasive. MicroGrants opened the door with a $1,000 grant that permitted his wife to enroll in the Kaplan test preparation program.

In the meantime she had begun attending Minneapolis Community College to become a nurse. Their oldest daughter, Pepe, 21, enrolled at the University of Minnesota and will graduate in 2009. The oldest son, Obarijima, 19, last year completed his freshman year at St. Xavier University in Chicago. Amebeobari, their 18-year-old daughter graduated from high school in 2008 and is attending the University of Illinois in Chicago. The youngest children, Ngochinyan, 15, and Ntonobari, 11, are living at home.

Although their older children received scholarships for college, Mercy and Godwin are still paying for textbooks while providing for their youngest two children. To ease their financial difficulties, they began saving money by using less air conditioning and paying more attention to their spending habits. Although the couple still have many bills to pay, they are thankful for the MicroGrant for providing Mercy the opportunity to do well on her examination and help the family with their expenses.

*Reported by Sarah Hill*
*July 9, 2008*

Cleaveroy Benjamin

# Planning and Progress

Cleaveroy Benjamin came to Rich-field, MN with a dream of owning an electrical business. He attends Minne-sota Community and Technical College (MCTC), where he is studying to become an electrician.

In 2004, prior to enrolling at MCTC, Cleaveroy studied at North Hennepin Community College. But tuition at North Hennepin was more than he could manage, so he had to drop out. He started classes at MCTC in 2007, and he recently completed the first year of a two-year program. Once he finishes his courses, he will try to find a job as an electrician at one of the companies that partner with the college to find new employees.

Cleaveroy applied for a MicroGrant in November 2007 to help cover his school expenses. He received $1,000 and used some of the money to purchase books and several tools he needed. He applied the rest to his tuition. The grant, along with $400 in financial aid that he received from MCTC, helped Cleaveroy pay the $2,000 tuition.

In order to cover the rest of his tuition and other expenses, Cleaveroy works part-time during the school year and full-time during the summer as a detailer for Westside Volkswagen in St. Louis Park. During the school year, Cleaveroy can only work for five hours or less a day because he must be at school from 8:00 am until 2:00 pm. Even with limited hours, he struggles to find time to complete his homework, which hurts his GPA. When he was studying at North Hennepin and not working, Cleaveroy's GPA was over half a point higher than it is at MCTC. Cleaveroy must keep his after-school job, however, in order to cover basic expenses during the school year.

Cleaveroy lives with his wife and sister in Richfield. In the summer their financial situation becomes much less stressful. His full-time income, along with the money his wife makes working part-time, allows the couple to save $600 to $800 every month. This offsets added costs when school is in session.

Cleaveroy and his wife both believe strongly in his ability to graduate from MCTC and achieve his goal of becoming an electrician. His wife explained: "Cleaveroy is good at making a plan and sticking to it, despite ups and downs." He is determined to earn his degree so that he will be qualified to do the work. If his life becomes too busy and his grades begin to slip, Cleaveroy knows he will need to put more effort into his schoolwork in order to bring his grades back up again. He knows it won't be easy.

The MicroGrant Cleaveroy received in November 2007 allowed him to stay on course with his plan. The $1,000 meant he did not have to drop out of school in order to find the money to continue his education, as was the case when he had to leave North Hennepin Community College. Before receiving the grant, Cleaveroy used to worry about how he would pay for school, but the money he received from MicroGrants lightened his financial burden. As Cleaveroy explained, the grant took off some of the weight, enabling him to continue to pursue his career goals.

*Reported by Berit Johnson*
*July 31, 2008*

Tasha Kirk

# Breaking a Cycle

Tasha Kirk grew up with her sister under the care of her single mother, Ruby Kirk-Powers. As Tasha explained, she is very grateful to her mother, who "gave up a lot to see to it that we were well taken care of and educated." Today Tasha understands first-hand the sacrifices her mother made, now that she has also become a single mother of two.

Having gone through this "cycle of sacrifice" that passed from one generation to the next in their African American family, Tasha and Ruby are determined to break the pattern for Tasha's children. They started their own travel Agency, MinneApple Travel, in hopes of establishing a self-sustaining business that will provide reliable financial support for their family. Tasha hopes that the new company will ensure that her children "don't have to give up on their dreams just to get by or to support their families."

In May of 2007, Tasha and Ruby applied for a MicroGrant in order to cover some of the start-up costs for their new business. They received $1,000, which they used to purchase promotional materials, including business cards and flyers, and to pay for the monthly hosting fee for their company's website.

Although MinneApple Travel is not yet the well-established business that Tasha believes it will one day become, the MicroGrant has helped her keep the travel agency to maintain its early growth. Tasha is reinvesting all of the agency's profits back into MinneApple Travel, while she is able to provide for her family with the $40,000 a year she earns working as an asset administrator for Ambergris Financial. Tasha is very appreciative of the MicroGrant because, as she explained, "it's allowing me to be an entrepreneur while maintaining a household and working full time." This in turn will allow her to break the cycle that Tasha and her mother have experienced as single parents.

*Reported by Berit Johnson*
*August 5, 2008*

# 4
# Art

MANY OF US TAKE art for granted, seeing it as a nice, entertaining frill—essentially a pleasant distraction, a diversion.

But is it?

The earliest humans painted cave walls, thumped on logs, and engaged in rituals that were the museums, symphonies, and theaters of our predecessors. The instincts that produce them rise today against other forces that counsel survival or avoidance of frills.

Art is irrepressible. It is the expression of the deepest urges of the human animal, and it is essential to survival.

In the pages ahead we find the stories of those who specifically try to escape their dilemmas through art. Art becomes the expression of irrepressible inner urgings. It is not a frill. It is a necessity.

Rev. Yosef Hunter

# Death, Life and Art

Rev. Yosef Hunter is an intelligent, 54-year-old nursing home chaplain with a great sense of humor. During a meeting at the local Perkins, he teased an intern about the amount of food he consumed during our short interview, joking, "God bless you if you can eat all that." While the intern devoured the "Tremendous Twelve," Rev. Hunter spoke eloquently, and as his story unfolded, it was impossible not to be caught up in his tale.

He grew up in New Orleans and attended Louisiana State University for his undergraduate degree. Then he moved to New York City, and in 1982 he graduated from Yeshiva University, an orthodox Jewish school, with a master's degree in counseling. After that, he returned to New Orleans, and his home was robbed twice. Although he had a good, secure job, he was fed up with the crime and the heat. In 1986 he decided to move to Minnesota to pursue his career in counseling.

Rev. Hunter worked as the clinical director of a large counseling agency. He advised a variety of adult clients, including middle-class suburbanites and people who were incarcerated or just coming out of the criminal justice system. At the same time, he worked as the director of social service for another agency, and was burning out fast. He wanted to go into the ministry, but money was stopping him. He was paid $75 per hour for counseling and didn't want to give that up.

The turning point came when his oldest daughter was dying of cancer. Only 25, she owned rental property, and even in the hospice she was on the phone making business calls. He sat by her side and listened to her conversations. When she got off the phone she said, "Dad, I know I have cancer. I know it's terminal. But God gave me a life and as long as I'm alive I'm going to live my life." Her example helped him make the decision to do what he felt called to do and to stop worrying about money.

Although he was ordained at Union Seminary in 1994, Rev. Hunter didn't begin working as a chaplain until 2002. He had always wanted to work at a nursing home, but initially he had doubts. Now he uses his counseling experience as well as his ministerial training when he is speaking with nursing home residents, and they appreciate his ability to listen. His responsibilities as chaplain include conducting worship services, Bible studies, and prayer groups. And Rev. Hunter administers pastoral counseling to residents of many religious backgrounds.

After his daughter died, he also began paying attention to his creative urges. He started making cut-paper silhouettes. He enjoyed this activity and found it therapeutic. He heard about MicroGrants from a friend and decided to apply. As a chaplain, he didn't have much spare money, but he wanted to continue his hobby. Rev. Hunter received a MicroGrant and used it to buy supplies: paper, knives, and frames.

Not long after that, he came to the conclusion that he was not as good making silhouettes as he'd thought. He met people in the field and realized he knew nothing about presentation. Eventually he learned how to make his artwork look more professional by matting his pieces and putting a white cloth on his table at craft shows to make his booth look more attractive.

One day when he was sitting in church, gazing at the stained glass windows, he had an inspiration. He thought, "what would it be like if I drew a stained glass window design on paper and cut it out?" Now, instead of making silhouettes, he does stained glass cutouts. First he draws the window design on paper. Then he cuts it out with an Exact-o knife. Finally he mounts the paper cut-out in a frame and puts a mirror behind it to give it a 3-D effect. The whole process takes from seven to ten hours.

So far, his new creations have been well received at art fairs and bring in around $2,000 a year. He knew he had to come up with a different approach because many people were doing silhouettes. At the moment, he doesn't know of anyone else making stained glass window cutouts. Rev. Hunter tries to go to four craft shows per year, and friends have encouraged him to enter the contest at the state fair. His artwork continues to bring him pleasure and wants to continue in the future.

Without the MicroGrant to buy supplies, Rev. Hunter would not have been able to explore this art form. He is gradually refining his technique.

He wants to go to more craft shows and is hoping that his artwork can become a substantial part of his income.

Rev. Hunter enjoys what he is doing. He is fond of his job at the nursing home and truly loves creating his beautiful cutouts. His daughter's death moved him to follow his true calling—to work as a minister, enriching the lives of nursing home residents. MicroGrants enabled Rev. Hunter to create beautiful artwork that not only has therapeutic benefits for him, but also is beginning to augment his income.

*Reported by Cathy Bader*
*June 21, 2007*

Heidi Arneson

# Dysfunction, Art and Progress

Heidi Arneson compares her life to a plate-spinning act. Like a performer who keeps several plates whirling simultaneously, Heidi moves quickly between projects, giving each the momentum to continue spinning on its own. "My life is like the eye of a hurricane," she explains. "Even though it sounds like I am doing a lot—and I am—I like to keep things really simple." Surrounded by the murmur of quiet conversation in the Second Moon Coffee Café, Heidi speaks a mile a minute as she tells her personal story.

For the past thirty years, she has enriched the Minneapolis area with artistic workshops and solo performance pieces. Although the life of a freelance artist has been spiritually fulfilling, Heidi concedes that she has faced a constant struggle to make ends meet. Thanks to the support of local organizations, including MicroGrants, Heidi is able to maintain a wide array of projects and continues to create new artistic outlets for herself and for the community.

Heidi has always lived in Minnesota. When she was just a child, her family's values as well as their vices inspired her to pursue an artistic career.

"Their love and creativity inspired me to be a trailblazer, while the alcoholism and violence inspired me to use my creativity to build a safe space for others to carve their own paths."

When she turned 18, Heidi moved to Minneapolis to pursue her artistic ambitions. After moving, Heidi got married and had her only child. But she soon divorced and was left to raise the young girl on her own. Then followed the usual struggle to support herself and her daughter. Tired of relying on government assistance, Heidi eventually found a "regular" part-time job as an actress and set designer at the Science Museum of Minnesota. Although she had to make some artistic sacrifices, Heidi enjoyed working for the museum and was grateful for the stable income.

In 1990 Heidi quit her job at the Science Museum to focus on her artistic goals. "I wanted to tell *my* story," she said. Drawing on her own experiences, Heidi created performance pieces and began offering workshops to help aspiring artists with the creative process. Although she received several grants in support of her efforts, Heidi continued to struggle financially during this time. "Sometimes I would tell my daughter, 'we need to eat brown rice for this week,'" she recalled. Undeterred, Heidi continued to expand her artistic programs within the Minneapolis area.

In 2006, she developed a plan to take her workshops to an entirely new community—the state prison system. Direct Action, an original program conceived by Heidi, is a performance workshop for inmates in correctional facilities. A $1,250 MicroGrant, approved in May 2006, helped set the program in motion.

When Heidi started the pilot workshop at Ramsey County Correctional Facility, she was unsure how the inmates would respond. "I was shocked at how willing they were," she recalled. "They just jumped right into it." Through Heidi's Direct Action workshops, inmates create spoken-word pieces about their lives that they perform in front of the entire prison community. Since finishing the initial pilot run, Heidi has completed four month-long workshops at the Ramsey County facility. She believes that Direct Action is helping the inmates to grow personally and spiritually by empowering them to tell their stories and gain insights in the process.

In November 2006, Heidi received a second MicroGrant that allowed her to reach more people with her workshops. With the second grant, Heidi created a new Direct Action program for local children, many of whom had immigrated to America recently from refugee camps. Heidi claims that without the help of MicroGrants, Direct Action "would not have been possible."

By contributing to Direct Action, MicroGrants has enabled Heidi to reach two unique populations and help them grow through personal expression. Today, she continues to pursue a wide array of artistic projects. In addition to Direct Action, Heidi is working on her first novel and performing solo pieces throughout the Twin Cities.

Although she does not earn a substantial income as an artist, Heidi is content to lead a simple life with very modest living expenses. With the financial support of local grants and organizations, she plans to continue creating artistic opportunities for herself and the community. Now 48, she has learned how central the link is between art and life.

*Reported by Jamie Kallestad*
*July 26, 2007*

TRICIA HAYNES

# Puppetry With a Message

"Terrific! Great! Excellent!" These are words used by Minnesota teachers to describe the Tricia & the Toonies Enviro-Show, created and performed by 51-year-old Tricia Haynes. Tricia's passion for music, her desire to make a difference, and her love for children inspired her to create an educational puppet show geared towards children from kindergarten to sixth grade. Tricia travels throughout Minnesota using her puppets and creativity to entertain and educate children about the importance of recycling and protecting the environment.

Tricia was born in Toronto, Canada, but her family moved to Long

Island, NY, when she was a year old. She lived there until she graduated from high school and then traveled around the country, eventually settling in Canada at the age of 19. It was there that she began her career of singing and songwriting. When she was 21, she moved to Dallas, TX, where she heard there was work in films and commercials. She got a job as an extra on the TV show "Dallas," then went to Dallas Community College for four years, but ended up with too many electives and not enough required courses to graduate. But the experience helped her deepen and define her true interests.

Tricia moved to Minneapolis in 1989, hoping to make a living in music, theater, and the arts, without being caught up in the nightlife that's often associated with those pursuits. She had no idea how to pursue that kind of career, however, and so she fell back on what she'd done in Toronto: singing and songwriting. She worked in dinner theaters and sang in bands. She was frustrated because this work did not seem meaningful to her.

"I began conceptualizing a fun and educational theater for kids, using puppets and music and comedy," she said. "I was imagining what would be a fun way to learn, and it turned into a path toward making a living for me." Tricia began what is now known as Tricia & the Toonies in 1991.

She wanted her program to teach children about self-esteem, kindness, and family values. She performed in parks, at company parties, and at libraries. She found out during the first year of library tours that "we had something unique that really made the kids laugh and learn." The business was touch-and-go in the beginning because it was unique, but people began to give her a chance.

When Tricia performed her first show in Crystal, MN, she realized that it was impossible for her to run the whole show on her own. She needed someone to work the puppets. After going through several puppeteers, she finally found Pete, who has been working with her for the last fifteen years. "We have done thousands of shows and we never tire of it. It's kind of a miracle," she marvels.

In the beginning, Pete worked the puppets onstage while Tricia, in addition to performing, handled all the finances offstage and ran virtually every other aspect of the business. She soon discovered that she was working 80 hours per week and was constantly trying to juggle her time. "Most of my clients were city, state, county, and school organizatioins, so they were all tax-funded programs. Due to all the budget cuts—and there have been many—sometimes two or three clients needed to split the bill for a performance. This added a lot of extra administrative complexity and time in the office.

MicroGrants stepped in when Tricia desperately needed a hand. Receiving a $1,000 MicroGrant gave Tricia the courage and the extra funds to hire someone to work for her on a part-time basis. Her assistant handles daily tasks, such as finding out where grant money is coming from, researching where to write letters of inquiry, and contacting fiscal agents. Working 15 hours per week, Tricia's assistant has been effective and efficient. She hired him in January 2007 and he is still working for her as of this report. She says, "MicroGrants continues to work, even though the money has been spent."

Tricia's current shows focus on environmental issues because there is funding for those kinds of programs. Funding for character education seems to be drying up. "It's become about the environment because that's where the focus is." Children and teachers alike are enjoying her shows. "Reviews we get from the teachers are off the map every year," she notes. And after the show, children even want to go out and clean the schoolyard!

In the future Tricia would like to develop a health and wellness show for kids. Tricia marvels that she has been able to keep her show going all these years. "Fortunately, it's still a joy to do," she says. Tricia is thankful for receiving the grant because it gives her more time to do projects she finds meaningful. She was able to volunteer at several hospitals and work with children. "I love to make them giggle when they're not feeling good," she says. "It's just the best thing in the world."

Tricia Haynes' work benefits the community in more ways than one. Her presence in the schools and her positive influence on Minnesota youth will be felt for years to come. By investing in Tricia, MicroGrants is making an investment in the environment and the community. She is a determined woman who will find a way to keep her program afloat. "People think I'm crazy to get up in front of 350 fifth graders," she says, "but it's just a joy." Hopefully, because of a boost from MicroGrants, Tricia can continue to be a shining light in the community.

*Reported by Cathy Bader*
*July 23, 2007*

Deborah VanderEyk

# Self-Expression and Growth

Deborah VanderEyk, single and "multi-cultural," has a passion for helping others. With over 20 years of experience in social services, she continues to devote her energy and talents to enriching her community. "I've always tried to maintain a balanced between social work and art education," she says. "Those are the two things that are most important to me." Deborah is 57 years old and currently works as both a substitute teacher and homecare provider in Sauk Rapids, Minnesota. In addition, she offers workshops for children from low-income and immigrant families.

Deborah is a painter and a published poet, but she wishes she could do more. Because she suffers from fibromyalgia, a chronic syndrome affecting the muscles and bones, Deborah has learned to live with limitations. "The only drawback is that I can't do as much as I would like to," she says. With the support of MicroGrants, Deborah has acquired important skills through computer, photography, and writing classes. As an artist, she appreciates the opportunity to grow and is eager to share her knowledge with the children she teaches.

When Deborah was growing up, religion was her major motivation for helping others. In recent years, she has adopted a more secular philosophy of social service. "We live in a society in which we need to work together," she says. "To be self-absorbed prevents the connections we need."

After earning a bachelor's degree in social research, Deborah moved to Minneapolis and embarked on a difficult, yet rewarding, career path. Deborah spent two years in the Peace Corps and ten years working with Native American organizations. During the 1990s she became seriously ill and moved to St. Cloud to recover. For three years, Deborah was incapacitated due to her illness. Finally able to work again, Deborah spent several years in Colorado before moving back to Minnesota in 2001.

Since returning to Minnesota, Deborah has worked hard to cultivate creative opportunities for children in the St. Cloud area. She designed workshops for children from low-income and immigrant families and believes that she has helped them gain self-confidence. "Its amazing how much kids can learn through the arts," she comments. "It helps them identify who they are." Deborah saw an opportunity to start a creative writing workshop, but she felt that she needed to deepen her skills. She wanted to take some classes, but couldn't afford them.

Deborah applied for a MicroGrant in November 2006. With the funding she was able to take computer classes through St. Cloud Community Education and pay for photography instruction with a professional photographer. Soon after completing the courses, Deborah got a scholarship to attend a writing workshop at the University of Minnesota Split Rock Arts program. After she had finished, Deborah began developing a creative writing program for children in collaboration with two college professors.

Deborah will use computers and technology extensively in this new workshop, and she is grateful for the opportunity to become more proficient in these areas. Without the computer and photography training, Deborah would not have had the background to teach the workshop that she designed. At the time of the interview, Deborah was looking forward to presenting the new workshop for the first time. She believes that it can help immigrant children to "feel comfortable learning English and at the same time feel good about themselves."

Deborah does not expect to be able to retire any time soon. She enjoys substitute teaching and providing home healthcare. Thanks to the help from MicroGrants, she has gained technological skills and experience that will allow her to continue providing workshops and artistic opportunities for the St. Cloud community.

*Reported by Jamie Kallestad*
*July 25, 2007*

STEVEN BROOKS

# An Artist and His Patron

Steven Brook's house is filled with art. The 50-year-old artist's paintings cover almost every wall of his small, South Minneapolis home. He has a passion for art and is eager to share the knowledge and appreciation he has gained over many years. Between explaining why people buy kitsch "art" and discussing Bach, Steven tells his story.

Steven has played music since he was a child. He played the piano and drums, and after high school he wanted to get a degree in music. Grooming himself to become a professional musician, he went to a junior college to study music theory. During this time he played percussion, including timpani, with five community orchestras. When funding for the orchestras was cut, Steven decided to go back to college.

He enrolled at the University of California, San Diego (UCSD), but after a while he realized that he wasn't happy playing music any longer. He took a studio art class out of curiosity. Up to that point, in his mind, art was limited to Picasso. Although he enjoyed drawing, he had little understanding of art beyond that.

One Saturday afternoon when Steven was writing out a score for full orchestra, he realized that what he really wanted to do was change his major from music to art. After he switched majors, he actually progressed faster through his coursework. He finished his degree and then applied to graduate school. His goal was to become qualified to teach at the college level. With a good G.P.A. he was accepted at four of the six schools to which he applied. He decided to go back to UCSD. A full scholarship made it an easy choice.

Steven eventually graduated and moved to Minneapolis, where he has relatives. His M.F.A. qualified him to teach college courses, so after finding a cheap apartment, he began teaching downtown. He also worked as a guard at Walker Art Museum, where he met his wife. They married two years later, in 1989, and now have two boys, 8 and 13.

Early in the marriage, when the children were small, Steven worked at temporary jobs. He taught art classes at the School for Communication Arts and at Globe College. He believes that artists piece their lives together, and that the different jobs at different times during his life are those pieces.

While raising his children, Steven stopped painting to focus all of his attention on his sons. He and his wife traded off staying at home to watch the boys. He worked during the day, while she attended the university at night. They job-shared at a library for a year, and his wife eventually found a job working for Health Partners. Steven began teaching piano and quickly acquired students. It was a perfect arrangement because he could watch the boys during the day, and his wife could take over when he was giving piano lessons.

Steven wanted to return to painting to see where it would lead, but he was apprehensive. His life had changed; he needed to look again at his influences and what inspired him artistically. At about that time, he and his wife launched their own website. Steven took on the persona of a French chef and wrote articles about art, film, and food. (The website currently has some of his writing in addition to his art.)

He continued to try to find a way back into painting. He had the time, but economically, it seemed impossible. In those days, he was staying at home and looking after the children, working only part time.

Steven applied for a MicroGrant in October 2006 and received $500. The funding enabled him to buy equipment he needed to make the panels on which he paints. He also purchased gouache, a chalky white paint that he applies to the panels to create a suitable surface. He used half of the grant for tubes of color. Steven also spent part of the money toward a digital camera, which enables him to make his artwork more accessible. In addition to posting his paintings on the website, he can burn images onto a CD, which he will take to galleries to showcase his work.

With the equipment Steven bought, he is able to build panels faster. He also uses a watercolor technique that doesn't require mixing colors and allows him to complete a painting in eight or nine hours. Consequently, Steven's artistic output has increased. Before receiving the grant, Steven was able to produce only two paintings per year. In the eight months since receiving the grant in October of 2006, he has done seven. The grant helped Steven speed up the process, and now he is building a body of work.

Steven had a small show at Betsy's Coffee Shop in December 2005 and is now preparing for a larger exhibit. He is not looking for wealth, but he does need to support his family. He plans to continue teaching piano and painting. He is beginning to look for spaces and galleries to store his paintings because they are overflowing his house.

MicroGrants enabled Steven Brooks to continue building his collection of work. Without the help of the grant, it would have taken him years longer. He will continue to paint because it is what he loves to do. MicroGrants is moving him toward an exhibition of his paintings and the beginning of public recognition.

*Reported by Cathy Bader*
*June 22, 2007*

The table below is typical of those created from the data collected for each MicroGrants recipient.

| | |
|---|---|
| Age | 57 |
| Home zip code | 56379 |
| Marital Status | Single |
| Dependents | 0 |
| Yearly Income | $13,000 |
| Change in income since receiving grant? | No |
| Education | B.A. social research, B.S. art ed |
| Race/Ethnicity | Multiracial |
| Obstacles to Employment | Health issues, lack of computer skills |
| Health Insurance | Medical assistance |
| Government Assistance | Disability, Social Security |
| Employer/Position | Self-Substitute, Homecare, Workshops |

DANIEL COLEMAN

# A Star Aborning?

Young and energetic, Daniel Coleman radiates charisma and charm. They emerge spontaneously, and his ability to entertain shines, enhanced by his undergraduate studies in acting and mass communication. At 20 he has just finished his second year of community college and is looking for ways to build a career. After he completes his degree at Normandale Community College, he wants to get a master's degree in mass communication and business, and to explore where he can go with his performing talent.

The youngest of six children, Daniel developed a passion for entertaining, keeping his brothers and sisters amused. He loves cracking jokes, making people laugh, and telling stories. He has done public speaking and has performed in many plays and improvisations. He contributes to the community by mentoring and counseling youth as a volunteer at a local YMCA. He also works as a credit adviser at Target Financial Services, which he enjoys because he can help people.

But there were bills to pay as a full-time student. He heard about the opportunity that MicroGrants offered, applied and was accepted. As soon as he received his grant, he paid off his bills and immediately signed up for acting classes. Through those classes, he was able to gain clarity on where his principal interests lie and focus on them. He said, "I was just very fortunate. I was very happy to actually have the time to pursue something I love without being stressed all the time. Now I know what I want to do." He excelled in his classes and became a member of Phi Beta Kappa.

But he reached an even more important goal. The opportunity to act motivated him to go deeper into his education. He started investigating master's programs at Arizona State and New York University. "If I didn't have the chance to take the classes or get a chance to be in a play, how could I know what I want?"

Daniel credited MicroGrants with inspiring "a belief that one can actually do something and proceed, instead of being in the same position all their life." It enabled him to develop his natural talent and pursue his love of performing. He doesn't know what the future holds, but he might be found soon performing on a stage or speaking in front of audiences. This young man, believes his future is unlimited.

*Reported by Daniel E. Geoffrion*
*June 8, 2007*

SHANNAN HUGHES

# Troubadour

Shannan Hughes has two "true loves" in her life—music and history. The first was instilled by her parents on the family's dairy farm in Southeast Minnesota. But the second wasn't realized until she began taking American history courses "for fun" when she was a student at the University of Minnesota.

Although Shannan found many ways to pursue these interests in her life through church choirs and community activities, she never planned to make a living in either area—until now. During the past few years, Shannan's determination and skill, combined with a boost from MicroGrants, have allowed her to begin developing a career that draws on her knowledge of both music and history. Her new path has opened doors that put her in touch with many communities.

After completing a master's degree in American history at the University of Minnesota, Shannon found herself tens of thousands of dollars in debt. She needed a way to pay back the money. Starting with clerical work, she spent several years in temporary employment, barely managing to pay the bills, rent, and college loans. She describes these years as "a series of dead-end jobs" that left her unfulfilled. When she finally was able to finish paying off the loans, Shannan realized that if she was going to continue to struggle financially doing boring clerical work, she might just as well face the struggle doing something stimulating and rewarding.

For the past ten years, Shannan has been exploring ways to support herself with her talents and knowledge. In order to combine music and history into a marketable package, Shannan created a "one-woman-show" that combines storytelling with the music and history of the 1920s, 30s and 40s. She takes the show across the state of Minnesota, reaching out especially to rural communities. She also spent one summer teaching a workshop at the Guthrie Theatre in Minneapolis.

Although she has years of experience singing and playing piano tocomplement her academic credentials in American history, Shannan believes the biggest challenge in this line of work is "billing yourself as an expert."

The "hand-up" from MicroGrants made a huge difference. Because her income was low, Shannan couldn't afford to buy a computer. She relied on the Minneapolis Public Library to access the Internet and to find musical resources. She never knew if she was missing an e-mail message from a potential client when the library was closed. Also her ability to advertise was limited. With the money from the grant, Shannan has been able to publicize her program on a web page. The grant also paid for software that makes the business side of her program more efficient, and for an Internet connection to maintain contact with clients and potential venues. She is also beginning to accumulate her own reference library of musical scores and histories.

Although Shannan realizes that her one-woman-show still falls short of being self-sustaining, she is moving in the right direction. The Micro-Grant helped her to develop her business and to market herself professionally to attract more high-profile venues. She wishes that our society were structured in a way to give artists an easier time making a living. But she is resigned to the way things are. With the help from MicroGrants, Shannan is looking forward to the day when she can finally support herself with the work that she loves.

*Reported by Jamie Kallestad*
*June 12, 2007*

# 5
# Altruism and Spunk

THROUGHOUT THESE PAGES we encounter the stumbling, but striving, human spirit in all its colorful disarray. We should entertain no illusions that the MicroGrants constitute a final cure—a sure way out. But they are a lift and a prod.

Progress is almost always incremental and difficult. Often it is accompanied by stumbles. But we also find success here, and there is beauty in that.

Desiree Smith

# Multi-Tasking

Desiree Smith is a 37-year-old, single mother who currently earns just over $15,000 a year. She relies on monthly child support checks for her two-year-old son, Brynnan. Her financial status is unstable, but she's a tough cookie and dedicated to improving her current condition through education. Confidently, she asserts: "I know that where I am today won't last for long."

Two $1,000 grants from MicroGrants have played a big role in helping her get on track. In addition to being a part-time personal care assistant (PCA) at Affordable Professionals, Desiree is a full-time student at Metropolitan State University. She has completed her associate degree, and is on course to complete her bachelor's degree within the next year.

The first of the two grants went towards necessities for school: a laptop computer and software. The second grant covered some rent and allowed her to set up a savings account with a program called Match, which contributes an amount of money equal to what the client puts away. Desiree tries to save at least $25 to $50 a month, gradually weaving a safety net for herself and her son.

Desiree's studies severely limit the amount of time she can spend as a wage-earner, but she is committed to getting an education that will one day allow her to have a job that is both fulfilling and will give her financial security. She acknowledged the importance of staying in school, explaining, "I know the only way to get out of this rut is to get an education."

Desiree is currently studying to earn a degree in social work and looks forward to a stable job in the field in the near future. Desiree's motivations extend beyond her personal security. She has a strong desire to help other people. Before beginning her studies at Metro State, she trained to become an alcohol dependency counselor, which provides an alternate way to earn a living if she has difficulty financing her education.

Desiree is grateful for the MicroGrants, which came at times when she desperately needed them. The grants have allowed her to stay on course with her education and career objectives. Although Desiree is highly motivated, she has faced challenging financial obstacles. "Sometimes," she said, "trying isn't enough. The program really helped me." She called it a "Godsend." The money from MicroGrants helped Desiree clear several hurdles as she continued to progress toward earning her degree. As a result she is now in her final year of studies, on track to achieve an improved lifestyle.

Desiree clearly understands the importance of looking toward the future. MicroGrants was part of a long-term solution, as opposed to a short-term fix. She noted that the people who work with MicroGrants ask questions and work with the recipients to make sure that they have a plan and stick to it. In Desiree's words, the "counselors make sure you're working for the grant. There's no room for error." This reflects the aim of MicroGrants—to make a *lasting* change. The money comes with guidance and follow-up that increase the probability of long-term success, which is Desiree's ultimate goal.

*Reported by Berit Johnson*
*June 9, 2008*

## Abdi Abdirahman

# Aiming Really High

Abdi Abdirahman had a big smile on his face as he introduced himself. As he sat down and began to talk about his experience with MicroGrants, to explain specifically how he had used the grant, it quickly became apparent that Abdi had every reason to smile. A MicroGrant is intended to help bring a person who shows potential to a new, higher plateau along the path to becoming self-sufficient; this is exactly what Abdi's $1,000 grant allowed him to do.

When Abdi applied for a MicroGrant at age 28, he was attending school at Lake Superior College and interning part-time at Children's Hospital in St. Paul. Because the small salary he was earning from the internship had to support his wife, daughter, and son, Abdi was not able to pay all of his tuition or purchase the books he needed for his classes. He applied for a MicroGrant in May 2007. After receiving the $1,000, Abdi bought the required books and spent the rest for tuition. He stuck with his studies over the course of the next year, working hard to maintain a 4.0 grade point average.

On May 16, 2008, Abdi's hard work paid off. He graduated from the Respiratory Care Practitioner program at Lake Superior College with honors. His mother, wife Miski, three-year-old daughter Ramla, and one-year-old son Ridwan all made the several-hour trip to the college to celebrate with Abdi on the big day. After the ceremony, one of his professors gave Abdi a lab coat as a gift to commemorate his success at Lake Superior. Surrounded by his family and close friends, Abdi spent the rest of the day celebrating his accomplishments.

After graduating, Abdi traveled with his wife to England, and then to

Austria to visit his brother who lives in Vienna. It was the first time the brothers had seen each other since Abdi moved to the United States from Somalia nine years earlier. Abdi put a lot of effort into planning the trip in a way that minimized costs. He arranged to stay at his brother's place instead of at a hotel, and he used public transportation to go sightseeing. While in Europe, Abdi snapped many pictures of the sites they visited and later compiled the photographs in an album.

Abdi and his wife returned home to Minnesota in June 2008. Soon after, he went back to work at Children's Hospital. With his newly acquired degree, Abdi has maintained a full-time position at Children's as a Respiratory Care Practitioner, and will get further training in the Neonatal and Pediatric Intensive Care Units. He will make over $38,000 a year, more than three times the salary he was earning as an intern.

With the increased income, Abdi will be in a better position to support his family, while also saving to fulfill his ultimate dream—becoming a medical doctor. Abdi has his heart set on going to medical school, perhaps specializing in cardiology. He explained: "no matter what, that's what I want to do." At the same time, he knows how difficult it will be. Abdi has signed up for classes at St. Paul College in order to begin preparation for the next big goal.

Over the next four to five years, he plans to work and save money for medical school. He is also considering schools outside of the U.S., where tuition is lower. However, he is worried about keeping his family together while continuing his training. Abdi knows he must be patient. "I am trying to make plans to avoid these kinds of problems," he said. "That's why I want to work for four or five years before I go anywhere."

Although Abdi has a lot of work to do before he can even apply to medical school, he has already come a long way since immigrating to the United States from Somalia in 1999. In the last nine years, he has nearly perfected his English by taking ESL classes and listening to radio talk shows, such as Minnesota Public Radio. He is now a college graduate with a full-time job and ambitious plans for the future. As he freely describes himself, he is truly a "workaholic."

Because of Abdi's strong work ethic and motivation, his $1,000 grant has made a significant and lasting impact on his life. He has reached a new level of self-sufficiency because MicroGrants gave him the financial means to complete his college education. As he said of the grant, "I appreciate it, and I will remember the help I got forever." For Abdi, the MicroGrant was so much more than a one-time gift; it allowed him to improve his financial status and progress towards his goal of becoming a doctor.

*Reported by Berit Johnson*
*June 30, 2008*

**The table below is typical of those created from the data collected for each MicroGrants recipient.**

| | |
|---|---|
| Age | 29 |
| Home zip code | 55418 |
| Dependents | 3 |
| Yearly Income | $38,300 |
| Change in income since receiving grant? | $26,700 |
| Education | Lake Superior College Respiratory Program |
| Race/Ethnicity | African, Somali |

ANTONIA APOLINARIO-WILCOXON

# Reaching for the Gold Ring

A ntonia Apolinario-Wilcoxon, wearing a vibrant scarf and colorful shirt, walked into the Headwaters Conference Room. She is
African, but she grew up in Brazil. She came to the United States in
1979 through an exchange program. Antonia is now 52 years old and
divorced, with two sons. Her hyphenated last name comes from her
Norwegian ex-husband.

At the time of her divorce, the family was bankrupt and Antonia could
not borrow money for a down payment on a car. She lives in Hopkins, a
suburb of Minneapolis, which is twenty miles from her job in St. Paul. She
needed a car to commute to school and work—and to be "an influential
voice in public policy on behalf of toddlers and their families who suffer
from infant mental health problems." She also needed the car to transport
her son to activities and to church. The $1,000 from MicroGrants allowed
her to make a down payment, take out a loan, and purchase a car. Antonia
felt that the car, which was "more reliable than public transportation, provided access to places that public transportation did not, in the time that
I had to get there."

Antonia needs reliable transportation because she works full-time
while studying. She is a mental health program consultant at the Minnesota State Department of Health. She is also pursuing a doctorate (Ed.D.)
in leadership, policy and administration at the University of St. Thomas.
This program focuses on critical pedagogy, a teaching approach that helps
students learn to question and challenge domination (racism, gentrifica-
tion, etc.) She loves mixing with younger students and loves the program
because it is so relevant to her job. Antonia's position at the Department
of Mental Health is unique. It gives her "some source of freedom" because
she is able to work on projects that she creates. In addition to her regular

job, Antonia has worked as a consultant for non-profit organizations for twelve years.

Antonia's educational history is impressive, considering that she paid her own way through a bachelor's degree in economics and a master's degree in administration. In one year, she plans to be defending her dissertation and sending her younger son off to college. He is 18 and will attend Hamline University in St. Paul. Antonia's ex-husband will end his child support soon. Antonia is still paying off her own school loans, but has already saved enough to pay for her son's first semester. Her son will help with his college expenses through work-study and scholarships. Antonia does not need to worry about her older son, 26, who lives in Minneapolis and is self-sufficient.

In five years, Antonia hopes to work in both the United Statesand Brazil. She grew up in poverty, so she knows what the mental healthcare problems are like there. She hopes to give aid without charging in Brazil. At home, she is frugal, and says she has "cut expenses as much as I could." Antonia controls her thermostat, packs a lunch, takes care of her own yard, and wears used clothing. Fortunately, her state job provides health insurance; Antonia has diabetes and is dealing with clinical depression. It is with great fortitude that she has gotten to the where she is now. She plans to keep on going.

*Reported by Winnie Tong*
*July 1, 2008*

# 6
# Single Parenting

POOR CHOICES, GULLIBILITY, and lack of education are signposts along the route to the underclass. There's more. But grit and a hand up sometimes work marvels.

In these pages we get particularly graphic examples of the realities behind the struggles.

We read of ghastly murders—escalation of "domestic violence disputes"—and wonder.

Wonder no more. The reality is revealed ahead.

And yet, people persevere. The human is undaunted. We ought to be casting medals, but it is probably best that we content ourselves with issuing grants.

Lisa Erickson

# Living in Fear

Lisa is a 39-year-old divorced mother with a four-year-old son. After learning a Bachelor's degree in history from Columbia University, she started her own business as a recruiter. With her husband, who was always the life of the party, the "golden boy," and an adorable little boy, Lisa thought she had the perfect family. Life was good, until it wasn't.

A few years after her marriage, her life changed abruptly and completely. Her husband began to insult her and threaten her. He never went beyond what was technically legal—it was always "one slap, one shove," that was meant to scare her. "It's like these men know exactly what is allowed by the law and what's not," she said. He also said cruel things to her, and she found that "Verbal abuse is worse than physical abuse." There were actually times when she wished he would just hit her instead of berating her.

When friends saw Lisa, no one thought to ask what was wrong. "They never thought there was something wrong with my husband," she said. "They thought it was me." At first, Lisa was influenced by her friends and told herself that she must be imagining things. But one day, searching the Internet, she found an article about borderline personality disorder. It seemed to fit. When she confronted her husband, he vehemently denied that he had any such problems. Lisa was alarmed. She contacted borderline personality disorder support groups online and discovered she wasn't alone.

She ultimately filed for a divorce. Her husband balked and the process was harrowing. Eventually, the divorce was finalized, and they have joint custody of their child. When she hands over her son Lisa worries about the father's influence on the boy.

Lisa's ex-husband continues to torment her. She described the day when he stole her extra set of house keys, then casually asked her if she was missing anything. She searched frantically for the keys until she realized that he had taken them. He hounded her in other ways as well. The worst episode occurred in the winter when Lisa took her son sledding. Her husband, seemingly angered by this, stole the sled. Lisa called the police, but he denied everything. Fortunately, the officer recognized that her husband, not Lisa, was the one with a problem. The next day Lisa found the sled dumped in her backyard, "like a carcass." She has had post-traumatic stress disorder since the divorce, and the harassment has led to depression.

Not surprisingly, Lisa's distress afffected her work. As a self-employed recruiter, she matches qualified people with high-level positions. Her clients are mostly small businesses that need new employees, and she has several reliable clients who have stayed with her through the years. Each search takes from 6 weeks to 6 months, and she is paid on completion. Her annual income ranges from $20,000 to $30,000. Before the divorce, the couple had a comfortable joint income. But alone, Lisa has had to rely on some governmental financial assistance in the form of food stamps.

Lisa felt humbled by her experience, but she is determined to get back on her feet. In five years, she hopes to have an office with several employees. Currently she is saving what she can and doing wihout cable and an Internet connection. "But my son and I look good, and we feel good," she said. "We laugh all the time and my son has no idea how we have struggled to get to this day. That matters to me. One problem is not going to ruin our lives."

Lisa needed help to get through a tough time. She received $1,000 from MicroGrants in January 2007, shortly after her divorce. Housing and transportation costs were her most urgent concerns. Her parents have helped her buy the home where she and her son are living, but her stepfather told her that he would sell the house unless she can pay the mortgage. In addition, her car broke down and she couldn't get a loan to replace it. The MicroGrant allowed her to make it to March 2007—when she received a check from a client. And now, with the worst behind her, she is on her way.

*Reported by Winnie Tong*
*June 9, 2008*

Lakisha Holman

# Surviving Job's Trials

L akisha Holman is a 30-year-old African American single mother with
two dependents—a 4-year-old daughter and an injured brother. As if
those responsibilities didn't provide enough stressin her life, she ran into a
series of misfortunes that might have defeated a person without Lakisha's
drive to succeed.

She got into an accident and her car was totaled.

Just two weeks before meeting with MicroGrant interns, she was laid
off her job as a guard with Twin Cities Security Company.

She had to appear in court to dispute an allegation that she had stolen
cigarettes from Walmart eleven years ago.

But sometimes the sun does shine. In 2005, Lakisha enrolled in the
LPN program at Hennepin Technical College in Brooklyn Park. After re-
ceiving a scholarship that pays full tuition, she made good use of her time.
She has attended every class for the past three years. In a year and a half,
Lakisha hopes to have her license so that she can work in a hospital and
earn more money.

The accident happened last year. Without a car, Lakisha had to take
the bus. This was time consuming and difficult, because she had to travel to three places every day. She lived and studied in Brooklyn Park, she
worked as a security guard at a library in North Minneapolis, and she took
her daughter to daycare in downtown Minneapolis.

Lakisha spent up to six hours a day shuttling from place to place.
This schedule was exhausting and stressful: "I was always running to be on
schedule for the bus. If I was just one minute late, I wouldn't make it to
the next place." She also worried that she would be marooned in the city at
night with her daughter because buses run from downtown Minneapolis
to North Minneapolis only at certain times of the day.

Desperately needing a car, she heard about MicroGrants through Project for Pride in Living. In January 2008, she received a grant and used the $1,000 to buy a used '95 Pontiac Grand Am. This greatly decreased her commuting time—and also her stress. Then she was laid off.

Despite the turmoil, Lakisha has great support. Her boyfriend and mother help her with expenses and help keep her spirits up such as Lakisha's mother offering to treat her to a relaxing pedicure and manicure at a salon. Since Lakisha can't afford these luxuries, this kind of treat from Mom is a nice morale booster. Lakisha's brothers, 24 and 25, take turns baby-sitting her 4-year-old daughter. Because of her brothers' generosity, Lakisha is able to save money she would otherwise have had to spend on daycare.

Lakisha knows that she's lucky to have such a supportive family. She reciprocates by cooking a big dinner for them on Friday nights. After gathering around the table for a hearty meal, they settle down to watch a movie. This family time helps Lakisha get through the hard times.

Still, Lakisha is financially burdened. Before being laid off, she was living from one paycheck to the next. Fortunately, she had earlier managed to save $470 and was able to pay some expenses, such as rent. (Since Lakisha qualifies for Section 8 Housing, her rent and utilities come to about $350 a month.)

Lakisha recognizes that education will help increase her income and lead to a more fulfilling and secure life. "Going to school is going to give my baby and me a better future," she said. "I can focus on what I have to do." When other friends want to party, Lakisha politely refuses, she would rather spend the time studying or playing with her daughter. She set out a plan five years ago, and has followed it step by step. Lakisha has never skipped a class, because she knows having a nursing degree will help her earn more money. She has overcome obstacles in the past, and knows she can do it in the future.

*Reported by Winnie Tong*
*July 1, 2008*

Iris Dixon

# Overcoming Bad Choices

Iris Dixon is an inspirational woman—a 43-year-old single mother of three who has beaten a lot of odds. Her road to education has been strewn with obstacles, yet she didn't let them prevent her from achieving her goals, and she is well on her way to graduating from college.

Iris grew up in Chicago in a rough neighborhood. A high school dropout, she went to beauty school and worked in a few shops. At 24, she was living with her mother when her first son, Ramon, was born. She wanted to change her life. She was tired of dealing with "the system."

Iris had a sister who was doing well in Minneapolis. Seventeen years ago, Iris left Chicago and moved in with the sister. She started out working at fast food places: Popeye's, Wendy's and Bruegger's Bagels. She wanted to be productive, and the county helped her out so she could support her baby. After a while, however, living with her sister did not work out, and Iris and her two-year-old son found themselves in a shelter.

Shortly after that, she found a place to live, completed her GED at Summit Academy OIC, and enrolled at Minneapolis Community and Technical College. It was during that time that Iris began going to church and joined support groups. She wanted to stop drinking and smoking. She wanted to be clean.

Also during this time, she met a man who became the father of her daughter Lynn. The relationship was detrimental to Iris, at one point becoming so violent that surgery was needed on her hand, and the father wound up in jail. Iris dropped out of MCTC after her first semester and moved into a shelter with her two children.

When Ramon started kindergarten, Iris volunteered at his school. She wanted to go back to school herself, but this wasn't the time. She reconnected with Lynn's father briefly, but he got into more trouble and went back to prison.

In 1997, Iris got a part-time job in a school, working through a "parent partner" program that allowed people in the community to work in the schools. She loved the job, and working with children changed her life. But funding for the program was cut, and she had no idea what to do next. She prayed—and managed to land a job in the resource center of the school where she had been working before.

In 2001, Iris went to Bible school and completed a two-year program. She got a ministry certificate in 2003. Her faith has helped her to stay clean, focused and happy.

By 2002 things were going well for Iris. Her daughter's father was released from prison and they got married. He worked as a job facilitator, and she worked in a school as a teacher's assistant. During this time, Iris had her third child, a son named Sam. Things seemed to be going well, but Iris began to notice changes in her husband. He admitted to her that he was using again. She wanted him to get help. He didn't, and is now serving a 15-year prison sentence. She divorced him, but they still communicate.

Iris decided it was time to return to school and go into the field of education. When her ex-husband went back to prison, her oldest son began to have problems. He wouldn't listen to her and began running the streets. In 2003, Ramon, then 15, was shot in the stomach. He had to have surgery, but survived.

Iris was under continuing stress. After her son was shot, he was charged with a felony. Iris had quit her job at the school and started a daycare in her home. She wanted to spend more time with her youngest son, Sam. However, she had to close the daycare because it is illegal for felons to live in a home providing childcare. She had to make a choice, and she chose her son.

She wanted to move out of the area, but did not have the money. She remembered hearing about a program called "All About the Kids" that helped families with children. The program helped her get a voucher for a Section Eight apartment, which meant that she was required to pay only a portion of the rent, and this eased the financial burden. Iris and her children moved into a new place, but the apartment was hardly ideal. One morning she woke up hear to her baby screaming because he had a cockroach in his ear. Iris and her family moved again.

A few years ago, they moved into the home the family now occupies.

Iris finally went back to school at MCTC last year and heard about the "Urban Teachers Program." She knew it was exactly what she wanted to do. She knew dangers of drugs and life in the streets and wanted to be able to help young people struggling as she had.

School has been tough for Iris. She is taking 13 credits a semester and working part-time, but MicroGrants provided a timely intervention. Iris received a grant in February 2007. This was shortly after her oldest son was in a car accident. He sustained serious injuries, but has made a full recovery. Iris continued to go to school to pursue her dream of becoming a teacher. She spent the grant on a computer, driving lessons, bills, and helping her son. A few months after the car accident, Ramon was picked up on murder charges. Iris is spending what is left of her grant to pay for a lawyer for her son.

Iris has struggled through school, working, paying the bills, and raising her children. But she kept going. She has had horrendous obstacles in the way of her education, but nothing will stop her. She believes that remaining focused is crucial to her success. Her 15-year-old daughter Lynn helps tremendously.

Iris is currently working part-time as a family liaison, providing services to parents and children within the schools and the community. Once she finishes her teaching degree, she will be able to work full-time with children.

In a few months, she will begin working in a juvenile center as a minister. She wants to help young people so they do not have to go through what she has been through. Iris expects to complete her Urban Teaching Degree in 2009. She also wants to complete her driver training classes to obtain her drivers license, and eventually purchase a car. In the long-term, Iris would like to own a house. She is trying to put money aside and improve her credit rating.

Setting an example for her children is what keeps Iris working towards her degree. She wants her kids to know that they can be what they want to be in life. She will be the first college graduate in her family. Iris is a proud grandmother and she also wants to set a good example for her granddaughter. She hopes the children who will be her students in the future will see the results of hard work and perseverance, and strive to achieve their own goals. She wants to convey the message that they do not have to be bound to the streets, drugs, and negativity.

With her MicroGrant, Iris was able to take care of herself and her family. She has overcome many obstacles to arrive where she is today. Through her hard work and dedication, there is no doubt that Iris will complete her college degree.

She deserves more than applause. She deserves the awe of everyone in the community.

*Reported by Cathy Bader*
*June 28, 2007*

The table below is typical of those created from the data collected for each MicroGrants recipient.

| | |
|---:|:---|
| Age | 39 |
| Home zip code | 55105 |
| Marital Status | Divorced |
| Dependents | 1 |
| Yearly Income | $25,000 (varies) |
| Change in income since receiving grant? | No |
| Education | B.A. history, Columbia U |
| Race/Ethnicity | White |
| Obstacles to Employment | Post-traumatic stress disorder |
| Health Insurance | Yes |
| Government Assistance | Yes (food stamps only) |
| Employer/Position | Self-employed/ recruiter |

Naomi Mohammed

# Filial Devotion

Naomi Mohammed, a single mother of five children, was among the
first to receive a MicroGrant. She used the grant she received in December 2005 to help improve her son's life.

Naomi, 45, was born and raised in the Minneapolis Phillips neighborhood. Today she works in the same vicinity at Welna Hardware, where she
has been in charge of the lock and key department for 20 years.

Naomi gets up at 4:00 a.m. to do household chores and starts work
at 6:00 a.m. She has arranged her schedule to finish at 2:00 p.m. every
day in order to be at home when her children return from school. Her
children's ages are 21, 18, 15, 13, and 8. She hasn't heard from their father in three years and is the sole provider for the family. "Sometimes divorce is a good thing," she tells us. "In my case, it was a fabulous thing."
The family is close, and they work together to make the household run
smoothly. They have dinner together every night; Each child has chores
to do and each cooks dinner one night a week. Naomi is proud of them.
She calls them "awesome kids." Because the family works cooperatively,
Naomi is able to take college classes.

Naomi is attending Minneapolis Community and Technical College,
working toward a degree in business. She loves being in school and has
been there for six semesters. After 13 more credits, she will transfer to
Metropolitan State University to complete her bachelor's degree. She has
been taking two or three credits a semester, making her graduation date
hard to predict.

Naomi is unsure about what kind of job she would like to pursue
once she completes her schooling. Education has been a long-term goal.
She wants all of her children to go to college and will do whatever it takes
to get them there. It is an important goal; she believes a degree opens the

doors to opportunity.

Naomi wishes she were as sure about what she wanted to do as her son is. He plans to become an emergency room doctor. It was partly for him that she applied for a MicroGrant. His car broke down, and he needed it to be able to attend Paramedic Training Classes in White Bear Lake, which is a long drive from Minneapolis. Naomi used the MicroGrant to pay for repairs on her son's car. He has since graduated first in his class and is working as a Paramedic.

Naomi also used the MicroGrant to pay for plumbing and household needs. She just moved into a house that had been vacant for four years, and discovered problems that needed to be fixed.

With the help of MicroGrants, Naomi was able to fix her son's car and make home repairs without spending money from savings. As a result, her son is working at a job he loves, and her home is livable. Naomi plans to continue working hard to finish her own education and support her other children as they continue in school.

*Reported by Cathy Bader*
*July 11, 2007*

LaVeka Belyeu

# Absent Fathers

In August 2007, LaVeka Belyeu, 26, had Malik, her only child. She loves children and was overjoyed when Malik came into her life. Having a child, though, has placed a large financial burden on her. Although LaVeka is saving significantly by having her mother take care of Malik while she is at work rather than putting him in daycare, it is still difficult to pay for necessities like diapers and baby food. Although she has been working as a nurse's aide at Fairview Hospital for over four years, she finds that her growing son gives her an incentive to do something else so she can spend more time with him.

LaVeka would like to start a day-care business. It would allow her to spend more time with Malik at the same time she is providing for him. But she needs a degree in childcare development to own and operate a day-care center. The degree would increase her knowledge and skills – and add to her credibility as a childcare provider. She would also be eligible to apply for a group family childcare license, which would allow her to care for eleven to fourteen children. Without the license, LaVeka can only get a family care license, for up to ten children.

In the fall of 2007, LaVeka decided to go to Minneapolis Community and Technical College (MCTC) to earn the one-year degree in childcare development. Before she could enroll, she had to find a way to pay for books and tuition of over $5,400. Although she had a steady job at Fairview, it was difficult to cover the entire cost. Fortunately, she qualified for a $1,500 scholarship through Fairview. To keep the scholarship, LaVeka must maintain a minimum GPA of 2.3 (a goal she is achieving). Still, even after receiving this assistance, she had to pay the remaining tuition before she could begin classes.

LaVeka heard about MicroGrants through Mary Jo Copeland, often called a certified urban saint, who is the founder and director of Sharing and Caring Hands. In November 2007, she applied and received $1,000. Shortly after receiving the grant, she enrolled in MCTC's childcare development program for the Spring 2008 semester. She used the Micro-Grant to cover the cost of the books for her courses as well as some of the tuition. Now she is on track to get her childcare development degree in January 2009.

After receiving the degree, LaVeka will apply for a license to open a day care in her home. She sees a high demand for one that has flexible hours. Parents who work in the fields of healthcare and manufacturing often need childcare at night and on weekends, and Laveka plans to offer childcare services at those times.

Eventually, LaVeka would like to go to school to become an occupational therapist. She would work with physically, cognitively, or emotionally disabled people to help them maximize their skills and abilities. Occupational therapy would allow LaVeka to earn a higher income while fulfilling her desire to help others. In the next five years, LaVeka hopes to have successful day care, and then a career in occupational therapy. She credits MicroGrants for the opportunity to attend MCTC and progress towards her dreams.

*Reported by Sarah Hill*
*July 2, 2008*

Jesse Oyervides

# Real Leadership

Jesse Oyervides is a 41-year-old Latino man who has always done his best to help his community. When he was 26 years old, Jesse worked as a janitor for the Los Angeles Federal Courthouse. When a protest group attempted to smash the windows of the building, Jesse and other janitors stopped the destruction by spraying the protesters with fire extinguishers. Shortly after that, an article in the LA Times praised Jesse's bravery and credited him with stopping the violence. Now Jesse works full-time as a maintenance manager at New Concepts Management Group, a private real estate and management company. He is also a board member for several community organizations.

Jesse hopes he will be a role model for his sons, 8 and 10. He volunteers at a program called Java that arranges activities for children and "gives them a positive place to go" after school. Jesse is also on the board of Whittier International Elementary School.

Jesse sends his sons to a private Christian school in Minneapolis called Hope Academy because he believes that faith matters. Hope Academy is focused on the youth of inner-city neighborhoods of Minneapolis. Its mission is to help urban families equip their children to become the leaders of the future. Jesse's boys have been there for six years.

Although Hope Academy strives to be affordable, the tuition is still a stretch for him. Jesse says, "if I have to work two jobs to keep them in school at Hope, I will." Jesse's older son is interested in science, and Jesse encourages his sons' academic pursuits. He enjoys spending his free time with his children, although his dedication to them limits the time he has for working.

Jesse had a high-paying maintenance job when he lived in Chicago. A graduate of the Technical School for Plumbing there, he had credentials.

He decided to move the family to Minnesota so that his paraplegic wife could be closer to her relatives. In the Twin Cities, Jesse started with low-paying maintenance jobs. He has worked at New Concepts for two and a half years.

Jesse divorced several years ago. For a time he was homeless, because he had been living with his wife's family. Through friends at church, he found another place. He eventually got full custody of the children.

He believes that he is qualified for a higher paying job with more benefits, but he chooses to do odd jobs as a maintenance manager so that he can spend more time with his family. Jesse has a strong relationship with his boss and his customers. His boss treats him well, and he's allowed to live in a condominium in the New Concepts building where he works. Recently, he received a $300 raise in his $30,000 annual salary.

His ex-wife once contributed to child support but will no longer be required to do so.

Jesse has been putting aside $80 per month to prepare for the reduced income. He saves money on gas by riding the bus or biking.

In February 2008, Jesse was struggling with the financial burden of being a single parent with two young children. He described himself as being "too proud to ask for help." Finally Adrienne Foreman-Jones of Project for Pride in Living referred him to MicroGrants. The timing was perfect. He used $700 of the MicroGrant to pay two months of tuition for his sons, $100 for glasses for his older son, and $200 for past due rent. MicroGrants allowed Jesse to maintain his work-life balance, and focus on his sons.

Jesse wants to get a higher paying job in about five years, when his sons are older. Laughing he said, "Maybe I'll even write a book about my experience. Who knows?" Right now, Jesse just wants to set a good example for his children. He often performs small acts of kindness; recently he volunteered to fix the plumbing in his ex-wife's apartment. Indeed, his main concerns are "kids and community, " and MicroGrants helped him continue on that path.

*Reported by Winnie Tong*
*June 13, 2008*

Marie Chante Flowers

# Scratch and Find a Poet

*"You feel it, don't you, the energy in the air, the drive and the ambition so vehemently, and of it we are aware. Wanting because of me to touch your clothes, your eyes, and leap. Bucking your head along the way; however, remaining on your feet. Don't you dare. Keep going. Here, take my hand, I'll show you the way. With an attitude like yours, you'll touch the stars some day. I see you shining, see you in the rainstorm. So for now, keep going, atta girl, a star is born."*

—Marie Chante Flowers' spoken word piece "Attagirl."

Marie Chante Flowers, 29, is an African American and a full-time student at Minneapolis Community and Technical College pursuing a degree in liberal arts. She has done spoken word performances at her church, local theaters, and coffee shops. She has met and studied with renowned spoken word artists to learn how to use her voice expressively. She compares poetry to the air she breathes. At first glance, Marie appears to be a typical artist, but in the slideshow of her life, this one frame is only a glimpse of who she is and what she has been through.

*Wanting because of me to touch your clothes, your eyes, and leap.*

Marie was raised by a single mother and grew up in a family of dysfunction and chaos. She became pregnant at 13. The next year, she dropped out of high school and had to grow up quickly to take on the responsibilities of being a mother.

Marie's mother, who never graduated from high school, was determined to have her daughters get an education. But since she was a dropout, she felt that it would be hypocritical to tell her children to stay in school. So she decided to go back to school herself. She studied hard and earned a GED.

The day she received her certificate, she told her daughters, "now there is no excuse. I got my GED. Now I can tell you to go back to school."

Marie was inspired by her mother's example. She worked at several jobs until she found a program called "Putting It All Together," which helped her complete her GED. She says, "I didn't want to be uneducated. I didn't want to feel like a liability to society." In the meantime, Marie's mother started taking classes toward her bachelor's degree. Marie wanted to follow in her footsteps, but her progress was slowed when she had two more sons with two different men. None of the fathers are actively involved in their children's lives. And as the sole provider for her three boys, Marie found it difficult to go to school and earn enough money to raise a family.

*Bucking your head along the way; however, remaining on your feet.*

Marie didn't give up. Inspired by Oprah Winfrey saying, "if you educate a woman, you educate a family," she saved enough money to begin her college education. She had a 4.0 GPA after her first semester. But everything ground to a halt due to health problems. She was tired all the time, no matter how many hours she had slept or how many naps she took. She finally saw a doctor; the diagnosis was narcolepsy. She dropped out of school and worked full-time to pay her bills and take care of herself physically. Seeing the impact of her mother's pursuit of an education, and being unable to provide the same kind of example for her sons, was overwhelming for Marie. The combination of her physical problems and not being in school developed into depression.

*Don't you dare. Keep going. Here, take my hand, I'll show you the way.*

Marie worked very hard to restart her education. With the help of her doctors, she overcame her depression and had the stamina to return to school part-time. But in short order, one of her close friends died, her father became ill and was hospitalized, and she lost her job. This led to a nervous breakdown and narcoleptic relapse. Still, she was determined to go on. She worked with a nutritionist, psychologist, physician, and physical therapist to devise a diet and exercise regimen that would improve her well-being. She lost 35 pounds in the first 15 weeks and felt well enough to work and go back to school. But she did not have the money she needed to do both.

*With an attitude like yours, you'll touch the stars some day.*

When she realized that she did not have the resources to continue her education, Marie sought help everywhere. A friend at church told Marie about MicroGrants, and she applied right away. She was accepted and used the $1,000 to pay bills and for day care for her youngest son. This made it possible for her to return to school full-time.

The change in her demeanor was extraordinary. Her youngest son said, "Who are you, and what have you done to my mommy?" Marie replied, "What do you mean?" He said, "I don't know. This mommy smiles more and laughs more. The other mommy didn't smile a lot, and she always was sad." By having the opportunity to be in school, Marie regained hope and balance in her life. The MicroGrant provided the help that she needed to pursue her dream of unlocking her potential and being a role model for her children. She wanted to see what lay within.

*I see you shining, see you in the rainstorm. So for now keep going, atta girl, a star is born.*

In June 2007, Marie's Mom received her degree, her sons had just finished eighth grade, fifth grade, and kindergarten, and she was at MCTC full-time. Seeing her oldest son graduate from junior high was particularly moving for her. When she was his age, she had been pregnant with him. Instead of worrying about being a parent, he is interested in film studies and is being mentored by a local professional.

Marie's goal is to graduate at the end of the school year. Even with the illness she suffered in the past, she has maintained a 3.4 GPA. She is proud to be self-sufficient and is currently very involved in the local art scene. She is adapting one of her poems into a book for children and another one into a motivational journal for teenage girls. Her life is a journey of twists, turns, trials, and triumph and as she is letting her light shine. Did someone say a star is born? Meet Marie.

*Reported by Daniel E. Geoffrion*
*July 10, 2007*

BRENDA CLEVELAND

# Educational Investments

B renda Cleveland is an outgoing 35-year-old woman living in St. Louis Park, Minnesota. One of the first in her family to graduate from college, she works at Project for Pride in Living through AmeriCorps. She's held a variety of jobs, but has always had a desire to help others. Her life experiences are the source of her altruism and she wants to pursue a career in social work.

Brenda was born in northern Minnesota and moved to Minneapolis with her family when she was fifteen. After graduating from Hopkins High School in 1990, she enrolled in Minneapolis Community and Technical College (MCTC) for one semester. During that time she met a man, became pregnant, and had a daughter. She married the father of her child three years later, and had another daughter with him in 1995.

Shortly after that, they divorced, and she had to go to work to support her children. She found a job at Supervalu in retail accounting and worked there for about a year. She couldn't advance because she didn't have a two-year associate degree.

She had applied for Section Eight Housing at the beginning of that year and found out she would begin receiving rent assistance in August of 1997. She gave notice to Supervalu and registered for classes at MCTC. She completed two years of liberal arts classes, then transferred to the University of Minnesota where she majored in history.

Brenda paid her own college tuition while raising two children. She graduated in 2002 with a bachelor's degree and wanted to get a master's in education. With a little research she discovered that the cost of her education would be around $50,000, and there were few jobs for social studies or history teachers. She considered law school, but saw no way she could do that and raise her kids at the same time. While she was deciding what career path to take, Brenda got a job at White Castle and worked there for four years. She hadn't intended to stay that long, but the flexible hours allowed her to spend time with her children.

Brenda began working at Project for Pride in Living as a Community Organizer in 2006. She facilitates relationships among the residents and helps them build bridges to the community. She is responsible for one apartment complex in St. Louis Park and one in New Hope. Her job duties include writing a monthly newsletter, taking residents to food shelves, taking them to Minnesota Family Investment Program appointments, helping them write resumes, organizing potlucks to bring them together, and bringing in outside resources, such as a volunteer lawyer from the Legal Aid Society. From the beginning, Brenda has introduced the residents to free resources and inexpensive family activities. She is working with AmeriCorps to get on track to go to graduate school.

Brenda heard about MicroGrants through her work at PPL and applied for a grant to pay for a statistics class in the fall. (She did not want to pay for tuition with money she needs to take care of her children.) After completing the class, Brenda will have finished the requirements to pursue a master of social work degree. She will apply at the University of Minnesota, the College of St. Catherine, and the University of St. Thomas and hopes to start classes next fall. In order to support herself and her daughters, Brenda plans to work part time at a social services job. When she obtains her degree, it will give her many career options—which appeals to her eclectic sensibility.

In the future, Brenda wants to open an individual counseling and therapy practice. She has also considered life coaching. She is good at motivating; she is the person her friends turn to when they are seeking advice. Because of her varied life experiences, she can identify with many types of people at different stages in their lives. But she is apprehensive about life coaching right now because she wants to finish her degree first. It will give her credibility. Brenda plans to focus her graduate studies on researching poverty and the benefits of self-sufficiency. She plans to write a book on the subject after completing graduate school.

Brenda also wants to write a book about her personal struggles. At one point in her life she weighed 320 pounds. Over the course of two years, she took off the excess weight by eating sensibly and exercising. She worked with a therapist to help achieve her goal, doing a lot of self-examination to try to understand why she was killing herself with food. She has successfully kept the weight off for another two years and is more active than she has ever been before.

Brenda wants to write about the regimen she followed to lose the weight, but also about the emotional side of it. Being overweight was hard on her self-esteem. She felt that people either looked at her oddly or didn't look at her at all. Brenda likes the way she looks and feels now. One motivation for staying fit is the attractive clothes she can buy. Another is setting a positive example for her children.

Her main goal is to make sure her children understand the importance of a college education. Showing them that they can have dreams and make them happen is the best example she can set. She wants to raise healthy, well-educated, and respectful young women.

Brenda has faced many obstacles on her path to educational achievement. She was among the first in her family to go to college. She managed to pay for college herself, while being a single parent and getting no child support—although she now owes $32,000 on loans.

MicroGrants is helping open opportunities for Brenda. She explains, "whether you're a single mom or any mom raising children, if you have to choose between paying $1,000 for a class or feeding your kids, it's pretty obvious what you're going to do." The grant will help her meet all the qualifications for graduate school without having to take money away from her children's needs. When she graduates, her earning potential will jump from $30,000 to $60,000 per year because of the license. She hopes to be able to continue to advocate for people and pursue her own dreams in the field of social work.

*Reported by Cathy Bader*
*July 2, 2007*

Ngozi Konan

# Seizing America's Opportunities

N gozi Konan's basement apartment is warm and welcoming. Morning sunlight, slanting through half-closed blinds, illuminates the living room, spotless and organized. Even as Ngozi invites her guest in, her three-year-old daughter races around to arrange the chairs for the meeting. This comfortable, but disciplined, household is one of Ngozi's points of pride.

Since emigrating from Africa, Ngozi has been working hard to create a stable, safe, and healthy environment for children. She believes that such places are not found, but rather made. She proudly states: "My own home, where I lay my head, is good for me." After four years in America, Ngozi has discovered that pursuing a long-term career is a challenge that takes years of patience and a disciplined work ethic. If the methods she uses to run her household offer any indication, Ngozi appears to have the right skills and mindset to build a successful career for herself, while she raises her children in a positive environment.

Although Ngozi appears confident and independent today, her life has not always been stable. "I'm originally from Nigeria, but I have traveled far and wide," Ngozi said. When she was a child, her parents were very strict and kept a close eye on their children at all times. When she grew older, Ngozi's natural curiosity made her wonder about the world outside her country. Eventually she traveled to the Ivory Coast. Due to Nigeria's collective "village" culture, Ngozi never experienced either the virtues or vices of personal independence and self-sufficiency.

In the Ivory Coast, Ngozi felt the freedom of independence for the first time, but also faced the consequences. Although she never intended to stay long, Ngozi explains that she was stuck there after marrying. She had four children over the course of eight years. The entire time she and her family had to contend with the country's hostile attitude towards foreign immigrants. She was traumatized by the constant fear of violence.

Finally Ngozi and her husband were able to immigrate to the U.S. under the sponsorship of her uncle. They hoped to find a better life and a safer environment. The first year in America was difficult for the transplants. In July of 2003, soon after arriving in Minneapolis, Ngozi separated from her husband and found herself supporting the four children on her own. The family lived in a shelter run by Sharing and Caring Hands while Ngozi looked for work.

Although she struggled during the first year to establish the basics for survival—housing and employment—she never lost sight of her long-term goal of entering the medical field. Asked what motivated her to pursue such an ambitious goal, she explained, "I always had this dream as a little girl growing up. I love meeting people, I love helping people."

By working through a temporary agency, Ngozi took the first step towards achieving her objective by becoming a nursing assistant. Soon she was able to move her family out of the shelter and into the apartment on Emerson Avenue where they now live. It is close to the children's school and the local library.

Once Ngozi and her children were settled in a safe, stable home and she had a job in a medical field, friends thought she would be satisfied. But she was just getting started. In 2005, Ngozi began taking classes at Minneapolis Community College to become certified as a Licensed Practical Nurse. When she completes the program, Ngozi will be able to earn a better living and work in higher-level positions. She will no longer have to rely on government medical assistance.

In order to attend the classes, Ngozi cut back her work hours to part-time. The decrease in salary left her with very little money to pay for child care while she attended classes. With no relatives or support network to help care for her children, Ngozi feared that she would never have the money or time to take the classes she needs while raising a family. With the help of MicroGrants, however, she has found a resourceful compromise that allows her to do both.

When Ngozi received the $1,000 MicroGrant in 2006, it was as though a great weight had been lifted from her shoulders. She knew exactly what to do with the money; she bought a laptop computer. With it, she has been able to enroll in online courses at Hennepin Technical College and is now working towards nursing certification at home. The grant also helped her pay for textbooks and course materials that financial aid at Hennepin Tech does not cover.

Today, Ngozi works at Efficiency Medical Center part-time, and is taking courses in ethics and interpersonal communications online. Most importantly, the online program gives her the freedom to be home with her four children. "I think I am doing well to teach them the best way I can," she says. She needs little encouragement to talk about her children's perfect attendance at school and good grades. All of her children are under 11 years of age. The money she saves by not having to pay for childcare makes it possible for her to go to school.

Without a "hand-up" from MicroGrants, this proud mother may have had to put aside her childhood dream of becoming a nurse. With the anticipated Nursing Certification from Hennepin Tech, Ngozi will soon be completely self-sufficient.

*Reported by Jamie Kallestad*
*June 24, 2007*

# 7
# Disabilities and Health

SOMETIMES LIFE DEALS blows that challenge the laws of probability without repealing them.

Some of the disasters of life are unavoidable, but we have to deal with the statistical probability that each of us gets roughly the same number of breaks and defeats as do others. So the difference becomes how we cope—and how we are equipped to cope—with opportunities and setbacks.

Now we meet even bigger heroes than appear on surrounding pages. Theirs was the grim, silent struggle to survive.

Life sometimes tempts us to surrender.

Ahead lie the accounts of those who chose to fight.

Diana Hobbs

# A Sentence of Death

Eight years ago, Diana Hobbs's then four-year-old daughter Akaysha was diagnosed with leukemia. During the three and a half years she underwent radiation and chemotherapy, Diana had to quit her job to care for the child. The stress of the cancer battle also took its toll on Diana's relationship with her husband, and ultimately they divorced. But Akaysha survived and has been in remission for five years.

While nothing can compare to her daughter's fight for life, Diana has had to contend with several additional stresses in her life. In December 2007, she had surgery to increase the blood flow in her legs. She didn't have enough vacation time accrued at work to cover the healing period, and as an on-site instructor for a company called Opportunity Partners, she didn't have the option to work from home.

Because of the work she missed, money became tight. At the same time, her car was falling apart; the radiator, alternator, water pump, front and back brakes, and clutch plate all needed repair. Diana applied for a MicroGrant to cover the cost. Some of the repairs were sloppy; she hears grinding in the brakes again, and the clutch is performing badly. Nevertheless, Diana was happy to be able to get to and from work, now that her car was at least drivable again.

Although Diana, 37, now has transportation, she also has had more problems. Recently she fell at her job and injured her knee so badly that she may need surgery. She is in so much pain that she is unable to spend more than four hours a day on her feet working. Her worker's compensation check was slow in arriving, so Diana has been struggling to make ends meet. She supports her daughter Akaysha, and two sons, D'Andre, 17, and Kelone, 10. She had some money saved for emergencies, but used all of it to replace a flat tire and to cover expenses immediately after her injury.

There was more. Financial support from her ex-husband dried up. Diana's older son has a different father who does provide support, but only for D'Andre. The other two children have not received anything from their father in four months. Diana looked for ways to cut expenses. The rent and utilities for her apartment total $860 per month. She considered moving into a less expensive town home, but concluded that it would be safer for her kids to stay where they are.

And there were more obstacles for Diana. She suffers from depression, anxiety, and a hypothyroid condition. The medicine she needs to treat these conditions is very expensive because she has no medical insurance. She feels overwhelmed with all of her responsibilities as a single parent of three, and her anxiety makes it even harder. At this point in her life, Diana would like to pursue other work opportunities. She would like to go to school to become a registered nurse. But she is so busy trying to provide for her family that she believes it would be "too much to go to school now." Diana feels stuck and has found that "doing everything on my own is very difficult."

While Diana is experiencing a very tough period in her life right now, she knows that past struggles—her daughter's battle with leukemia—have prepared her for the challenges she is facing now. She is confident that she and her family will find a way through this, noting that they have "made it in tougher situations." She truly appreciates the MicroGrant she received because it allowed her to fix her car at a time when she would not have been able to pay for the repairs on her own. Although Diana has many difficulties she still needs to overcome, clearing the transportation obstacle was an important first step.

The struggle continues, but she is a woman who is hard to defeat. What lifts her now is knowing that someone cares.

*Reported by Berit Johnson*
*July 7, 2008*

119

Valerie June Brown

# Real Heroism

Valerie June Brown is a remarkable 54-year-old African American woman. She was dependent on drugs, primarily crack cocaine, from the age of 15 to 41. Now, she has been drug-free for 13 years, and she supports five dependents. Her friends see her as one of life's scarred and battered, yet undaunted, heroes.

Valerie was trapped in a vicious cycle. She would do anything to get money to buy drugs, including forging a check. After using the drugs, Valerie would drink alcohol to blot out her problems and the shame. Emerging from a blackout, she'd repeat the cycle. The years passed in a blur.

Valerie finally broke the cycle after 26 years. Church helped the most. Valerie's former drug dealer, now her husband, also encouraged her to stop using drugs—one of life's many ironies. He told her "you're better than that," and eventually Valerie believed him.

Sister Joan Tuberty, who referred her to MicroGrants, provides support, listening to her talk about the daily struggles. Initially, Valerie saw herself as a bad person, but slowly, with Sister Joan's help, her self-esteem grew. She burst into tears as she described how understanding the nun had been. She said, "There have been a lot of changes in my life that I'm real grateful for."

Valerie takes care of her disabled sister, two nieces, and her mother, who has Alzheimer's disease. Following an incident of domestic violence, her sister had a stroke and seizure, which left her unable to work. She now lives on a government pension. Nevertheless, her sister's daughters are doing well. One niece is 19 and studying to be a certified nursing assistant. The other girl, 20, works in the retail business. Valerie does not have any children of her own, but she tells her nieces that although they are not a traditional nuclear family, they are still a family. Valerie's husband now repairs and sells cars for a living.

Valerie's yearly income, about $28,500, is supplemented somewhat by contributions from the rest of the family, but she is the main breadwinner. She saved bit by bit and bought a house in 2007. She was led to believe that she was getting a fixed-rate mortgage, but in fact she had signed a contract for an adjustable rate, which meant that in time, Valerie would have to pay more—and more.

She applied for a MicroGrant to help her with the increasing costs. Her paycheck was not enough to keep up with the mortgage, but the MicroGrant helped with the payments.

But even after receiving the $1,000 grant, Valerie found her money stretched tightly. Fortunately, her job at Catholic Charities provides a steady source of income. Valerie has worked as a resident assistant since September 2002. She contributes to the community as well, volunteering with a transitional housing program. She helps others find housing, but she knows that she's "not too far from where they are."

Valerie has a couple of luxuries—a cell phone and cable—but she rarely shops and always buys clearance clothing. Before the MicroGrant, Valerie said, "I was destitute." Now, she manages to save $25 every month.

As for her old problems, Valerie says, "I was my own worst enemy." Now, however, she believes that "My worst days sober are better than my best days high." As a person who clearly recognizes the importance of long-term goals over short-term benefits, Valerie has set solid goals for the next five years. She plans to refinance her home and continue taking care of everyone in the family. Her goal is to keep the family together. She thanks MicroGrants for helping her keep the house where the family lives. She feels that MicroGrants has been there for the people that need help. In Valerie's words, "I just felt blessed."

*Reported by Winnie Tong*
*July 3, 2008*

Gwendolyn Jones

# Gaining With Pain

Gwendolyn Jones is a single African American woman who works in a predominately male industry—construction. She is employed as a laborer by Bolander & Sons, a highway road construction company.

Gwen, 44, is frequently laid off in the winter. However, her biggest problem is not the seasonal nature of the job. She has degenerative disc disease, which involves the soft, compressible discs that separate the vertebrae in the spine. The problem can be caused by a variety of factors. In Gwen's case, it was a 1992 car accident that led to the disc ailment. She is in constant pain.

Gwen is usually able to pay the medical fees to treat her spine, but during the winter of 2007, she was laid off and did not have any income to cover her treatments. Gwen decided to apply for a MicroGrant.

She'd heard about MicroGrants from Lora Stone at Project for Pride in Living. She received a $1,000 grant in February 2008, a time when she sorely needed medical attention. Her situation is better now because she takes medication—strong painkillers, including morphine. It's risky, but the alternatives may be worse.

When Gwen works, she takes less medication than the prescription calls for. She is afraid that the presribed dose for her pain would cause her to "fall asleep in a corner somewhere." As a result, she is often in agony while at work. Gwen does not want to lose her job because of her disability; she has not told her coworkers or employer about her condition.

It's not the life she had envisioned when she was young. For two years she majored in journalism at the University of Arkansas. Then she moved to Minneapolis and worked at Target headquarters in accounting. But she wanted a more "hands-on" job with a higher pay, so she switched to construction. She has been doing this work for eleven years. Though Gwen earns a high salary—up to $60,000 a year if she is fully employed, she would like to change occupations in the near future.

In a year, Gwen would like to go back to school to become a registered nurse while she continues working in construction. In that way, she will be able to make a living without putting so much strain on her body. Switching careers would also increase her opportunities for the future. "There's not a lot of advancement in this field," she acknowledged.

Although her job is difficult, Gwen is determined to keep on truckin'. She has a good relationship with her coworkers and strong support from her family and church. Money is still tight, but Gwen can now pay off her medical bills. She credits MicroGrants for "enabling me to see a doctor," when she was struggling financially. In Gwen's words, "I'm glad there's something out there for people in need."

*Reported by Winnie Tong*
*July 28, 2008*

ARLETHA WILSON

# Easing It

Arletha Wilson's husband, Willie, was remarkably healthy for most of his life. He had never faced any serious medical problems until August 15, 2007. In the middle of the night, Willie, 58, had a stroke. The next morning, Arletha woke up to find him unable to speak properly or to walk without losing his balance; his mouth was twisted to one side. Arletha immediately drove him to the emergency room.

She remembers praying a lot during the next several days, as the doctors ordered tests to determine the cause and extent of the stroke. She made phone calls to out-of-state family members to explain what was happening. It was a stressful time. She tried to keep her mind on her job from 8:00 am to 4:00 pm, skipping her lunch breaks so that she could leave early. Then she drove straight to the hospital to spend four or five hours with Willie.

Slowly, he began to recover. With progress, however, came numerous visits to the hospital for various types of rehabilitation. Willie needed speech, occupational, and physical therapy. Each visit to the hospital meant a $60 co-pay, parking fees, and money for gas. Within four weeks, the money the couple had saved was gone.

Then, in the early winter of that same year, Arletha, 55, desperately needed dental work. Their health insurance didn't cover it, and they couldn't afford the expense. Arletha tried to just live with the intense pain until she could pay for the dental work, but it was hard to wait. Her job as a receptionist at Project for Pride in Living (PPL) became very difficult. She told a friend, "it is hard to keep your mind on your job and someone else's problems when the side of your face, head and ear are hurting." Even answering the phone could be agonizing. If a caller spoke loudly or slammed down the phone, it hurt her ear. Meanwhile, the pain was keeping her awake at night. Lack of sleep made matters worse.

Arletha's dental problem extended beyond her health and personal comfort. It affected her job performance, and thus her ability to support herself and her husband. The $1,000 MicroGrant Arletha received in November 2007 meant that she could get the dental work she needed and—freed from the relentless pain—continue to work. The grant allowed the couple to avoid the downward spiral that unemployment would have caused.

Six months later, a thankful Arletha recalled her trauma and rescue: "The quick response from MicroGrants was the key." After applying for the grant, she did not have to wait long before she received the check, and this allowed her to have dental surgery quickly. She kept her job, and her husband has continued to recover. Arletha's positive outlook on life has helped. The experience of her husband's stroke gave her a new appreciation of how important it is to live in the present and to enjoy every day. "I live one day at a time," she said.

Arletha appreciates that the grant helped her conquer the financial stress resulting from her dental bills and Willie's rehabilitation. Meanwhile, she has learned an important lesson while working at PPL. There, she has encountered some disadvantaged people with bad attitudes; they believe the world owes them something. For Arletha, however, these negative attitudes remind her that there is another outlook, the one she has chosen. She does what she has to do to get by. "We owe ourselves. The world doesn't owe us anything," she said. "I strive each day to be the best I can be."

Arletha explained how thankful she is for the life she leads. When many people might focus on their trials and ask, "why did all this have to happen to me?" Arletha appreciates what she has: her job, her husband, and her faith. Her positive attitude, along with the help that MicroGrants provided, enabled Arletha to get through hardships that would have defeated someone with a more negative outlook.

*Reported by Berit Johnson*

BERNIECE MERCHANT

# Building From Ashes

Berniece Merchant is a 47-year-old African American woman who owns a hair salon. She is a mother of two and grandmother of one. Growing up was hard for Berniece,She came from a rough neighborhood where drug peddlers and prostitutes were everywhere. People around her were constantly selling themselves and using.

She was one of them. From the age of 18 to 34, Berniece used drugs and was a prostitute. She says she did it to survive. That was then. She changed course completely when she went to WomenVenture and learned the skills necessary to live a different kind of life. She learned how to operate a hair salon and run a business. Today she owns Dias Hair Studio on Lake Street in Minneapolis.

The city has been repairing the road in front of the salon for some time, and her business has suffered. The street is torn up and the air is full of dust. Traffic is often detoured; the road is sometimes narrowed down to one lane, and there is nowhere to park. It's a hassle to drive in the area, and some of her customers have started going to other salons. She got some money from the government as compensation for the negative effect on her business, but in the long run, it will not make up for the reduced income or the loss of regular clients.

Berniece wanted to make her shop more appealing by renovating it. Through WomenVenture she heard about MicroGrants, applied for a grant, and received a check for $1,000. She was shocked when it arrived. "Not a lot of people help small businesses," she said. The money paid for a new paint job for the salon, a new floor, and new furniture. She also used part of it for the rent. She believes that if she hadn't gotten the grant, she would have lost her shop.

Whether the redecoration has made a difference to customers remains to be seen. Berniece says she's noticed more people coming in. However, Lake Street used to be a dangerous place. Berniece can show you bullet holes in her window from four years ago. "It's gotten better," she says, "but Lake Street wasn't very safe in the past." She fears that people may be reluctant to get their hair done in an area they perceive to be a "tough neighborhood."

Berniece believes that her strengths—persistence and faith—will eventually prevail. In the future, she wants to market her own product line called "Series 6 Treatment" and to open a bigger salon to expand her business and generate more income. Today, she thanks MicroGrants and Joe Selvaggio: "He didn't know me, but he helped. It meant the world to me."

*Reported by Nick Nhep*
*July 22, 2008*

Estelle (last name withheld by request)

# The Power of Knowing

Estelle didn't understand what was wrong. She couldn't read maps or remember conversations. She took three times as many notes as her classmates in college to memorize new concepts, and still spent more time studying than they did. For most of her life, Estelle rehearsed her daily schedule over and over in her head, lest she forget an important appointment or deadline. "I thought I was losing my mind," she said, looking back on many stressful and frightening moments. Although she spent most of her life with this fear, Estelle now understands the cause and is learning to cope with the long-term effects of a traumatic brain injury.

After finishing high school as class valedictorian, Estelle left for college with a presidential scholarship and high hopes for a successful career in the sciences. But after only one year there, her education ground to a terrifying halt. Estelle was assaulted in her dorm room and sustained a brutal head injury that left her hospitalized and in a coma for ten days. Despite the severity of her injuries, Estelle believes that the physicians treating her never tested for neurological damage. The doctors told her, she said, that the partial facial paralysis and hearing loss would "go away" in time.

Estelle eventually graduated from college, but for almost 30 years she suffered from the long-term effects of the injury without knowing their cause. In 2005 Estelle's brain damage was properly identified and diagnosed by a physician for the first time. She has also found a support network at the Courage Center, a rehabilitation and resource center that specializes in treating brain injury and other conditions that can create barriers to health and independence.

With a better understanding of herself, Estelle, now 51, has been developing a new career in writing. With the help of MicroGrants she is now accumulating the tools and portfolio necessary to market herself as a professional writer.

Her greatest challenge in the past thirty years has been dealing with the label "mentally ill." Before getting an accurate diagnosis of her disability, Estelle couldn't explain her frequent memory loss or depression. Doctors and counselors settled on "mentally ill" as the explanation. Although Estelle is well educated—she has a master's degree in social work—her supposed mental illness has cast a shadow over every job opportunity. After ten years working at a Fortune 500 company, Estelle lost her seemingly secure position after taking a mental health leave in 2002. She filed a lawsuit against the company for illegal and discriminatory practices, but settled out of court.

After the layoff, she began experiencing severe neurological problems that were further consequences of the brain injury. For the next two years, Estelle was homebound, living with a partner who suffered with a mental disability. She tried to support herself with the retirement and severance packages from her former employer, but in 2005 she lost her home and assets, and also ended a long-term relationship.

Estelle sought help at the Courage Center, determined to understand what was wrong.

After she discovered that the problems she had been experiencing were caused by brain damage, she was able to use the information to choose a more appropriate career path. Calling on her interests and natural talents, she decided to pursue freelance writing. Thinking back to her high-school ACT results (97th percentile in the English section), Estelle thought, "I've always loved reading. I've always loved writing. What was I doing in business?"

Today, Estelle writes for several local and community newspapers. She applied for a MicroGrant to purchase a digital camera for her work as a freelance journalist. Often publications want photographs to go with the articles she submits. And she is accumulating a substantial portfolio of articles and photographs to demonstrate her abilities. She would like to get reporting jobs for higher-profile publications in the future. Although her freelance career seems to be heading in the right direction, Estelle understands the reality of her situation. "I love journalism, but it is simply not a viable career option," she comments. To supplement her freelance earnings, Estelle is planning to take a course in grant writing in hopes of finding a more stable career.

With the remaining grant money, Estelle bought art supplies and a design table on the advice of therapists at the Courage Center. Her art projects are a therapeutic release for her. But her drawings have another purpose. She is writing a children's book and creating illustrations to go with the story.

Estelle receives disability support from Social Security because of her brain damage, and this is a vital part of her income. However, she has demonstrated great potential and is moving towards self-sufficiency. MicroGrants helped Estelle during a crucial transition in her life as she re-enters the workforce and begins a new career path better suited to her unique situation and talents. In addition to her freelance work, Estelle has been writing promotional pieces for the Courage Center, as well as assisting with community programs at the Minneapolis Urban League.

Living with brain damage has been a challenge, but as Estelle reminds us "it's only the executive functions that are affected; my intelligence is intact." Based on all the valuable work she does for the community, she's not the only one who is thankful her persistence and her gifts.

*Reported by Jamie Kallestad*
*June 20, 2007*


Argian Dee

# A Figure from Dickens in Modern Times

Argian Dee is a man of few words. He speaks quietly, yet firmly and succinctly. Argian has faced numerous struggles not only in his home country, the Philippines, but here in the United States as well. However, this young man is determined and will not give up. Through the help of MicroGrants, Argian is attending Minneapolis Community and Technical College (MCTC) full-time to become an X-ray Technician.

His parents were dead by the time he was 12. Argian lived in an orphanage until he was 16, adopted at when he and his two siblings were adopted by a couple who brought them to Minnesota. Now 24, Argian stays in touch with his adoptive parents, who provide strong support for him.

He arrived in Minnesota in December 1997 and saw snow for the first time. Coming to America was a culture shock. Because he did not know English, he was placed in ESL classes at the 9th grade level. It was challenging for the first year, but through hard work and determination, Argian graduated from high school in 2002.

After high school, he got a job making cabinets and pool tables for two years, but he was struggling with drug use. He experimented with drugs for the first time in the United States, giving in to peer pressure from his friends. Two years ago Argian quit drugs and joined the Victory Church in St. Paul.

In the summer of 2005, he began to have health problems. "I had bone deterioration," he said. "I was really weak, and my bones got soft." Temporarily disabled, he was hospitalized for a month. During that time he decided he wanted to pursue a career in a medical field. "You know, people always get sick," he observed. When he recovered and regained his strength, he was able to begin his plan, which was to go to school to "get back on track," and "start over," as he put it.

But he had no money for tuition. So Argian wrote a letter to Joe Selvaggio, requesting a MicroGrant. The funding helped him pay for books and tuition. He is currently attending college full-time and hopes to finish the X-ray technician program in two years.

Argian hopes to become an X-ray technician, and eventually a radiologist. He is currently living in a group home because of his past drug history. But he does not plan to stay there long and is currently looking into other living options. His citizenship papers are being processed. With these, he will be able to apply for a Social Security card and find a job. He is happy to be in America because there are "a lot of opportunities." He values his education and is enjoying his current semester at MCTC.

*Reported by Cathy Bader*
*July 23, 2007*

# 8
# A Dog's Life and Other Tales

THE WAYS OF ADVERSITY are strange. We live in a society where pets are pampered and humans discarded. And yet we will see how this peculiar human devotion to pets can spell salvation. And plants can become routes to the literal, as well as figurative, flowering of dreams.

Enterprising people seem better bets to make it because their investment seems larger and the roots they extend go deeper. We will meet some of them on the pages ahead.

## Lisa Gomzales

# Anything But A Dog's Life

Lots of Love Pet Grooming is a cozy salon in Ramsey, Minnesota. Its owner, Lisa Gomzales, opened the business in February 2007 with the help of a Micro-Grant. The salon is filled with sounds of dogs barking, a hairdryer whirring, and the phone ringing. Lisa is the only employee, so it is difficult to find a moment when she is not busy. This Friday afternoon, she is cutting the hair of a cocker spaniel while she talks with a visitor.

Lisa is a 44-year-old single mother of five daughters, ages 28, 21, 18, 16, and 14. Lisa's two youngest girls still live at home, and she is also helping to raise her 10-year-old grandson. Lisa said she "basically gave up everything to raise kids."

In 2001, when Lisa's youngest daughter was in school full time, Lisa went back to school herself. She wanted to be a child protection worker, but she needed a 4-year degree. She was on public assistance and could get tuition assistance for only a limited period of time. She decided to go for an associate degree in human services, hoping to connect with a non-profit organization. In the meantime, her family was struggling. She was still getting public assistance and working part-time jobs, but she couldn't find anything to adequately support her family.

In 2003, she completed her degree and began looking for work. After graduating, Lisa accepted a position in a group home working with people who had traumatic brain injuries. The job was stressful. She was required to stay overnight, and ultimately realized she couldn't manage that with five children. She continued to search for human service jobs without luck. She tried to come up with enough money to support the family by working odd jobs.

One day Lisa was trimming her dog's hair when she suddenly realized that she was relaxed, enjoying herself, and feeling artistic and creative. Her love of animals led her to enroll in a pet grooming school. She studied hard and became certified as a pet groomer. Working at three salons, she gained valuable experience and knowledge about running a business.

Lisa had found something she loved to do, yet she was still struggling financially. She needed a bit of luck. Lisa entered her name in a raffle on a computer at the welfare office. She won. The prize was an opportunity to participate in a program called "Project Gate." The program paid for business classes, linked her with a business consultant, and directed her to WomenVenture. Through WomenVenture she learned about MicroGrants.

With the help of MicroGrants and a small loan from WomenVenture, Lisa opened her pet salon. She began in February 2007, and the business is taking off. Lisa used the MicroGrant to buy some grooming tables for $600. The rest of the money was spent on a phone for the office, new clippers and blades, advertising, and related expenses.

Lisa's business is currently turning a profit. Her advertisement just came out in the Yellow Pages. She is expecting new customers and is usually completely booked for at least three days a week. The price for each pet depends on its size. Lisa can groom around 5 pets a day, and make between $150 and $200 dollars a day. The cost of running the business ranges from $900 to $1100 a month, which means that Lisa is gradually earning a living. Right now Lisa works Tuesday through Saturday, but if she is booked through the week, she is willing to work on her days off. Her love of animals is evident in the way she carefully grooms each animal, taking special care to avoid the warts or other lesions common on older dogs.

Because of her past experience, Lisa knows what to expect throughout the year and can plan accordingly. Business usually picks up in the summer and again around the winter holiday season. But she believes that she can stay busy year round because her business is in high demand. People who live in the area are grateful because it was inconvenient to drive all the way to the Twin Cities to get their dogs groomed.

When Lisa opened her salon, she bought an extra table with the idea of having another person working there in the future. The second groomer would be self-employed, but would split his or her earnings with Lisa in payment for the space, equipment and clients. When she gets to that point, Lisa will know that she has really succeeded.

Lisa's long-term vision is to open a pet boarding and grooming facility. She would like to offer "doggie daycare," boarding by the day or week, while continuing her grooming business.

She would like to work out of her home in the future, but she realizes that leasing a different space is probably a more realistic plan. She needs a yard large enough for kennels and for the dogs to run around. Her original business plan was for doggie daycare, but she could not get a permit to do it in her home. It is a goal she can work towards. She is considering taking a part-time job at an animal boarding center to learn about the trade.

Lisa has goals and is willing to work hard to achieve them. Without the help of MicroGrants, Lisa would not have been able to open her salon. Banks would not loan her money because her income was low. She struggled to start the business, and MicroGrants was there with a helping hand. Before Lisa received the MicroGrant and opened her business, her family was constantly moving. They have lived in Minneapolis, Columbia Heights, and Brooklyn Park. She plans to stay in Ramsey for a long time, because she is finally secure and self-sufficient. MicroGrants enabled Lisa to gain financial stability, and in the end, happiness for her and her family!

*Reported by Catherine Bader*
*June 15, 2007*

## Linda Lake

# Flowering Hopes

Linda Lake owns a small flower shop in Maple Plain, Minnesota, a town not far from Minneapolis, but still touched by the embrace of rural America. The small flower shop is located at the end of a strip mall.

Linda is outgoing and warm. Her easygoing manner immediately relaxes visitors. She openly discusses her shop and her family. She has two children ages 21 and 16, and two grandchildren. Her 21-year-old daughter attends Crown College and has an internship in Las Vegas. Her 16-year-old son often works at the flower shop with her, trimming the trees around the business. He recently got a job working for the owner of the mall.

For the past eight years, Linda and her family have lived in subsidized housing—not an ideal place for children. She did not let her kids stay there alone. Her building seems safe enough, but last year one of the buildings nearby was the scene of endless parties and possible drug dealing.

Linda was married, but she divorced in 1994 and is the sole supporter of her children. There were aspects of the divorce that were infuriating and lingered. But rather than being absorbed by the fallout, Linda looked for something fulfilling that could move her in a new direction.

When she was married, Linda was virtually a full-time mom with a small landscaping business. She enjoyed the work and intended to do something similar, but on a smaller scale, after her divorce. But she realized it might be too physically strenuous, and decided instead to go to school for retail floristry. She was aware that it probably would not be a lucrative business, but she felt it was something she would enjoy.

She completed the retail floristry course in 15 months and interned in a flower shop. She then went to work at the popular Bachman's garden store in the Twin Cities. Linda enjoyed this job, but found that the long hours and the commute precluded spending as much time as she'd like with the children. As a compromise she opened her own shop.

Linda was able to start "Flowers by the Lake" with the help of WomenVenture, where she took classes and wrote a business plan. She applied for a loan through the organization to start her business and opened her shop in 2003.

Her first location, just down the street from her current location, was in a rickety old building that was expensive to heat in the winter. When Linda realized that she would have to move, she was upset and frustrated, because her business was just getting established, and the move set her back quite a bit. Many of her customers are men coming home from work, and the old location made it very convenient for them to stop and quickly pick up flowers for their wives on the way home.

She found her new location by chance. Someone who worked in the strip mall came into her shop and told her about the empty spot in the building. She is happy, but still struggling. Many flower shops are going out of business because places like Costco and Home Depot buy flowers in bulk, which is much cheaper. Linda wants to educate people about the fact that the flowers they purchase at the larger stores may have been flown in from South America, where child labor is often used.

In order to compete with the large companies, Linda made a large sign that advertised her "Flower of the Week" for a dollar a stem. Unfortunately, somebody ran over the sign and destroyed it. To replace the old sign, Linda wants to put a new one by the road, with neon green lettering for visibility.

Linda's financial difficulties have made it difficult to keep her business running smoothly. Her daughter has been paying the rent to help keep the business running, because Linda has no other sources of income. She heard about MicroGrants through WomenVenture.

Not long after, she applied for and received a $1,000 grant. She used it to buy bedding plants this past spring. She put them on racks near the road so when people drove by they would see a splash of color. When she sells the plants, the money will go towards the big sign for her shop. Linda also purchased parts for a large cooler and assembled it with her children. The cooler saves money by keeping the flowers fresh longer.

In the short term, Linda wants to make her stock more profitable.

When she has reached that goal she wants to find different ways to tweak her business because the industry is going through changes. She believes she will stay in business because she can do things that large businesses can't do for their customers. Her flower shop is able to customize orders to fill different niches. She also wants to get more standing orders to help pay the bills.

Since the opening of "Flowers by the Lake" four years ago, Linda Lake has been increasing her sales every year. After the shop moved, profits were down for a while. But thanks to MicroGrants, the shop is back on track. Without the grant she wouldn't have been able to buy the bedding plants, which served as advertising and helped new customers to locate Linda's store. The business would otherwise probably have taken a drop in sales this year. MicroGrants enabled Linda's shop to keep its pace of steady growth and hopefully made things a little easier on this small business owner.

*Reported by Catherine Bader*
*June 20, 2007*

The table below is typical of those created from the data
collected for each MicroGrants recipient.

| | |
|---|---|
| Age | 44 |
| Home zip code | 55303 |
| Marital Status | Unmarried |
| Dependents | 3 |
| Yearly Income | $24,000 |
| Education | HS, associate's degree, pet-groomer cetificate |
| Race/Ethnicity | Caucasian |
| Obstacles to Employment | Lack of work history, daycare, raising children, lack of education |
| Employer/Position | Lots of Love Pet Grooming/owner |

Antoinette Williams

# Fighting Scary Obstacles

Antoinette Williams radiates energy. It's impossible to suppress a smile as she punctuates every remark with an infectious laugh and a beaming grin. Yet beneath the liveliness and vigor resides a spirit in tune with both herself and the traditions of her unique ancestry.

Born into a mixed family of African and Native American heritage, Antoinette has drawn strength from the rituals and healing practices of both cultures, marveling at how similar the two actually are. Combining her own creative energy and traditional wisdom with a degree in elementary education from the University of Minnesota, Antoinette has supported her seven children by working as a counselor in local public schools for the past 30 years. Very recently, this active lifestyle was dramatically slowed. In 2002, Antoinette was diagnosed with colon cancer and began extensive chemotherapy and radiation treatment.

Although the cancer weakened her body, Antoinette's resilient spirit grew. She found strength in her ancestral traditions and wisdom. With the support of her many children, Antoinette resolved to open her own small business after leaving treatment. After a small "hand up" from MicroGrants, and hours of hard work, Antoinette's fine soap store, Rituals, is steadily gaining momentum.

She decided to move to Minnesota in 1972. "I was running,"she explained, Having been shuttled from New York to Florida to Chicago, she had a lot to run from. Beneath Antoinette's lighthearted laughter is the memory of her childhood's physical, sexual, and emotional abuse. After living through an abusive relationship with her father and encountering blatant inequality in the still segregated South, Antoinette knew that she did not want to raise her children in the same environment.

Minnesota was the home she had been looking for. Antoinette remembers Minneapolis as a very peaceful place in the 1970s, which surprised her because, "unfortunately, violence had been the norm for me." She instilled in each of her children a strong sense of values—honesty, tenacity, and spirituality. She is proud that six of her seven children have attended or are currently attending college.

Antoinette learned the art of making soap from her grandparents and elders while growing up. She described her young self as "a very precocious child" who always asked questions at a time when children were expected to speak only when spoken to. Over the years, soap-making has become an important part of Antoinette's life, although she had never considered taking her talents beyond her family and circle of close friends.

During her cancer treatment in 2002, Antoinette realized the true value of her product. "One of the things that I learned from my experience with cancer is the importance of maintaining and exercising healthy rituals in our daily lives," she said. Since recovering, Antoinette has devoted herself to her business in order to share both her fine soaps and healing wisdom.

Antoinette has known Joe Selvaggio since the 1970s from her work in counseling. She applied for a MicroGrant when she was "just barely making it." After spending almost all of her savings on the cancer treatments and opening a new storefront, she had very little left to support herself. Expanding the business was imperative to the future of Rituals, but Antoinette's limited resources were an obstacle to development.

Thanks to MicroGrants, Antoinette was able to purchase a computer that she says has "opened up a whole other world for me that I didn't even know existed." With the computer Antoinette created a website to expand and market the business. She created spreadsheets to analyze the price of selling and making the soap. And she saved her original soap recipes to ensure that the products will survive for generations to come.

The computer also allows Antoinette to keep track of her store's inventory. She laughs, remembering that, "last year if someone asked me how much inventory I had in my store, I couldn't have told them!" Another important development is the creation of an online shopping cart that will soon allow her soap to be sold beyond the Minneapolis region. Indisputably, the computer has transformed Rituals into a rapidly progressing business, though it still retains the personal, familiar qualities of a homegrown operation.

Thanks to the computer, Antoinette's business is growing faster than ever. She now has three part-time employees (including her daughter) and reaches new people every day with her "necessary luxuries" and life advice on the importance of rituals. Although she still works part-time as a counselor, Antoinette predicts that Rituals will begin to turn a profit by the end of the year. Now cancer-free, Antoinette is as strong as ever and brimming with renewed energy. She hopes to soon devote herself to Rituals full-time, and today continues to share her talents, wisdom, and contagious laughter with anyone who takes the time to stop by the store.

*Reported by Jamie Kallestad*
*June 14, 2007*

The table below is typical of those created from the data collected for each MicroGrants recipient.

| | |
|---|---|
| Age | 37 |
| Home zip code | 55116 |
| Marital Status | Single (engaged) |
| Dependents | 3 |
| Yearly Income | $24,960 |
| Change in income since receiving grant? | No |
| Education | Some college |
| Race/Ethnicity | African American |
| Obstacles to Employment | Misdemeanor—check forgery, poor rental history, past drug and alcohol addictions |
| Government Assistance | No |
| Employer/Position | TwinCitiesRISE!/Administrative Assistant |

Mollie Mosman

# Purposeful Progress

When you drive down her street in residential north Minneapolis, Mollie Mosman's bright red door immediately catches your eye. The brightness matches her greeting and personality. With a friendly hello, she welcomes a visitor into the home that she shares with her lively four-year-old son, Grey, and their cat, Pointy Rocket. The place is neat and comfortable.

Mollie tells of her life. She and her twin sister were adopted when they were six months old. She has lived in Minneapolis most of her life. She moved to Arizona with her family while she was young, but eventually they returned. She graduated from Eden Prairie High School, then took classes at the University of Minnesota, but did not finish her degree.

Instead she began working as a medical transcriptionist. A friend who ran a clinic needed help. She worked there for a few years and eventually began writing grant proposals for a living, but stopped when her son Grey was born. When he was three she went back to work, again at the request of a friend who needed someone to run a non-profit organization.

When Mollie and her husband divorced, it was a turning point in her life. She began a new career in bookkeeping. She provides services mainly for non-profits, but she works with a few small businesses as well. Bookkeeping provides a flexible career, which is important to Mollie because she is the main provider for her son. She likes having a job that makes it possible for her to work from home and spend time with Grey. Mollie expanded her business and began saving more money when she received a MicroGrant.

In addition to working with MicroGrants, Mollie is a client at

WomenVenture. She is in her first year of FAME, a two-year program for women in business. The participants set savings goals, and WomenVenture matches the savings 2:1. WomenVenture paid for Mollie to update her computer, but not the software. That is where MicroGrants came in. Updated software enabled her to expand her business, attract more clients, and become more technologically capable. When Mollie learned she was receiving a MicroGrant she was grateful and practical. She immediately called her sister and went out to buy the software. Her enthusiasm for her work, and her motivation to support her son drives Mollie's success.

She considered going back to school before she began the bookkeeping business, but the time and financial commitment were too great for her at the time. She could make more money working without a degree. Molly is being mentored by two CPAs and has enrolled in workshops at the University of St. Thomas to add to her skills and knowledge.

Mollie plans to continue with her bookkeeping into the future. She maintains that her career choices tend to evolve as she does. The nature of the work makes it a challenging career. She is always looking for new clients, but strives to maintain a positive balance of work so as to not to be overloaded. A supportive network of family and friends reassures her.

Mollie's bookkeeping business is rowing. With the upgraded software programs, Mollie is able to work more efficiently in her home while being a single parent to Grey. The beautiful flowers in Mollie's front yard are in bloom in early June. Leaving the house, you cannot help but think that Mollie's new business is beginning to bloom as well.

*Reported by Cathy Bader*
*June 7, 2007*

# 9
# Hitting Bottom
# and Bouncing

CHEER UP, THEY SAID. Things could get worse.

I cheered up and, sure enough, they got worse.

Welcome to the world of losers. Ye shall have them with ye always.

The fight to escape. Fishes on hooks twisting to escape cruel fate.

Prison, debt, hospitals, morgues await. Life among the ghetto dwellers—not the lotus eaters. Ease and pleasure are not in the cards.

The pull of family, the crippling disabilities of racism, the darkness of ignorance, the devotion to loved ones, the entertainment of hopeless dreams, and the moments of redemption lift the lives of the heroes, and, especially the heroines described here.

LAVELLE COLLASO

# Driving and Driven

L avalle Collaso describes himself as a hardworking man with a lot of kids. This father of six, ranging in age from six months to 13, works hard to support his family. His job consists of transporting disabled people to and from their appointments. As the main provider for his family, Lavelle struggles to pay the bills. He knew he needed help, and in January 2007, he applied for and received a $1,000 MicroGrant.

Lavelle described the grant as a "restart button." Before he received it, his bills were piling up. He had family and friends who provided much needed emotional support, but minimal financial support. When Lavelle received the MicroGrant, he was ecstatic. He told his children that he was going to buy them a computer. They weren't sure he was serious. When he walked into the house carrying the big box, their faces lit up. Their joy made Lavelle feel as though it was Christmas. He finally had enough money to pay his bills *and* buy a computer to help his children succeed in school!

The grant had more than just a financial impact on Lavelle's life. It showed him that people do care about one another. Seeing that people were willing to help him when he needed it most was something that stirred him. Lavelle loves his current job of taking disabled people to their destinations. He enjoys helping people. He is very grateful that Micro-Grants gave him a grant, which enabled him to pay his bills and continue with his job.

In the future, Lavaelle would like to start his own transportation business. Because the MicroGrant paid all of his past bills, Lavelle is now able to keep up with his current ones. Each month he puts aside the money he doesn't have to spend paying past due bills. It is a safety net for his family—or, he may try to save enough to start his own business in the future. He imagines starting with two or four vans, increasing the number each year. He dreams of expanding the company to other states.

Lavelle's strong work ethic and belief in his own ability will be crucial to his future success. He is a man driven by his need to provide for his family. Lavelle knows what he needs to accomplish, and MicroGrants has enabled him to begin to reach those goals. With the love of his family, and his end goals in sight, he is on his way.

*Reported by Cathy Bader*
*June 4, 2008*

RAQUEL SOSA/JOSE AMEGON

## Babel's Challenge

Raquel Sosa came to meet with MicroGrant interns to talk about what her life has been like since she received the MicroGrant. She brought her fiancé Jose Amegon and their youngest daughter, 5-year-old Amy. The family received two MicroGrants, each for $1000. The first came in August 2006, and the other in December 2007.

Raquel is a Mexican American, born in Los Angeles. She grew up in New York City and attended school there. She dropped out of high school in 9th grade, partly because she was embarrassed when other children teased her about her broken English. She could get by, and even find work, because Spanish was the primary language in the Hispanic community where she lived. Raquel met Jose in New York, and they moved to Minneapolis to be closer to his family.

Now she is going to school and is enrolled in an ESL program. Language, cultural barriers, and the lack of a high school diploma prevented her from getting good jobs in Minnesota. Raquel considers herself a hard worker and she hopes to complete a GED, and get a promotion or a better job when she is more fluent in English.

At work Raquel's limited language skills isolated her. Although she is doing manual labor as a line worker and forklift driver at Miller

Manufacturing, she would probably be more successful if she could interact with co-workers. She earns $9.30 per hour, or about $19,000 a year. Jose is earning a higher salary at $15.15 per hour.

Even though they are both employed, it is hard for them to make ends meet. The family does not receive any government financial assistance. They are working on budgeting and trying to build up a savings account. Their older daughters, ages 7 and 12, want to wear brand-name clothes, like their classmates. But Raquel and Jose cannot afford such luxuries. Raquel said sadly, "they want to wear Ecko, but I can't provide that."

PPL's Tina Wombacher, who referred them to MicroGrants, notes that the family does not spend beyond their means, except for cable TV. Since their jobs are already stressful, they feel that economizing is better than trying to earn more income. Raquel says that with help from MicroGrants, their living situation is definitely better than it was before.

Raquel and Jose were among the first MicroGrants recipients. Initially, the family lived in Minneapolis with Jose's sister in very crowded conditions. Jose commuted to his job at Miller Manufacturing in Glencoe, about 60 miles west of the Twin Cities.

The family used the first grant to move to Glencoe. Raquel quit her job a Wendy's in Minneapolis when they moved. Tina described the grant as a supplement for the gap in income while she looked for another job. The family found that living in Glencoe was less expensive overall and better for the children. Jose described the neighborhood where children can play out on the streets. "It's safe, not like in Minneapolis," he said.

Now the family rents a spacious apartment and lives more comfortably. Because Jose doesn't have the long commute any more, he can spend more time with their daughters. Raquel and Jose would like to buy a house one day, although saving money proves difficult.

Raquel and Jose used the second MicroGrant to pay off immigration expenses and taxes. Jose had some tax debts. He had paid off around $10,000, but could not afford to pay any more while his other bills, including car payments, rent and utilities were piling up. The MicroGrant helped the family pay off most of the bills, and they used some of the remaining money to buy a Christmas tree and gifts for their daughters.

Tina Wombacher described the grants as a way to help stabilize people so they don't fall backward. She feels that although the family lacks higher education, it is not lacking in spirit and work ethic. They are moving ahead little by little.

*Reported by Winnie Tong*
*June 4, 2008*

LAKEISHA TURPIN

## Ghetto Reality and its Lessons

A women lies sprawled on the ground. Her body is swollen and covered with bruises. The inside of her mouth and tongue are black and blue. She has stopped breathing.

This was the sight that greeted 17-year-old Lakeisha Turpin as she entered her house just after Lakeisha's father had argued with her mother, then beat her and choked her until she couldn't breathe. He ran out of the house and turned himself in to the police.

Lakeisha, a junior in high school and the second-oldest of seven children, seemed to be left with one parent dead and the other about to be locked away for decades. However, as the rescue workers arrived, her mother miraculously began breathing again. Even though her mother survived, the terror and chaos from the day was crushing.

Until the age of 12, Lakeisha had lived in Chicago amid a culture of gambling, drugs, and abuse. When she was young, her father took her to gambling dens, and they would stay out until two, three, or four o'clock in the morning—even though Lakeisha had school the next day—and she was the only girl in a room full of drunk and high men.

If her father won, the next day would be great, but if he lost, he would take it out on Lakeisha's mother, Tichelle. Although he didn't beat the children, Lakeisha says, "all of my life, as I grew up, I was scared of my father because of what he did. We had respect for him because we were afraid of him. He was a bad husband, but a good father."

The only thing that he feared was Tichelle's family. He didn't start abusing his wife until after her father died. He was also afraid of her brother, but the day before Lakeisha's uncle was to be released from prison, he told police he had seen the uncle shoot and kill someone in order to keep him behind bars.

Tichelle gathered her children and moved to Milwaukee to live with her extended family. But not long after that she and her husband moved their family to Minneapolis. The husband began to get into more trouble. He was arrested for domestic violence. He claimed to have problems with their pastor and began going to a different church. He stopped attending services with the family.

In 2001, after years of frequent separations and extramarital relationships and relapses into drug abuse, Tichelle and her husband called a family meeting to discuss the situation. He took Lakeisha for a walk, told her about his past problems, and apologized for his actions. It seemed like everything was going to be all right. Lakeisha and her sister went out to do a quick errand. When they returned 15 minutes later, they found the house surrounded by neighbors. They rushed inside to find That their father had tried to kill their mother.

Lakeisha was devastated. She had been an honor student all through high school, and she had a scholarship to play volleyball at Michigan State. After the attempted murder, Lakeisha felt alone and entered into what she describes as her "don't care mode." She started drinking and smoking. She skipped classes and her grades fell. She became pregnant and eventually lost her scholarship.

Yet, even though it seemed like all hope was lost, when she found out that she would be a mother, she knew she had a decision to make. "I was either going to be the best mom I could be, or I was not." She decided to turn her life around. She stopped smoking and drinking and stopped seeing some of her old friends who were bad influences. She started working harder in her classes, and graduated from high school the next year. She wanted to be able to make a life where her daughter could succeed.

In the five years since that time, Lakeisha has worked hard to create that kind of life. She went to the University of Minnesota and took a webpage design class. She completed courses in English and math at Minneapolis Community and Technical College. She went to Summit Academy

OIC to learn how to become an administrative assistant and took nursing classes at Midwest Career Institute. She has worked at numerous jobs while receiving financial support from the Minnesota Family Investment Programs (MFIP).

She also found time to create, organize, and run a program to empower teenage girls. Lakeisha says that the goal is "to encourage the women to do right; keep going and don't give up, don't make the mistakes I made and learn from other people's mistakes." Lakeisha wants to be a mentor and to guide young women towards success.

One day in late 2006, when Lakeisha was driving, she was pulled over by a police officer. He told her that she owed over $2,000 for unpaid parking tickets. Her driver's license was suspended and she had to turn down job offers because she couldn't drive. She no longer received assistance from MFIP and was having financial problems.

She applied for a MicroGrant to help her get out of the hole. She went to court and the judge ruled that she could pay $1,000 and do seven days of community service to pay for the balance. In July 2007, she will have finished her community service work and hopes to re-take and pass the driver's exam by the end of the summer. Being able to drive again will increase her opportunities for employment.

Lakeisha wants to become a registered nurse. She took classes at Midwest Career Institute, but failed the certification exam twice. If she passes on her third attempt, she will be able to find a good job with flexible hours. This, in turn, will enable her to pursue her long-term goal of earning a master's degree in counseling within the next six years—by the time she turns 30. She plans to go to school full-time and work part-time in nursing until she graduates.

She wants to be a counselor. She says, "I just want to help people. Let them know don't give up—you can't get anything just sitting down. You've got to get up and go get what you want." Lakeisha's story might sound like a melodramatic novel to people living comfortable lives, but it represents much of the reality facing the underclass. Some of them are lost in the morass. Lakeisha's vow: "I'm going to make it."

*Reported by Daniel E. Geoffrion*
*June 24, 2007*

Lubakare "Lu" Matayo

# Trekking Toward The Dream

Lu Matayo, 35, had experienced several lifetimes worth of excitement before he found himself sitting in a quiet Minneapolis coffee shop.

In the early 1990s, the Sudanese government made it mandatory for classes in all schools to be taught in Arabic. This outraged English-speaking southern Sudan. They protested by boycotting the schools.

In 1991, after more than a year of protests, Lu Matayo, then 18, obtained a visa to enter another country. Predictably, the Sudanese authorities refused to grant him an exit visa. He attempted to walk out, but he was arrested near the border, imprisoned, and tortured for attempting to leave. Lu was finally released when church leaders from the country negotiated the prisoners' release on the condition that they would not leave the city.

An exception was permitted for Lu. His pastor convinced the Sudanese government that he needed to go to northern Sudan for training. After many bribes and other hurdles, Lu made it to a refugee camp in Ethiopia. From there, he immigrated to St. Paul, Minnesota in 1996. After five years of running, Lu was finally safe.

Lu enrolled in the seminary at the University of St. Thomas. He has held a wide variety of jobs to pay for his tuition while supporting himself and his family. After four years, he left the seminary and decided instead to complete his B.A. in peace and justice studies at St. Thomas.

After graduation he began working for the Minnesota Council of Churches in the area of refugee resettlement, and he enrolled in the master of social work program at St. Thomas.

In the fall of 2007, Lu started an internship at the Interprofessional Center for Counseling and Legal Services at the University of St. Thomas. His caseload included immigrants applying for asylum status and elderly people who were referred by county protection agencies.

His managers were impressed by his abilities. George Babolia, a licensed independent clinical social worker at St. Thomas, said, "Lu quickly demonstrated his skill at connecting with clients and putting them at ease. His potential contributions to the field of social work are huge."

However, in late fall 2007, Lu was laid off. Then came a struggle to make ends meet. Without a job or income, he was unable to pay his tuition balance at St. Thomas or continue his internship without financial hardship to his family. The University of St. Thomas put a hold on Lu's registration, and he was unable to continue his schooling. Lu needed to come up with $2,000 for the unpaid balance in order to register for the few remaining classes he needed to complete his master's degree.

"The most painful part was that I had just started my internship," he said. "But because I didn't have the money to pay for school, I had to leave it."

In January 2008, Lu received $1,000 from MicroGrants. He used it to pay for half of his remaining balance at St. Thomas. Later, he got a job as an advantage services coordinator for Commonbonds and was able to pay off the remaining tuition while supporting his wife and two children. At Commonbonds, Lu worked with senior citizens and their families in a capacity similar to that of a licensed social worker, but with a smaller paycheck. The grant enabled him to complete his master's degree.

"MicroGrants," he said, "has allowed me to get the knowledge that I needed for my future."

After receiving his master's degree, Lu intends to become a licensed social worker so he can make enough money to support his family while following his passion of helping others. He hopes to work as a social worker for Hennepin County and eventually for an overseas charity organization.

"MicroGrants gave me hope," Matayo said. He's come a long way from Sudan.

*Reported by Sarah Hill*
*May 30, 2008*

Matthew Busby

# Family

Matthew Busby is a 53-year-old grandfather supporting four people on $39,000 a year as a maintenance manager at Project for Pride in Living (PPL). Today his financial status is unstable, but with his motivation and dedication, he will move ahead. "Nothing's impossible with hard work," he believes.

Matthew has had to deal with health problems, including weight and liver difficulties and hypertension. He needed gastric bypass surgery in July 2007, an expensive procedure that he and his wife could not afford. Matthew applied for a MicroGrant and used it to pay for the surgery. Since then, he has lost 25 pounds. His blood pressure is down, and he says that the MicroGrant has had a "positive impact on his stress level."

Right after his surgery though, Matthew faced additional financial burdens. His wife lost her job, and they were living from paycheck to paycheck. Matthew was financially supporting two grandchildren who live in Arkansas with their mother, and also his 17-year-old granddaughter who lives in Minneapolis.

His granddaughter stayed in their apartment intermittently, but when the landlord found out, he told them they would either have to move out or to pay additional rent. In fact, the Busbys really needed a larger place. The one-room apartment was too small. But the rent for a two-room apartment was $893, compared with $500 for the one room. Matthew could not afford to pay the higher rent and support his family.

Matthew applied for and received a second grant. It enabled Matthew to move into the larger apartment and fix up his battered car so he could transport boxes and furniture from the old place to the new.

While they were moving, Matthew's granddaughter had to stay at the homes of friends. Matthew hated that. He wished he had the money to give her a nice place to live, buy her new clothes, and provide her with quality food. In five years, Matthew dreams of owning a house and having all of his grandchildren live there while he and his wife work full-time.

Matthew has been working as a maintenance manager at PPL for four years, and he would like to continue. His motivations extend beyond the personal security that such a job provides. He has a strong desire to see the work he does brighten other peoples' lives. When he is fixing up a property for a new tenant, he imagines, "I'm moving in here." He gives each apartment detailed, personal attention. Matthew has a pleasant relationship with the tenants and says he learns a lot from his coworkers.

He feels blessed to have received money from MicroGrants. To him, it was the "difference between day and night." The grants gave him peace of mind through his surgery, car repairs, and move. Although he is highly motivated and hardworking, he needed the assistance and security that the grant provided.

As a person who knows how hard it is to earn a little bit of money, Matthew praises Microgrants for reaching out to people in need while inspiring them. He likes the fact that the MicroGrants are accompanied by follow-up. He believes that this increases the likelihood of long-term success for the recipient.

On the surface, he is one more African American confronting daunting challenges. Beneath the surface he is a dedicated family man who takes his responsibilities seriously—with surprising effects on those around him.

*Reported by Winnie Tong*
*June 8, 2008*

Tanya McCaleb

# Modern Emancipation

Tanya McCaleb is a 47-year-old mother of five, and she has struggled. But she will not give up her quest for a college degree and a home.

When Tanya was married, she was trapped. Although her husband was not working, he discouraged her from getting a job outside the home. They were barely getting by on government assistance, yet he would not allow her to get training so that she could contribute to the family income. "He didn't want me to attend college. He probably wanted me to depend on him all the time and be on assistance, and I didn't want to be on assistance" Tanya said. She finally divorced him.

Starting life on her own was hard. Her ex-husband did not contribute any child support. So it was up to her to raise the five children on her own. She began taking classes at Minneapolis Community and Technical College in 1993 and played volleyball on the school team.

After three years, she decided that she wanted to pursue a bachelor's degree in accounting at a four-year college, and she applied to many different programs. Public assistance would pay for courses, a bus pass, and day care—but only if she were enrolled in an associate degree program. She decided to forego the financial assistance to go to Augsburg College.

Tanya succeeded at Augsburg. She found an inexpensive day care at a local park that had a sliding fee scale. She didn't drive, so she rode the city bus for over two hours to get to school. During a bus workers' strike, she walked for hours to and from school and day care. On the way home, she would stop to buy the children ice cream cones saying, "Wow, we walked this far in an hour!" knowing that they were only halfway there.

She had to find the strength to stay motivated. Tanya did not have enough money for both tuition and living expenses and had to take out loans. But she managed to complete all of her courses except her internship credit. She marched with her graduating class in 1999.

By searching databases, Tanya found a job in the accounting department at Project for Pride in Living (PPL). She was hired for the job in spite of the fact that she had not quite completed her degree. She moved into PPL housing in the suburb of Crystal in 1999 and was happy to have found a safe neighborhood for her family.

Tanya learned how to drive and found a car through the McKnight Foundation. She has now worked at PPL for the last eight years. In 2003, to make ends meet, she added a part-time job—working between 14 and 22 hours a week at Kohl's. (She continued to work 40 hours per week at PPL.)

It was not until 2007 that Tanya was able to start the internship she needed to finish her degree. Her finances had been stretched too thin to be able to afford it. (It was the kind of internship that she had to pay for, not one that offered a stipend.) She was grateful that Augsburg agreed to pay for it. Now she is working an additional 12 hours a week, a total of 74 hours of work each week.

Tanya received her MicroGrant in a time of great need. Someone stole a box of checks from her mailbox and wrote a check for $500. She called the police when she discovered that a check had been forged. But since the incident involved her mailbox, it became a federal investigation. The process takes months, precious time that Tanya did not have.

She paid the bills, but did not have enough money to cover her basic necessities. She called creditors and ask them not to charge her late fees because of the theft. She lost her car because she couldn't afford the monthly payments. On top of that, the credit card companies claimed that she owed $2,700, even though she had spent only $1,000 on those accounts. Tanya was struggling in quicksand, overwhelmed. It was then she learned about MicroGrants.

She applied and received a check for $1,000. Tanya went to a police auction at an impound lot and bought a car for $200. It was the middle of winter, and she needed the vehicle to get to work and to drive her daughter to school. The car was old but it served its purpose at the time. Tanya also went to court and settled with the credit card companies; she used the remaining $800 to start paying off her settlement. This has enabled her to begin to restore her credit, which, when the settlement is completely paid off, will open up more opportunities.

When Tanya was initially considered for the grant, she was $2,000 away from being able to buy a house. When the theft occurred, her plans for homeownership had to be put on hold. She needed to start saving money again while she completed her accounting internship. Finishing her degree will open up job opportunities that will allow her to work for a higher salary, work fewer hours and have more time for herself and her family. Tanya wants to own a home so that her grandchildren can have a safe place to visit. This is part of her vision to encourage her grandchildren to graduate from high school and attend college.

Tanya has faced and overcome many obstacles to reach her goal of a college degree. She went through a divorce, eight years of being only one credit away from graduation, while trying to raise five children without any child support. By working up to 74 hours a week, she has just about goals. It's been tough fight, but this mom is winning it.

*Reported by Dan Geoffiron*
*July 17, 2007*

The table below is typical of those created from the data collected for each MicroGrants recipient.

| | |
|---|---|
| Age | 55 |
| Home zip code | 55419 |
| Marital Status | Married |
| Dependents | 1 |
| Yearly Income | $22,000 |
| Change in income since receiving grant? | Slight increase |
| Education | GED, theology classes 5 years ago |
| Race/Ethnicity | African American |
| Obstacles to Employment | No |
| Health Insurance | Yes |
| Government Assistance | No |
| Employer/Position | Project for Pride in Living/ receptionist |

LACOTREF BIBBS

# Charity Begins at Home

Lacotref Bibbs is a 28-year-old African American single mother of two. She has a 6-year-old daughter and a 3-year-old son. Both currently live with their grandmother in Tennessee. Born and raised in Chicago, Lacotref came to Minnesota in 1990 and now lives in a one-bedroom apartment in North Minneapolis.

Lacotref is moved by the plight of people in need. She believes "there is no greater joy than helping others." She works as a personal care assistant at Hennepin Home Healthcare where she aids people in nursing homes. "I really love helping the elderly," she said. Although the pay is not high, it gives her a sense of fulfillment. She helps the seniors to take their pills and perform other daily functions. Nevertheless Lacotref desperately needs to help her own family. With two children to raise, she needs a place to call home.

When Lacotref came to MicroGrants looking for help, she didn't know what to expect. At the time, she was living with her mother and her two children. But there was an unexpected problem. Her mother had to move to Tennessee to help other family members. Lacotref suddenly needed money to move into her own place. Although she receives child support, it is not enough to provide for her family. She applied for a MicroGrant and a check appeared promptly. She was able to rent a one-bedroom apartment. "The grant allowed me to find a place to live. Without it I might have been on the streets," she said.

The one-bedroom apartment in North Minneapolis proved unsuitable for the family. Lacotref decided it was best to send her children to Tennessee to live with her mother, where they can have a better life. Moving to a new neighborhood, Lacotref had been worried about finding reliable baby-sitters. And in Tennessee her 3-year-old son can go to pre-school. "This grant," she said, "allowed me to focus more on saving money for a better place to live, and I am grateful to for that."

Moving into the place where she is living now is hardly the last of Lacotref's goals. She is looking for a three-bedroom apartment in a nice neighborhood. In the near future she wants to bring her her children back to Minnesota. When she talks about them, she glows wih warmth and pride. In five years she hopes to own her own home.

Lacotref spends all her free time working, hoping to save enough money to bring the children back. "I work for my kids," she says. "They are my pride and joy. That is the reason why I work so much." Indeed, Lacotref shows a great passion for her kids. She thanks MicroGrants for giving her this chance of a lifetime.

*Reported by Nick Nhep*
*July 2008*

## Natissja Skinner

# Dreaming

Isolated, unemployed, and without hope, Natissja Skinner was desperate. With two sons, aged 2 and 3, and a daughter on the way, she thought that she might soon be homeless, thrown out on the street. Then she learned about MicroGrants and that someone might be able to help her.

She applied and received $1,000. "It helped in the time of need," she said. "I was really in trouble and had nowhere else to turn." The Micro-Grant helped her bridge the gap while she was pregnant until she could become self-sufficient again.

Natissja is an independent woman. She has been working since she was 15 and had her own apartment when she was 16. She was taking business courses at the local community college and working as a beverage server at a casino when she became pregnant for the third time. Due to illness from the pregnancy, she couldn't get the hours she needed. Then her car broke down. Without enough money to get it repaired, she couldn't get to work and had to drop out of college. "Everything," she said, "just fell on me at one time."

Not being able to support herself and her children was a new and frightening experience. She had never needed help before; she had been totally self-sufficient. Her extended family was over a thousand miles away in Arizona and California. Friends in the area had told her to seek assistance from the county, but she discovered that she couldn't get financial assistance until she had received an eviction notice. After that, it would take 30 to 60 days before her request could be processed, leaving her on the streets, pregnant and with two young boys.

She said, "I didn't know who to go to for help, I didn't know where to turn." Her children's father did not provide any economic help. She was the sole provider for her family and for the first time, she couldn't provide. Yet, with the MicroGrant she was able to make it through. Her daughter will be born soon, and she is looking forward to returning to her job soon. She is also excited about returning to college. She wants to get back on her feet to take care of herself and her family. She wants to get on a path that will ensure her economic security and eventually enable her to do what she loves: writing poetry and making documentary films.

*Reported by Daniel E. Geoffrion*
*June, 5, 2007*

Rhonada Valentine

# Bumping Along the Bottom

Colorful streamers hang down from the ceiling of Rhonada Valentine's apartment to celebrate her 4-year-old son's birthday. As Rhonada starts talking, the little boy runs around the room in circles pretending to be a superhero. Whenever his 12-year-old sister catches the shirtless adventurer, he calms down, but after five minutes he begins to bounce about again.

Rhonada Valentine is 29 years old and, including her superhero son, has four children. Her daughters are 12 and 8 years old, and her sons are 4 and 1. She is struggling to make a better life for herself and her children. Even though her life has been filled with obstacles and hardship, she keeps persevering and tries to create opportunities for her children.

Rhonada has been working since she was 13. She would often work for a short time, and then quit when she found herself with some walking-around money. This hurt her employment record and made it difficult for her to find good jobs. When she was not working, she liked to to party far into the night, which made it hard to get up and hunt for jobs the next morning. Rhonada has been on and off welfare for the past 12 years

She can sometimes get help paying the bills from Willy, the father of her three youngest children. Rhonada has a complex relationship with him. She and Willy are not married, but they have lived together on and off for many years. In the past, there were some domestic violence issues, but Rhonada says they understand each other a lot better now.

On Valentine's Day 2005, Rhonada and Willy went to Las Vegas for a vacation and to get married. They were so busy enjoying themselves that they didn't get around to tying the knot. When they arrived at the airport for the return flight two hours late, they had gambled away all of their money and couldn't pay the $50 transfer fee to be rebooked on another flight. They called family members, but no one was willing or able to give them the money they needed to come back home. They ended up at the airport for the next two days, and decided—are you ready—to make a new life in Las Vegas!

They didn't know what to do, but a guardian angel came to their rescue. A woman who worked for an airline company noticed that Willy and Rhonada, who was four months pregnant at the time, had been at the airport for two days, sleeping on the chairs. She let them use her phone to get information about where to find a shelter. Then she took them to her house and cooked them steak and eggs. She told them how to get jobs and paid for them to stay at a hotel overnight. The woman's generosity helped Rhonada find her way in Las Vegas.

Willy and Rhonada moved into a motel-like place where they had a room for sleeping and shared a communal shower and bathroom for a little over $20 per night. Willy got a job, and Rhonada began working at Burger King. They struggled to make ends meet and by the time summer came, Rhonada was ready to go home. She was eight months pregnant and hadn't seen her other children since she had left them with her mother for what was supposed to be a one-week vacation. She used assistance from Nevada social services to purchase a bus ticket back to Minneapolis just in time for her older son's birthday.

Las Vegas was an important turning point for Rhonada. When she and Willy were stranded at the airport, she had called all of her family members to ask for money to pay the rebooking fee. Her mom didn't have it. Willy's mom had said that she could send enough for Willy to come back alone. But Rhonada and Willy wanted to stay together.

Rhonada had then asked her father for help. He told her that he had the money, but assumed she was doing drugs—as he had done for 33 years—and didn't want to enable that kind of behavior. As it happens, she was not using, because she had seen the damage it had caused in her family. Nevertheless, her father was convinced, and he had called other family members across the country to tell them not to give her money.

She had never felt so alone. She had helped her extended family financially from the time she got her first job. But it became clear that she would have to find a way to take care of herself without their assistance. She was broke, pregnant, and hundreds of miles away from the rest of her family. Experiencing homelessness and poverty, she became determined that she was not going to live like that, or subject her children to that kind of instability. She returned to Minneapolis in June 2005.

When she returned, she found a job at a laundromat. Even though she was struggling to make ends meet, Rhonada found time to help others in need. She volunteered at a nearby school teaching English to native Spanish speakers. She taught a class in the morning, and then had to hurry to her job. She would do one or two hours of laundry and then go back to the school, to teach more classes in the afternoon.

Rhonada applied for a MicroGrant in September 2006. Due to "some issues" involving Willy, who was not living with her at the time, the light bill had not been paid and the energy company turned off the power at her house. For the next two months, Rhonada and her children moved in with her mother while she resolved the issue.

The MicroGrant paid her rent, and she was able to use part of it to negotiate a repayment schedule with the energy company. "The MicroGrant made me keep pushing forward," she said. "It didn't let me give up and I was this close to giving up. I would have to start all over again, or go crazy." MicroGrants enabled Rhonada to keep her apartment and create some normalcy for her children.

A steady living situation allowed her children to open up and bloom. During times of turmoil, they were reserved, but now they are able to express their feelings and emotions. They had been very quiet, but now Rhonada can't get them to stop talking. She encourages them to work toward their highest aspirations saying, "whatever you see on TV, commercials, whatever you see outside, anything that you see on earth, we made it. If you see that any human made something, you can make it, too."

Rhonada knows that she won't be able to do everything that she wants because of decisions that she made in her earlier life, but she is trying to reach the highest level she can and wants her children to reach their full potential.

Today, she no longer receives welfare money and is working toward being an air traffic controller. She completed one year of training and needs to go back to school for the second year to complete the program. She no longer has the time to teach, but she is still working at the laundromat. The atmosphere is hot and the work is exhausting, but the job gives her a source of income. Her car broke down, which limits her options to find a higher-paying job. Her stepfather works at the same place, and she can rely on him to keep her job until she can save enough for another car.

Rhonada has been through a lot in her life. She hit bottom when she was broke and eight months' pregnant in Las Vegas, with the rest of her family unable or unwilling to help, and over 1,000 miles away. Yet, she came back to Minneapolis and has started to make her household into a stable and nurturing place for her children. She is still looking for that breakthrough that will enable her to make more money. But until that time, she is continuing to work hard.

*Reported by Daniel E. Geoffrion*
*June 28, 2007*

MERCEDES CRUZ

## Family Dreams and Nightmares

Mercedes Cruz is not one who looks to outside support for help. She grew up as her family underwent a difficult transition from a life in the Philippines to living in America. Mercedes began working when she was 7 years old and learned the importance of self-reliance early.

Confronted with a challenge today, she still holds to the theory that, "I'm going to do it myself, and it's going to work." As a recent graduate of the Carlson School of Management at the University of Minnesota, she has seen that her determination has certainly paid off. She is confident, capable, and ready to tackle almost any problem. However, she has spent most of her life tackling other people's problems.

Thanks to her rapid adaptation to American culture, her resourcefulness, and her naturally dependable character, Mercedes has grown into a position of great responsibility in her family—especially since her stepfather left the picture seven years ago. She is devoted to her mother and brother, and the constant need to stabilize the family's finances has prevented her from striking out on her own and pursuing her own goals.

To ease the financial burden on herself, Mercedes applied for a MicroGrant on behalf of her mother, Antonieta, in order to help her achieve self-sufficiency. With the help of MicroGrants, combined with plenty of encouragement from her daughter, Antonieta now has a plan to support herself. And Mercedes hopes to finally be able to pursue a career in show business.

Mercedes remembers, "I've always been very independent, always the one to take care of the finances for my mother, my brother and myself." During her senior year of high school, Antonieta was going through a divorce. In order to make the down payment on a house for the smaller family, Mercedes sacrificed all of her college savings, $13,000, which she had been building up since she started work at age 7. Fortunately, Mercedes' grades and financial need qualified her for grants and scholarships that allowed her to attend the Carlson School of Management.

While Mercedes has been quite successful in her own right, her mother has struggled with financial problems ever since coming to America. Although Antonieta continued to run the family vacuum business after the divorce, she couldn't keep up with the mortgage on the new house. She began working long hours in a new job with Sterilmed, Antonieta's $11-per-hour wage still was not enough to keep up with mortgage payments, electric bills, and insurance bills. In 2003, she filed for bankruptcy.

Mercedes identifies the house as the primary source of the family's financial woes. She recalls, "my main goal was to get her out of the house, because it was kind of like the black hole of finances." However, in order to sell the house and move into a more affordable place, Antonieta needed to pay off outstanding bills. At that point, Mercedes knew that she couldn't single-handedly shoulder the family's financial problems any longer, so she sought out MicroGrants for a "hand up" from the difficult situation.

Receiving the $1,000 MicroGrant was an emotional experience for Antonieta. Mercedes recalls that her mother found it hard to believe there were "strangers" out there who would want to help them. When the check came, both Mercedes and Antonieta cried for joy as they realized that the debt would finally be paid. Thanks to the MicroGrant, Antonieta completely paid for both car insurance and electric bills. Had she not made these essential payments, she could not sell the house, and she would not have been able to commute to her job in Apple Valley every day.

Moving out of the expensive house into an affordable apartment in Brooklyn Park has been an invigorating change for Antonieta. Before receiving the grant, Antonieta wasn't aware that there were opportunities or programs that could help improve her living situation. Since moving out of the house and paying off her bills, she has become more motivated and much more independent.

Mercedes said her mother has recently applied to technical college on her own initiative. She has begun looking for less expensive loans, and signed up for computer courses. Now that Antonieta is beginning to manage her own finances, Mercedes finally has the freedom to pursue her own passion: show business.

Although Mercedes had good jobs at Insight and Glaceau with her degree in marketing, she has found much greater fulfillment working with local comedy shows. "It is my release," she says. Mercedes plans to move to Los Angeles sometime soon.

The fact that Mercedes is finally moving to Los Angeles suggests that she has confidence in her mother's ability to support herself. With a little help from MicroGrants, both Antonieta and Mercedes have gained independence. Antonieta has gained the independence of self-sufficiency, and Mercedes has finally gained the independence that a young person seeks—the freedom to chase a dream.

*Reported by Jamie Kallestad*
*June 19, 2007*

Makeba Stevens

## Fitful Progress

A dimly lit and noisy hallway leads to Makeba Stevens's third-floor apartment, A young boy pokes his head out, looks at the visitors, then shuts the door. We eventually go in, meet Makeba and her family, and learn why the boy suddenly closed the door in our faces.

Makeba is a 34-year-old African American certified nursing assistant (CNA). She was born in Mississippi, and later moved to Chicago, where she lived for 20 years. Four years ago she moved to Minneapolis to change her life and find a better environment for her children. When she arrived, she lived in a shelter and began working with a neighborhood agency. But they were not helpful to her, so she began working with Project for Pride in Living (PPL). She appreciates everything PPL has done for her.

When Makeba received her first MicroGrant she was working at the Family Dollar Store. Someone had used her car without permission. They parked it in a tow-away zone and it was impounded. She used the first grant to retrieve her car. She needed it to get to and from work, and it allowed her to keep her position as an assistant manager.

When she started at Family Dollar, she made $7 an hour as a cashier and was constantly yanked around in the company. She was transferred to another store as an assistant manager—but without the title or pay increase. She went back to the first store and worked again as a cashier. Eventually she earned the assistant manager position at a pay increase of $.50 an hour. Finally Makeba was fed up. She remarked, "They're not going to keep using me. I'd rather spend time with my kids." She told off her boss and was fired, which didn't bother her because she was planning to quit anyway.

Makeba worked at temporary jobs from January until May of 2007. She worked 12-hour shifts for AmeriSource. Tired of the long days, she went to work for Rockwell Automation, assembling motors for Disneyland rides. She had worked at Rockwell for about a month when her car broke down. She could no longer get to her job because bus routes did not go anywhere near the company.

Frustrated and jobless, she thought about going back to CNA work. She had taken the certification test five years ago in Chicago and had been working as a CNA before she left Chicago. But she was unable to obtain a similar job in Minnesota because of a criminal record. She was convicted of a felony when she was 24.

In May of 2007, PPL and MicroGrants helped Makeba get the felony expunged. She used her second MicroGrant to pay for a trip to Chicago to clear her record. She also paid for rent, school uniforms for her children, and the electricity bill for her apartment. MicroGrants came at the perfect time for her. The second grant enabled Makeba to remain in her apartment without being evicted, clear the felony from her record, and it allowed her to submit applications for positions as a CNA.

Makeba applied for a position as a CNA at Edina Health Care and was hired. She is now a permanent employee. She enjoys her job and prefers working the 3pm-11pm shifts because she likes talking to the residents. However, right now she is working the 11pm-7am shift because it is the most convenient for her and the children.

Makeba is now stable. She can pay her bills, keep her apartment, and keep food on the table. She is the sole financial provider for four children, three of whom live with her. During the time Makeba was not working, she got behind on her bills. Now she is trying to catch up.

The job at Edina Health care significantly increased her pay and is motivating her to pursue further education. She would like to become a pharmacist technician or an LPN. She enjoys the healthcare field and wants to go back to school full time in the fall. "School is where it's at right now and I know I'm capable of doing it," Makeba said. She does not want to work as a CNA for 30 years; she wants to climb higher.

In order to fund her education, Makeba will need to continue to work while she goes to school. Her plan is to work at Edina Healthcare from 11pm-7am. Then, when her kids go to school in the morning ,she can go to class and do homework. She can spend time with them when they come home from school, and when they go to bed she will go to work.

This sounds fine, except that there is no time in the schedule for sleeping. Makeba insists she can get by on two or three hours of sleep and still be able to function. But she is also considering working part time.

Makeba's immediate goal is to move away from the area where she currently lives. She says that there is a lot of "riff-raff" in the building and there have been a number of incidents. Some of the other residents leave the outside doors open, which allows anyone to walk in. This is dangerous, especially for her children. (Which is why her son shut the door in our faces when we arrived.) Makeba's main focus is keeping her family safe.

Since receiving the two MicroGrants, Makeba has become self-sufficient. She is able to provide for herself and her three kids. MicroGrants helped Makeba get a fresh start. Although she struggles with rent, she has a secure job that will help her keep up with her current bills and pay off old ones. With a steady income, Makeba will be able to pay for school to further her earning potential and jumpstart her career.

It's an uphill climb but she looks capable of handling it.

*Reported by Cathy Bader*
*July 11, 2007*

The table below is typical of those created from the data collected for each MicroGrants recipient.

| | |
|---|---|
| Age | 49 |
| Home zip code | 55412 |
| Marital Status | Divorced |
| Dependents | 4 |
| Yearly Income | $32,000 |
| Education | HS, 2 years at Macalester College |
| Race/Ethnicity | Self-described human being |
| Obstacles to Employment | No |
| Government Assistance | No |
| Employer/Position | Project for Pride in Living/ Environmental specialist |

Tyanna Bryant

# Redemption

In the fall of 2006, Tyanna Bryant, a 25-year-old single mother of one, was struggling both with her personal life and her finances. She had just broken up with her son's father, Mike*, who neglected to pay child support or do much else to support their son, 4-year-old Tavoris. Tyanna was paying off student loans while supporting herself and Tavoris by working as an operations clerk at Wells Fargo Bank. Although money was tight, Tyanna managed to make ends meet.

On September 17th 2006, Tyanna made a big mistake, which made her financial situation even more difficult. That night, she decided to go to a party with a few family members. Before the party, she made arrangements for a designated driver to bring her home because she knew that she would be drinking alcohol. After the party, things went as planned; she and her family members made it home safely.

Once Tyanna got home, however, she called Mike. Inebriated, Tyanna decided to drive to his home. This was the first time Tyanna had even considered driving drunk. "I was always the one who made sure no one drank and drove," she said. Although Mike tried to talk her out of it, she resolved to go anyway. Still intoxicated, Tyanna took the wheel while her brother got into the passenger's seat. She was soon pulled over by the police and charged with drunk driving. The court took away her license, fined her, and required her to attend a DWI class.

Tyanna could not afford to pay for the fines and reinstatement fees— and keep up with her other bills and expenses. Because of this, she did not drive for over a year. Without a license, Tyanna relied on public transportation to get to work and pick up Tavoris from daycare. But she became fearful after seeing a man gunned down on the bus she was riding. She

---

*Not the man's real name.

resolved to get her license back.

In February 2008, referred by Twin Cities RISE!, Tyanna applied for and received a MicroGrant. At the time she applied, she had access to a car and would be able to drive it after she had her license. She used the grant to pay the $680 license reinstatement fee, $125 for court fees, and $130 required for the DWI class.

Currently Tyanna has her license but is not driving because she has no car. She is saving money to buy one and is actually thankful for her DWI. She believes losing her license was a small price to pay when the consequences of her drunk driving could have been injury or even death. Now, she is just glad that "everyone is safe." She also feels like she has become a better person because she has more understanding and appreciation of the "values of life" since the DWI.

*Reported by Sarah Hill*
*July 3, 2008*

Tina Caples

# Emerging From Darkness and Despair

Tina Caples, 37, has made big mistakes in her life. At the age of 8, she began a drug addiction that lasted until she was 34. She's used many kinds of drugs, but her favorites were alcohol and crack cocaine. Tina was willing to sacrifice anything and everyone to feel the euphoric rush of crack cocaine and the numbing effects of alcohol. As a result of her chemical dependency, two of her three children were taken away from her. Beginning in 2000, Tashianna and Ellis Jr., then 8 and 7 years old respectively, began living with their father. Her third child, Lashayla, 2, remained with Tina.

In the depth of her addiction, Tina tried to steal money from the company where she worked by forging checks. She intended to use the money to buy drugs. When the plan failed, Tina was charged with a felony and ordered to go through drug treatment. Tina said, "I knew I had a real problem when that happened." After treatment, Tina was placed in transitional housing, which she found to be filled with addicts who continued to abuse drugs. She slipped back into that world, risking jail and losing Lashayla.

Determined to stop, Tina decided to stay away from people who had been bad influences in the past, including family living in Minnesota. She has now been clean since August 9, 2005. The following year she went to Twin Cities Rise! (TCR!) to start a new chapter in her life. At first, Tina was reluctant to join one more organization that promised to help former addicts. But there she found people who helped her rebuild relationships with her children and others in her life. They also gave her an internship at TCR! as an administrative assistant. The manager was so impressed by her hard work and dedication that he offered Tina a full time position.

In November 2007, Tashianna, then 15, and Ellis Jr., 14, were placed in child protection because they were abused in their father's home. While working full time, supporting Lashayla, 9, and paying child support, Tina was battling the court system to regain custody of her two oldest children. One of her challenges was getting to work and to court on time. Tina had no car and relied on public transportation—reliable, but time-consuming.

In January 2008, Tina received a used car as a gift. The car needed repairs and insurance before she could use it. She used a $1,000 Micro-Grant to pay for insurance and some of the repairs and maintenance the car needed. With a reliable car, Tina was now able to travel to meetings at other TCR! locations as well as go to court. In June 2008, Tina regained custody of Tashianna.

Tina has held her position at TCR! for over a year. While she is still struggling to get custody of her son, Ellis Jr., who is now 15, she has other goals in mind as well. She hopes to turn 26 years as a drug addict into something positive. She would like to be a coach at TCR! Her understanding of chemical dependency would be invaluable to TCR! clients.

Eventually Tina would like to go back to school to become a social worker. She continues to attend Narcotics Anonymous meetings to get emotional support and stay clean. This is her support group. Since receiving the grant, Tina's life has turned around. Without it, Tina may not have been able to gain custody of her daughter. She is very thankful for the MicroGrant. "The grant program is awesome," she said. "It gives people second chances."

Today, at 37, single and engaged, she earns $24,960 a year and has discovered a new life.

*Reported by Sarah Hill*
*June 10, 2008*

# 10
# Existentialists and Other Oddities

THE PEOPLE IN THESE pages are true existentialists. They know they live in a sometimes hostile and indifferent universe, and they know they're going to have to fight their way into the sunlight.

But then, amazingly, a hand is extended to pull them up to the next rung.

Even as these folks help others—and the altruism on these pages is remarkable—they don't really expect help themselves, especially a gift with few strings attached. But sometimes it comes.

Rudy Collaso

# Finding Ways To Help

His disheveled hair is graying and unkempt. His eyes do not shine with the energy and promise they once had. His face is a map of past hardship. As Rudy Collaso shows the way into his house, a visitor quickly becomes surrounded by seven screaming grandchildren, cartoons blaring from the TV, and air filled with the smell of smoke. There are toys everywhere, and the floor has been ruined even though Rudy refinished it only a year earlier. Even in the midst of the chaos, Rudy remains calm and begins sharing his hope for the future of the neighborhood and family.

Rudy, 66, is in the midst of having all of his teeth replaced and recently undergone prostate surgery. He calls himself an alcoholic, but has been sober for the last sixteen years. He held many promising jobs during his life, but his struggle with alcoholism always prevented him from advancing or even retaining his positions. Rudy says that he always provided for his wife and eleven children, but any extra income went straight to booze. He would go on binges where he would drink alcohol until he had to get a blood transfusion to stop internal bleeding from having not eaten for a long time. Although he once had a promising future, Rudy has resigned himself to the idea that his time for achieving success is long past. But he remains steadfast in his belief that success is achievable for the younger generation, and that he can help.

Rudy's belief in the future is demonstrated through his community service. When his mother was ill and would have had to enter a nursing home unless someone cared for her, Rudy welcomed her into his house. She disapproved of his drinking, so he quit while she stayed with him and hasn't had a drop since. After his mother passed away, fourteen years ago, he moved from his hometown of Chicago to Minneapolis.

Many of his family members have since joined him. The money that

Rudy makes goes to provide for his grandchildren, and their presence is what started his community service. He began cleaning up trash and candy wrappers from the sidewalk while he watched them play. This helped to earn him a service award for his efforts, which inspired him to continue, and think of other ways to help the community.

Several years ago, Rudy worked with the police and neighborhood leaders to drive out gangs. According to him, their work has made the troubled area around 33rd Street and 4th Avenue 99 percent drug-free. Today, Rudy is as active as ever, working to make sure that the neighborhood remains safe, and also attractive. He planted flowers along sidewalks and has done handiwork such as refinishing a floor.

He applied for a MicroGrant to buy two snow blowers. With these he earned money to help support his numerous grandchildren, and also continued to help people. He worked for the managers of affordable housing complexes in his neighborhood, but stopped asking for payment after the first two months. He also clears the snow from walkways, a school lot, and a business lot so that people can be safe during the winter. Without the MicroGrant, he wouldn't have been able to do this work—or would have had to do it with a shovel, which would have been hard on his 66-year-old body. The snow blowers enabled him to do his work more easily, which, in turn, enabled him to help more people.

Will Rudy's MicroGrant cause a drastic change that will catapult him into the middle class? No, almost certainly not. But, it motivates him to continue his community service and it gives him the means to help more people. There is no doubt that Rudy has been and will continue to be a positive force in his neighborhood.

*Reported by Daniel E. Geoffrion*
*June 12, 2007*

SAM RILEY

# Catalyst For Peace

A visitor walked in the front door of Project for Pride in Living and asked for Sam Riley. The receptionist turned on the intercom and said, "Sam, could you please come to the front desk?" With those nine words, the whole atmosphere changed, like some kind of red alert. A woman's face suddenly appeared in the window of a locked door. She peered through the glass, slowly investigating all of the people and assessing the environment. Once she determined that there seemed to be no imminent danger, she cracked open the door to the main office, and through the narrow slit, asked if everything was okay. Five seconds later, two big men over six feet tall rushed through two different doors to offer support, if it was needed, and to make sure that everyone was safe. The receptionist assured them that she only intended to page Sam, but the tension remained. It was obvious that when the big guns are needed, the call goes to Sam.

Sam Riley walked through the door. He is an impressively large, African American man. His big hands still have knuckle-cracking strength even though he is 49 years old. Born and raised in Minneapolis, Sam has spent most of his life in the city. He graduated from Minneapolis North High School and went to Macalester College.

After college, he tried his hand at many different things including the military, wrestling, and being a bodyguard. As a professional wrestler, he worked for the American Wrestling Association, where he wrestled legends such as the future governor of Minnesota, Jesse "The Body" Ventura. After wrestling, he became a bouncer. One of his most exciting assignments was working for a musician known most famously as Prince. After the stint with Prince, Sam worked at several nightclubs as the head bouncer. He managed about 15 other bouncers and became skilled at reducing criminal behavior and violence.

For the past 15 years, he has worked for Project for Pride in Living as an Environmental Specialist. His responsibilities include resolving conflicts and teaching conflict resolution skills, negotiating with tenants, addressing tenant concerns and policy concerns, and interacting with the property management division. He tries to revitalize neighborhoods that have become entrenched in a cycle of poverty and destructive behavior. He works to ensure that a community that has improved continues to be a "breath of fresh air" in the inner city.

When Sam's daughter was born 16 years ago, he thought: "There needs to be change, or she is going to grow up into a world that is really bizarre. What can I do to help clear a path where she can possibly walk some sidewalks without being accosted, pestered, or propositioned by hopheads?" This concern motivated him to strive to make Minneapolis a safer place.

In addition to his job at PPL, Sam began to work at night in conjunction with the Minneapolis Police Department. Sam led a team of seven other volunteers who conducted night missions to places where illegal activity was going on. He would break down the doors of drug dealers' houses, and often forcibly wrestle them to the ground and handcuff them. The police officers typically followed his team inside.

Every person on Sam's team and on the team of police have been shot at one time or another. But Sam keeps doing this work, in spite of the danger, because he believes it is right. He says that after his biggest fear was realized, when his mother died, he was never again afraid. In his mind, getting shot at is just part of the action. His strength and bravery have allowed him to confront people that no one else would, and he has been instrumental in driving criminals out of neighborhoods.

One of his major successes was in the troubled area around 33rd Street and 4th Avenue. In the past, gangs would drive down the streets firing guns into the air to intimidate the people who lived there. Drugs were sold throughout the neighborhood. Fights would break out frequently at the nearby mall and in the streets. Sam and his team worked for years, together with the police and community leaders, to regain control of the area. The gangs broke into the cars and smashed the car windows of the people who were trying to clean up the neighborhood. But the area eventually became 99 percent drug-free, according to one of the local residents.

When Sam applied for a MicroGrant, Christmas was fast approaching and his car was falling apart. It needed extensive repairs, and he needed to be able to drive to fulfill his job responsibilities. It seemed that the only way to pay for the repairs would be to neglect other bills and expenses, and to forego presents for his three children. This meant debt and demoralization. Besides needing money to fix his car and pay for presents, Sam wanted to go to school to get certification as a bartender to supplement his income and earn a living after he retired from PPL.

MicroGrants was there. "The children had a wonderful Christmas," he said, "the car ran, and bartending school was paid for. A lot of goals were met, and that would not have happened without the grant." This was an important tipping point in Sam's life. It allowed him to continue to be self-sufficient, and provided a way for him to earn income in the future.

Sam is an intelligent, eloquent speaker who communicates a passion for helping others and making the world a better place. "Once I had children," he said, "I realized that the world just isn't yours anymore. You've got to live through, for, and by other people. You can't afford for them to fall."

He feels compelled to do all he can to make Minneapolis a safer place. When a homicide occurs, he goes into action and respectfully helps the families, whether they fall under his responsibilities for PPL or not. He tries to defuse the situation to avoid retaliation attacks. By being a strong force in times of chaos, he has helped combatants to resolve their differences peacefully. He has been successful in preventing many revenge killings that would otherwise have drawn out the cycle of violence.

The former ring opponent of Jesse Ventura and bodyguard of Prince has dedicated his life to making Minneapolis a safe environment. Sam is a person who continues to realize his potential, and has been instrumental in allowing communities to flourish. The MicroGrant proved an investment in community safety and stability.

*Reported by Daniel E. Geoffrion*
*June 20, 2007*

# 11

## And How Did It All Turn Out?

At this point a lot of people have been helped. The gifts have been used. We've read the stories. We should now consider the financial outcome.

But where is the beef?

We need to know the outcome.

Can people really be helped?

How many lapsed? How many climbed?

We need to know the outcomes—or at least get a sense of how the gifts mostly worked out.

### A statistical analysis by John Mauriel, Ph.D.

After reading these gripping and often poignant stories about the struggles of people attempting to move out of poverty, feed their children, overcome addiction, start businesses, enhance their education, and just survive in a world that often drains their inner strength and limited financial resources, what have we learned? Many will see the human imperative about which all religions speak so profoundly: it is our moral obligation to try to share our abundance with people who are much less fortunate than we are, many of whom lack the ability to obtain the basic necessities of a normal life, often through no fault of their own. These people will say, "We must try to help them. We must not abandon them," because it is the right thing to do—a moral imperative.

The stories in this book portray a very satisfying social return on investment through awarding MicroGrants to people who have a desire and strong motivation to move out of poverty, but just need a little "leg up." Reading about the lives of the 80 people interviewed for this book, one cannot help but be moved by their spunk, concerned about their inadequacies, upset about how often they do not progress as we would like them to, and deeply touched by their bravery in the face of huge obstacles. But some may still wonder about whether a small grant of $1,000 can enable a sustainable, positive impact on their lives. Others might speculate over those stories not included in this book because the individuals have moved or left town or for other reasons and were unavailable to interview. For readers who are satisfied with the human returns described in the stories of the people whose reports filled the earlier chapters of this book (and the many dozens of other, like recipients who were not interviewed for the book), and believe these alone are enough to justify more than $1 million in grants made over the last several years, you need not read any further.

For the readers who, even if impressed by the wonderful successes presented in the earlier stories, also have some curiosity about the hard measurable returns obtained for the money invested in the people who received MicroGrants, the next pages are an attempt to begin to quantify an answer to the Return-On-Investment (ROI) question in financial terms. This chapter is for those who may ask, "Are we really helping people in ways that benefit them and benefit our society and our economy as well? If so, how effective is this help? Are the funds donated to MicroGrants working effectively to reduce poverty and dependence on public assistance? Is there also a dollar return to society—that is, measurable financial returns from MicroGrants—that accrue to every citizen in this community? What is the bottom line, financial return to society from the award of Joe Selvaggio's MicroGrants?" In other words, what is the financial return on investment achieved by MicroGrants?

We have already seen the impressive social and human return that MicroGrants can bring about in terms of improved education levels, greater confidence, improved outlook, happier and healthier families, etc. Presumably these benefits will be converted into increased income and self-sufficiency. Is there also evidence that these social and personal gains also include long-run financial returns to the community?

In assessing financial outcomes, we do not use the term ROI lightly. Unlike the more widely known microlending programs made popular by the 2006 Nobel Prize winner Muhammad Yunus, MicroGrants, as conceived by Joe Selvaggio, is equity investments in people (i.e. in human capital), not loans that must be paid back. As Joe says, "The last thing the people I am trying to help need is another burden of interest and debt repayment."

The financial impact of MicroGrants can be measured by dividing the Investment Return on the total number of MicroGrants awarded by the annual cost of the program. The denominator of the MicroGrants' ROI calculation is relatively basic. It is the annual cost of the MicroGrants Program, the sum of the dollar amount of the grants plus the very small administrative cost of operating the program.

The tougher metric to calculate is, of course, the numerator—the investment return. While we cannot answer the investment return question as precisely as a natural scientist can measure velocity, weight or temperature, we may answer it with more precision than the economists' predictions of the future timing of economic cycles. Given the economic meltdown of late 2008 and early 2009, for which only a few economists gave us even small warnings of its severity, I need say no more.

As far as we know, no organization has even tried to calculate a full economic return to society, in purely financial terms, of giving unrestricted funds to people for the purpose of pulling themselves out of poverty or keeping them from falling back into poverty.

We know of no nonprofit organization that does all three of the following:

a) calculates the actual reduction in public assistance funds that their grantees save the tax payer (food stamps, cash, earned income tax credits, costs of policing and incarceration, etc.);

b) calculates the added tax revenues obtained by various levels of government when these people become employed again or increase their pay levels; and

c) subtracts out the benefits that were provided by partner agencies, thus eliminating the double counting that often exists when the few nonprofit organizations that try to document their results report their actual outcomes.

Despite the impossibility of getting an exact answer, we feel that this is a valuable snapshot of the last 18 months of MicroGrants' financial outcome performance. Readers who are only concerned with the results of our ROI calculations and not about the technical aspects of our analysis may skip the following section about our methodology and sample selection process and move right to the findings.

## A Word about Our Methodology

In making our calculations we had to make some simplifying assumptions and many educated estimates of impact. We tried to be very conservative in doing this. There are certainly other ways to approach these assumptions, and we welcome feedback and critiques as we continue the quest for more accurate measures of financial ROI to the taxpayer.

We also recognize that the self-report data are not accurate in all cases. Most recipients of MicroGrants are followed by social workers, coaches, or employment specialists for at least a year after they receive their grants. When possible we verified the self-report numbers obtained from grant recipients by questioning the social workers who were working with them. It is difficult to keep track of all people who are on the move out of poverty for much more than a year or two. Over time many of them will change residences, have different phone numbers or change jobs (hopefully for the better).

But we were able to track a significant sample and get some fairly good estimates. Furthermore, we can say that even if no benefit were to accrue to the grantees we were unable to include in this study, the resulting impact on those for whom we do have data can be reported to funders and agencies whose donations support these grant recipients. Given this information, funders may assess whether the financial gains are more than enough, when added to the non-financial benefits, to justify the cost of the entire MicroGrants program now and into the future.

In coming years, we hope to further improve the breadth and quality of our data. We also hope to set up systems to track a larger portion of recipients over a longer period of time to verify the sustainability of the gains they have made. In the interest of economy and because of limited resources, this first attempt is limited in scope.

## POPULATION AND SAMPLE SELECTION

For purposes of this limited study, we defined our population as:

1) Applicants who received MicroGrants between January 1, 2007 and June 30, 2008.

2) All of the applicants who had been recommended by one of the four agencies that were the focus of grant making during that period. They are Project for Pride in Living (PPL), Summit Academy-Opportunities Industrial Corps (SA) TwinCities Rise! (TCR!), and WomenVentures (WV). A few grantees who did not apply through these agencies were not included in the study.

3) People who received grants of $1,000 or more. (Many smaller grants were made during the study period, but we did not include them in our analysis.)

By January of 2007 the MicroGrants Program came to scale and began keeping records that were amenable to summarizing and analyzing. This was also the approximate time that Joe Selvaggio introduced a more systematic vetting process for approving grant applications.

We did not examine the progress of those who received grants after June 30, 2008. The time period between July and November, when we concluded the analysis, was too short to see results or measurable changes for those recipients. We also did not include recipients from some of the newer agencies that MicroGrants began working with in 2007 and 2008. In the future, our database will add these people and include other kinds of outcome data.

Beginning in late 2006, a MicroGrants applicant had to be recommended by a caseworker from a selected group of agencies that screened applicants and recommended them for receiving a MicroGrant. Our sample includes records of 144 grant recipients from these four agencies who received grants of $1,000 or more over an 18-month period and for whom useful follow up information was available from the referring agencies.

For the people we did include, the investment was $153,000 including grant amounts and related administrative costs. Of this amount, an estimated $56,000 went to applicants from several PPL agencies, $36,000 to people recommended by SA, $16,000 to people from TCR!, $40,000 to people recommended by WV, and about $5,000 to administrative overhead.

We relied on the grant application data provided either by the Micro-Grants applicant with verification by a caseworker, or application information provided directly by his or her caseworker within the agency. If an application had the approval of the caseworker it was sent to MicroGrants and was almost always funded.

The application form, which was modified in 2007 to include data needed for future evaluation research, contained salary information and estimated amounts of public assistance the applicant was receiving (if relevant), and other information about family circumstances and employment history that allowed us to ascertain the reasonableness of the financial information provided.

Time one for our analysis of ROI was the date the grant was made. Our follow-up data were collected in October and November, 2008. In order to be conservative in reporting outcomes, we included a period during which extensive job losses had begun to occur. To obtain follow-up information on salary and public assistance level for each grant recipient, we relied on the caseworkers in each agency to get this data from county reports and directly from the applicants they were following.

We have reasonably accurate data for 91 of the 92 grant recipients from three of the four agencies. In other words, in the case of these agencies, we were able to track 99% of their MicroGrants recipients and discover what their financial circumstances were at the time of the grant, and then at the time of our study. The chief reason for this unusually high percentage is that these agencies only refer people to MicroGrants who are nearing completion of an extensive and disciplined training program; people who may need just one final boost to be able to obtain successful employment in a new job, or successful launch or development of their own business.

In calculating the investment return, we give credit to the MicroGrant for a specific and limited portion of the income gains of people from two of the agencies (TCR! and SA) using a formula explained later. For the third agency (WV), the analysis of the micro-grant outcome was measured by ascertaining the success of the business ventures that MicroGrants helped to fund. At this time it is difficult to get useful data on financial outcomes for WV recipients, since most of their very small businesses do not have complete financial statements and some may not even have a meaningful revenue figure. However, we were able to estimate the probability of long-run success of these businesses using data on their current status collected for us by WV. The findings are summarized in the next section of this chapter.

In addition to the status reports, WV developed a system for classifying the purpose for which MicroGrants were made to their clients. Their categories include marketing and promotion, training, equipment purchases, start-up costs, website development, and cash flow. In the future we hope to be able to analyze the relative impact of these grant uses, as well as evaluate the financial position of the various businesses operated by past MicroGrant recipients.

For the fourth agency, PPL, two factors limited the amount of follow-up data we could obtain from their applicants. First, their candidates seem to be more mobile, since many of them were not part of a structured, longer-term educational/training and job placement program (though such programs do exist within PPL on a customized basis for many of their cases). PPL also intervenes for clients much earlier in their cycle of moving out of poverty, people who are often at a much needier and more vulnerable stage of their development, and then refers people to MicroGrants whom they deem very promising, but whose current situation may be very critical, requiring an urgent boost to prevent them from falling back into extreme poverty.

Since the other three agencies are focused for all of their participants more directly on one objective, either job training and employment (SA & TCR!) or business development (WV), it is often easier for them to track their various grantees. Most importantly, these three agencies refer only people who are already poised to move into a job or a new business development for which they have been recently trained, only needing a boost that the MicroGrants can give them to make the jump sooner.

For those PPL applicants for whom we do not have follow up data, it is either because they have become self-sufficient and ceased having to report back to the agency or because they have left the area or were unavailable for other reasons. In the future we hope to be able to interview a sample from this population to determine the degree to which our sample data is biased up or down.

So the 144 people who make up our sample include 91 of the 92 people from the three agencies and 31% (53 of 171) of the people from PPL agencies. Overall then we have tracked 55% of approximately 262 people from these four agencies who received $1000+ MicroGrants between January 1, 2007 and June 30, 2008, and for whom we feel we have reasonably accurate data.

## ASSUMPTIONS

To quantify the actual financial return, we made the following assumptions for recipients of awards from MicroGrants who were referred by PPL programs:

1. We assumed that the MicroGrant was fully responsible for their

later improvement in salary and reduction in public assistance because only those who would have fallen back into poverty without a grant were funded (perhaps because they could not pay a bill or get day care or buy a car and this event would then cause them to lose a job or promotion opportunity. These were typically people who PPL caseworkers had already helped to get to the point where they could go to school or hold on to a job or get their car repaired in order to drive to work, but just needed that last leg up that a MicroGrant could give them.

2.   Our calculation included the full amount of any change in public assistance they received and a fraction of the amount of any upward change in income they obtained to allow for additional taxes that would be paid to various governments on the additional income earned. We arrived at 20% as an estimate of the amount of his or her additional earnings that a lower income person still must pay back in taxes (7.35% FICA tax, 1.25% in Medicare Tax, an average federal and state marginal tax rate after exemptions and deductions of about 7% on the incremental income, and about 4.4% in state sales taxes and local property taxes paid, even if indirectly through rent).

3.   We could not measure such other potential savings to the taxpayer as reduced costs of incarceration and crime prevention, the cost of drug rehabilitation for those who might otherwise have fallen back into drug use and other criminal activity had they not received an award from MicroGrants.

4.   Finally, we annualized the monthly savings to the taxpayer, even though some recipients had received their increased monthly salary for 22 months so far, while others may only have received the increases for 4-6 months so far.

5.   We did not include any future increases in salary and benefits, assuming that these might be offset by some reductions or job loss by some people. In the future a more sophisticated time adjusted return on investment could take these variations into account.

Next, we made a different kind of calculation for TCR! and SA recipients based on the following assumption: The MicroGrant allowed SA and TCR! recipients to begin their new employment at a higher wage on average two months sooner than they otherwise would have without obtaining the grant. Therefore, MicroGrants should take credit for a one-time payback equal to the first two months of salary increases and public assistance reductions these employees obtained.

These two agencies have extensive training and job placement programs that are available only to those clients who agree to and maintain a strict discipline of work and satisfactory classroom performance over an extended time period. We found such agencies providing very strict and disciplined training and job placement programs to have the highest success rate with their MicroGrants clients, leading to the greatest average salary increases for the grantees. This is in large part due to the rigid initial selection process and the self-selection that this inevitably provides. In this case, the agency is fully responsible for the eventual increase in earnings, as well as the decrease in public assistance of their clients, and they deserve full credit for the subsequent financial returns to society after the two months following the receipt of the micro-grant.

However, in the case of these agencies, the MicroGrant was typically an investment in someone who could use it to begin work two or three months sooner than he or she might otherwise have been able to. MicroGrants' contributions to these people were intended to get them over a temporary hump (e.g. an ex-felon who can't get a loan to buy work clothes and equipment for the job or to fix his or her car to drive to work, or to reinstate or obtain a new driver's license), and thus the MicroGrant can take credit for a brief initial period of the first year's increase. Case managers from each of these agencies testified to this fact.

The estimates we obtained from case workers were that these people were able to begin their jobs two to three months earlier than if they had had to wait until they saved enough money to accomplish these required purchases (perhaps because they needed their car repaired, driver's license renewed equipment or clothes for work). See one testimonial below. In our calculation, we gave credit to Micro-Grants for two months worth of the salary increase and two months of the decrease in public assistance data in making this calculation. Many of these people might have fallen back into crime and addiction if the MicroGrant boost did not help them in transitioning more quickly into their newly obtained job, so we feel we are being conservative in giving the MicroGrant credit for only the first two months of their salary increase and public assistance decrease.

The employment director at one of these agencies stated the following:

*Suspended driver's licenses are a significant barrier for our partici-
pants who are ready for a Final Placement job. The vast majority of our
Customer Companies (employers) are located outside of the bus lines,
and this often requires our candidates to have independent transportation. It is not unusual for a candidate to miss out on a job offer(s) solely
due to a revoked or suspended driver's license. It is very frustrating for
the candidate and the Employer Services team to be stuck in a "holding
pattern" that often lasts months, waiting until the candidate can save
the money required for a driving license reinstatement.*

*The ability of our candidates to use a MicroGrant to get their driv-
er's license reinstated is a significant and important step in the process of
lifting people out of poverty and on the road to self-sufficiency. For many,
the MicroGrant accelerates the path to a living wage job with benefits
by months. In these cases receiving a MicroGrant provides the final boost
that propels the individual out of the poverty hole onto stable ground.*

In summary, we calculated the financial returns for TCR! and SA recipients on the following basis:

1.  Two months' salary is credited to MicroGrants for the increases
obtained by recipients
2.  Our calculation included the full amount of any change in public
assistance they received over those two months and 20% (rationale for the
20% was explained earlier) of the amount of any upward change in income
they obtained during that time.
3.  Fringe benefit data were not easily available and are not included
at this time, but most recipients also obtained health care benefits after
receiving a MicroGrant that they did not have before the grant. In future
research we will attempt to gather more information and quantify gains
from fringe benefits.
4.  As in the PPL calculation we could not include potential savings
to the taxpayer as reduced costs of incarceration and crime prevention,
drug rehabilitation, etc.

## Findings

Before examining the financial outcome data, it is useful to note how the grants were used. In the PPL portion of our sample (53 people), those who used their grant money for furthering their education were the largest block (15) followed closely by people who used their grant money for paying back rent or utility or other vital bills (13) and those who used it to buy or repair a car or get their driver's license reinstated (12). Another use of grant money was for buying clothes or tools needed for work (8). Five respondents could not be classified into one of these categories or their actual usage was unknown.

All of TCR!'s 16 recipients except one used their money for transportation to work—either repairing or purchasing a car or paying for reinstatement of their driver's license. The other one person used money for tuition and then lost his job. Similarly 26 of the 35 recipients from SA used their grant for transportation for work. The other 9 needed the grant to pay bills (6), education (1) and other uses (2). The grants made to WV participants were chiefly for helping them in developing their businesses.

The chart on the next page shows the breakdown of the various purposes for which the grants to all agencies were used and also a breakdown by agency of the grant purpose.

## Financial Outcomes—ROI to the Taxpayer from PPL MicroGrants

Examined in purely financial terms, the annual projected ROI for the $58,006 invested in the 53 clients in our sample from PPL who obtained MicroGrants was an impressive 9.1% /year.* When we look at the returns obtained for each purpose for which the grant was used, we find that the largest return was obtained from grants made to pay for education toward a degree or a certification that would qualify someone for

---

* The $58,006 includes $56,846 in direct grants and 2% overhead. When referring to PPL MicroGrant recipients, we will always mean the 53 who were part of our sample for this study. The method of calculating the net return is fully explained on page 185.

## RECIPIENT'S PURPOSE FOR REQUESTING GRANT BY PROGRAM

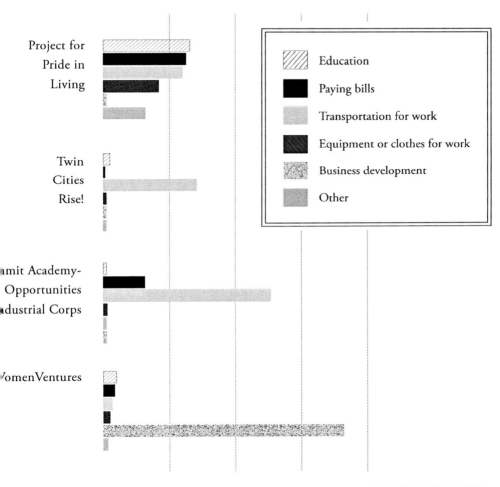

Project for Pride in Living

Twin Cities Rise!

mit Academy-Opportunities dustrial Corps

omenVentures

Legend:
- Education
- Paying bills
- Transportation for work
- Equipment or clothes for work
- Business development
- Other

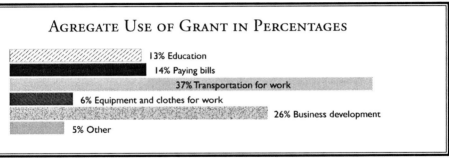

## AGREGATE USE OF GRANT IN PERCENTAGES

- 13% Education
- 14% Paying bills
- 37% Transportation for work
- 6% Equipment and clothes for work
- 26% Business development
- 5% Other

a higher level job (21.4%)*. This is probably not surprising since these recipients tended to have a focused goal and some long-term commitment to better their lives. A return of 12.5% was gained from grants to help people obtain transportation for work by repairing a car, getting a driver's license or paying back car insurance bills owed. The other uses to which grants were put did not yield such high returns. Using grants to pay bills owed only yielded a 4.3% return and interestingly there was a slightly negative return in the cases of people who used grant money to buy tools, equipment or clothes for work (-2.9%). Grants to people who did not seem to declare a specific purpose or whose purposes were vague also netted a negative return (-8.4%)

The following table indicates the annual dollar and percentage return on grants made to PPL participants in our sample by purpose of grant.

| | Net reduction in Public Assistance | 20% of Salary Increase | Net $ Return | Investment | Return in Investment |
|---|---|---|---|---|---|
| **NET TAXPAYER BENEFIT AND ESTIMATED PUBLIC ROI BY GRANT PURPOSE — PPL RECIPIENTS** | | | | | |
| **PURPOSE OF GRANT** | | | | | |
| Transportation (12) | $600 | $ 929 | $ 1528 | $ 12245 | 12.5% |
| Pay bills, rent (13) | $700 | $ - 82 | $ 618 | $ 14286 | 4.3% |
| Education (15) | $1830 | $1991 | $3821 | $ 18210 | 21.0% |
| Tools, clothes (8) | 0 | $ - 234 | $ - 234 | $ 8163 | - 2.9% |
| Other (5) | $-200 | $ - 228 | $ - 428 | $ 5102 | - 8.4% |
| Total (53) | $2930 | $ 2456 | $ 5305 | $ 58006 | 9.1% |

When examining the ethnicity of grant recipients in exhibit two, we find that African Americans, who comprise 34 of the 53 PPL persons in our sample (64%), also gave us a very high return on investment (14.4%), surpassed only by the recent African Immigrants who were mostly Somali. The 6 members of this group in our sample returned 16.2%. Those

---

* All ROI percentages for PPL grant investments are recurring annual returns and this number could increase (or decrease) as future salaries increase (or decrease).

13 people in our sample who identified themselves as other than African American or recent African Immigrants actually showed a negative return (-5.4%). Specifically, the seven Caucasians in our sample also gave us a negative return (-12.2%). Since there were very few who identified themselves in each of the ethnic categories other than African American, and since there were many people from the PPL client sample for whom we do not have data, we hesitate to draw any definitive conclusions about ethnicity, except to say that African Americans, including recent African immigrants, are by far the largest group included in our sample (75%) and they seem to have made more profitable use of their MicroGrants during the time period studied.

There was no significant difference between genders in the PPL group, but later we will see a large difference between genders in the SA and TCR! recipients. Further study of the reasons for these results will be needed as will an analysis of a larger sample of PPL recipients and more rigorous calculations in future evaluation research on MicroGrants. The table below shows data for some of these early results and the table on the next page shows all the data in chart form:

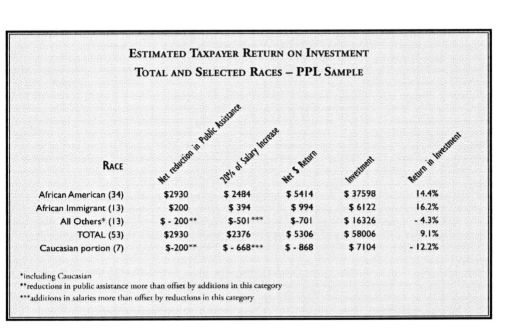

### ESTIMATED TAXPAYER RETURN ON INVESTMENT
### TOTAL AND SELECTED RACES – PPL SAMPLE

| RACE | Net reduction in Public Assistance | 20% of Salary Increase | Net $ Return | Investment | Return in Investment |
|---|---|---|---|---|---|
| African American (34) | $2930 | $ 2484 | $ 5414 | $ 37598 | 14.4% |
| African Immigrant (13) | $200 | $ 394 | $ 994 | $ 6122 | 16.2% |
| All Others* (13) | $ - 200** | $-501*** | $-701 | $ 16326 | - 4.3% |
| TOTAL (53) | $2930 | $2376 | $ 5306 | $ 58006 | 9.1% |
| Caucasian portion (7) | $-200** | $ - 668*** | $ - 868 | $ 7104 | - 12.2% |

*including Caucasian
**reductions in public assistance more than offset by additions in this category
***additions in salaries more than offset by reductions in this category

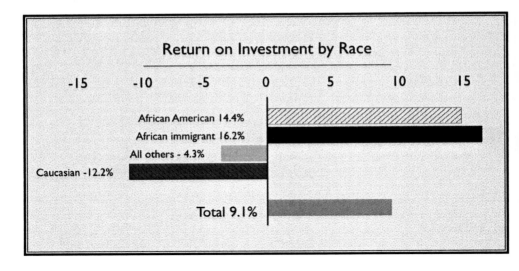

Return on Investment by Race

Since there were a number of people from whom we do not have data, we decided to calculate what the return would have been if all of the people from PPL who obtained MicroGrants during the period studied obtained zero increases in salary and zero reductions in public assistance. The denominator of our calculation would then be $176,509 instead of $58,006. The return from this population still comes to slightly over 3 percent annually and will probably increase in future years from this same group as their net total salaries rise.

### Financial Outcomes - Portion of MG returned to taxpayers from SA & TCR! Recipients

Next we begin our examination of the financial outcomes for recipients from SA & TCR!. WV, the fourth and final agency, is dealt with separately later. Based on the assumption we used that an average of two months of the net taxpayer savings these groups of participants provided for the taxpayer, the cash return to taxpayers for grants to the 35 participants from SA was $26,183 and from the 16 TCR! participants was $12,294. Thus, using our two-month assumption—namely that MicroGrants should take credit for just two months of the financial gains provided by these participants—these two agencies gave taxpayers an almost immediate one-time repayment averaging 77 percent and 75 percent respectively of the cost of providing them MicroGrants. This result is shown in on the table below, which also breaks down the total one time return to taxpayers by gender.

As stated earlier, it would not be appropriate to give credit to the MicroGrant for any future benefits to taxpayers since the programs of job training and placement at SA and TCR! were the chief reason for those results. In the TCR! sample the scores by gender showed a significant gap in favor of females, probably because five of the males in the sample had not yet completed the program and moved on to their upgraded job. Further study is in order on these findings.

We should emphasize that the returns we credited MicroGrants with are one-time paybacks during the first few months after the grant was made, and we credit the work of the other agencies (TCR! and SA) with all the future benefits. Parenthetically, we should report that in its recent e-newsletter, TCR! reports a documented Return on Investment of 295 percent to just the State of Minnesota in the form of reduced reliance on state subsidies and increased tax receipts. In addition their programs provide increased taxes to the federal government.*

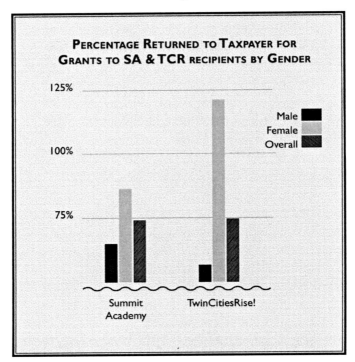

PERCENTAGE RETURNED TO TAXPAYER FOR GRANTS TO SA & TCR RECIPIENTS BY GENDER

[1] Twin Cities RISE! Electronic Newsletter Volume 1, Issue 1, February 2009

### Findings for WomenVentures (WV) clients starting new businesses or obtaining help for their business operations

In the case of an organization like WV, which provides aid to entrepreneurial women and a few men starting or building new businesses, we expect to see the most unpredictable outcomes. Although this type of grant making has a high risk of failure, when it leads to a successful enterprise it can mean a life-changing event and significant economic benefits to society.

As noted earlier, financial information is often not available from new small businesses, and even if it were, a few months to a year is too short a period to determine the ultimate success of a new business. However, we did obtain some information on the short-term post grant status of the businesses that were supported by MicroGrants through awards made to WomenVenture clients. The rate of success of the women in this organization that used their MicroGrants to assist them while developing their new small businesses is higher, and their rate of bankruptcy in the first year is lower, than for small businesses in general as reported by the Small Business Administration, whose statistic includes a large percentage of middle class entrepreneurs. This is illustrated in exhibit five in chart form below:

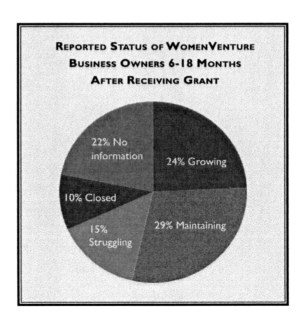

REPORTED STATUS OF WOMENVENTURE
BUSINESS OWNERS 6-18 MONTHS
AFTER RECEIVING GRANT

22% No information
24% Growing
10% Closed
15% Struggling
29% Maintaining

## SUMMARY & CONCLUSION

The return from grants awarded to recipients referred to MicroGrants by PPL came to slightly over 9% annually for PPL participants in our sample and will probably increase in future years from this same group as their net total salaries rise. Even if we assume no benefits went to all the PPL grant recipients not included in our sample, we come up with a respectable return of 3%/year resulting from the awarding of MicroGrants to the 171 PPL recipients who received grants between January 1, 2007 and June 30, 2008. It should be noted that if just one person of the 168 people (including those on whom we had no data) to whom MicroGrants made an award was, as a result of that award, kept out of the criminal justice system for just three months, even that initial ROI for PPL recipients would double or be about 6%/yr. *

Obviously, many of the recipients whose records we do not have also received substantial benefits and could add significantly to our numerator and thus enhance the ROI. Even if absolutely no benefit was accrued to the 118 MicroGrant recipients whom we were unable to locate information on, the financial return is still reasonably good. When one also considers the non-financial returns reflected in the stories presented in the preceding sections of this book, one can make a judgment about the efficacy of the MicroGrant program for PPL clients. When one adds the non-financial human benefits to the financial return presented here for these recipients, it is easy to say the program has been very successful for PPL recipients.

We also conclude that society received most, though not all, of its money back for the MicroGrants issued to those recipients from TCR! and SA. Furthermore, returns in future months could also be included for some of the people who might have lost their jobs and slipped back into poverty if they had not received the MicroGrant.

Finally, we can say that early returns from the WV clients who received awards from MicroGrants indicate that they may be doing somewhat better than the typical new small business owners in general and this might well be due to the additional "equity boost" they obtained from their grant.

But what are financial results, except a means to an end—namely reducing the number of people in poverty and moving them into self-sufficiency?

---

* Based on 2006 estimates of $24,000 as the public cost of incarcerating an individual

We have evidence that this has happened in many cases. While our data includes many estimates, we feel the return calculation is somewhat conservative at worst and perhaps significantly understated at best. Furthermore, we can be sure that our sample of lower income people who benefited from MicroGrants will usually spend almost all of their incremental earnings and thus benefit the economy in other ways. Whether the outcome measures we documented are adequate to justify the continuation of MicroGrants' program is a judgment each funder or participating agency must make.

An important result of this preliminary evaluation process is that the data we collected could help direct future grants to people whose needs and planned use of the money foretell a higher probability of financial return. It has also helped us start on a path toward more complete and accurate measures of the financial benefits to society. The process used in producing these outcome measures is only a first step toward a more sophisticated and complete calculation that can come from a rigorous longitudinal study. We might also consider some statistical measure of reduction in incarceration rates based on statistical probabilities. If even one MicroGrant recipient who would otherwise have been incarcerated for 2.5 years was prevented from falling back into drugs and prison, the government would save over $50,000 in the cost of incarceration, increasing the financial returns reported here by a factor of two. Other savings in cost of drug rehabilitation, or in helping family members and future generations could also be substantial.

Although the value of a venture that is trying to move people out of poverty can not be measured only in financial ROI terms, funders and volunteers should demand some report on quantitative outcomes achieved by the work they are supporting, even where guestimates, statistical probabilities and some realistic assumptions must be used in providing the outcome data. This is only a first step for MicroGrants in quantifying the social and financial benefits of its grant making.

Readers of this chapter must make their own judgments on how much the measurable financial return adds to the value of the program, and whether or not this financial return, in combination with the other outcomes described in the stories provided in previous chapters, makes the MicroGrants Program a worthwhile investment and even a better investment than their other philanthropic donations. We think the data we have presented supports the belief that the benefits of MicroGrants' work exceed its costs.

# Part II
# Commentaries

No SOCIAL PROGRAM, successful or not, is viewed thorough the same lens by everyone. All perspectives are influenced by one's educational background, philosophical leanings, ideological and political preferences, community, and intellectual and emotional temperaments among other factors. Knowing that, we asked people of divergent views and sympathies to comment on the MiroGrants program as it is presented in this book. On the following pages you'll find commentaries from a conservative, a liberal, a woman of color, and an entrepreneur.

# Culture, Compassion, and Conservatism

## A commentary by Mitch Pearlstein

Perhaps the greatest single moment in the history of Center of the American Experiment was when Margaret Thatcher keynoted our Annual Dinner in May of 1997. Sharing a dais with arguably the most important woman of the twentieth century, belting out a duet of "God Save the Queen" and the "Star-Spangled Banner" accompanied by almost 2,300 people at the Minneapolis Convention Center, was pretty terrific.

But as good as that moment was, it wasn't that much better than one seven years earlier when, after carefully adding up all of the Center's then-extant resources, I concluded that yes, we did, in fact, have enough money to buy our first electric coffee pot. Still, in a spirit of full financial disclosure, readers deserve to know how that happy moment occurred within months of a less giddy one, when I regretfully determined we still weren't rich enough yet to shell out $50 for a used IBM Selectric typewriter that I had discovered and coveted at an estate sale.

It's not that I've never recalled these latter memories over the last nearly two decades, as I have every year or so, especially around our anniversary in March. It's just that they never percolated up in the evocative and lesson-rich way as when I started reading the vignettes in this book. Especially during current days of cosmically huge numbers—billions of dollars in business scandals and trillions of dollars in "rescue plans"—it's invaluable, even joyous, to confirm how heroic entrepreneurism is not the least bit dependent on heroic budgets. I hope the following analogy works, but in the same way that writers like Bernard Malamud can make a loaf of bread, a chunk of cheese, and a bottle of inexpensive wine sound as bountiful as an evening at the new Manny's in downtown Minneapolis, the stories here make it clear that true-blue capitalists reside in all stations and come with all-sized bank accounts.

It's easy to lose sight of how pivotal relatively small, even tiny amounts of money can be for small start-ups. I've long been a fan of micro-grants, albeit primarily as used elsewhere, in less economically prodigious parts of the world. I suspect it never adequately occurred to me that comparably modest sums could be put to such productive commercial use in the most affluent nation on the planet, where G-Notes regularly run, not only like tap water, but the fancy bottled kinds, too. I stand happily corrected and eager to congratulate all involved with this venture, starting with my old friend Joe Selvaggio—through whom I met my wife at about the same time I was pondering whether to buy a secondhand typewriter, though that's a glorious story for a future day.

The quiet brilliance of MicroGrants notwithstanding, most people, it should be readily understood, are neither interested in, nor perhaps equipped to, start or run their own business. I take this limitation to be implicit in my charge of spotlighting (other) "conservative" and right-of-center ways of understanding poverty and lifting people out of it. So beyond acknowledging how MicroGrants captures the effervescent spirit of the late Jack Kemp and the possibilities and power of free enterprise, permit me to make several additional points, starting with the importance of striking benign balances.

A quick and important note, though, before proceeding about Kemp's mostly on-target conception and proposals. The former congressman, HUD secretary, and presidential aspirant had long been inherently right about the virtues of capitalism and how it can be made to help people in need. But at the same time, he never gave adequate weight to broader and problematic matters of culture, and how destructive strains can overwhelm and nullify the best of intentions and programs, especially in inner cities. This is a sobering caveat, overarching in consequence, that must be taken into full account always. More on this below, particularly as it applies to family fragmentation.

Center of the American Experiment's inaugural event was a day-long conference in 1990 titled "The New War on Poverty: Advancing *Forward* This Time." That was where, in fact, I first met Mr. Selvaggio. As the final afternoon session concluded, and the last of 300 ideologically and otherwise eclectic attendees filed out of the old Radisson St. Paul, he introduced himself and said something along the lines of, "Well, I've seen your program, now you've got to see mine," which at the time was Project for Pride in Living, another major Minnesota asset which is still doing superb life-enriching work. I took the tour and I quickly recognized that Joe succeeded in getting a very hard, yet imperative, balancing act pretty close to perfect, as he at once practiced a palpable faith in low-income men and women, while simultaneously recognizing that some people wind up in rotten spots in life because they personally and irresponsibly do themselves in. We have all heard him stand up for the least among us. But at least some of us also have heard him harshly criticize those who are lax, uncivil, and sometimes violent. The shorthand for this kind of warm heartedness, uncompromised by naiveté, is tough loving. It's likewise a good shorthand description of Joe's uncommon gifts and contribution.

An example of tough loving writ large in policy script was welfare reform legislation in 1996, which had been pushed mainly by congressional Republicans, but signed into law, to his large credit, by Democratic President Bill Clinton. Suffice it to say, the Temporary Assistance for Needy Families Act has succeeded extraordinarily for a governmental program, with the number of welfare recipients across the country falling remarkably, all the time without (as some opponents feverishly predicted in the '90s) American streets degenerating to those of Calcutta.

TANF's success highlights the now obvious timidity with which great numbers of politicians, scholars, journalists, social workers, and others (and in some ways myself) viewed welfare and its amenability to serious reform. Or, more pertinently, it's fascinating to note the degree to which inside players underestimated the ability of people to escape welfare if only they were pushed and prodded in the right ways. In other words, too many well-off folks had too little faith in poor folks.

The lesson here is that we needed to be bolder than we had been— bolder, not colder—in reining in welfare and eligibility for it. We needed to do so, not just in the interest of public treasuries, but much more to the heart, on behalf of millions of families, mostly mothers and children, who had been enwrapped, not in compassionate public arms, but in a well-intentioned dependency that not a single person reading these pages would wish on anyone he or she loved.

Frankly, I don't know what Joe thought of welfare revamping back then, or even now. But at the risk of irritating the hell out of him, it was the likes of Newt Gingrich and the Heritage Foundation which gave concrete policy life to Joe's belief in the God-given worth and strengths of poor people. And in conjunction with Bill Clinton, it was the former Speaker and others, mostly on the right side of the aisle, who calibrated a new and benign balance between holding feet to fires and touching hearts.

Several times during the Center's inaugural conference in 1990, I was accused of advocating "middle-class values," as if doing so was somehow unloving, to the point of bigoted. I didn't respond that day, but shortly thereafter wrote a column in the *St. Paul Pioneer Press* in which I conceded that yes, the secret was out: I had indeed been trafficking in such dastardly norms.

I defended myself by explaining that all societies have rules, and that when it came to radically increasing the chances of avoiding poverty, American ones really weren't all that unreasonable, and that all I meant by middle-class values were a half-dozen quite basic and mundane expectations: (1) Go to high school, work moderately hard, and graduate; (2) if you can work, work; (3) be married before making babies; (4) if you're married, try to stay that way unless circumstances are abusive; (5) don't do drugs or drink too much; and (6) don't commit crime. That was it; that's all I meant by middle-class values, which my critics condemned as bourgeois bull.

Reaction to the column frankly amazed me. I thought it was a rather well written piece, but praise (in most quarters) was far more enthusiastic than it inherently deserved. After all, what had I said that was so insightful or brilliant? All I had argued was that people ought to be commonsensical; not exceptional, not heroic, just responsible. Nevertheless, many responded as if I had broken new ground—when, in fact, I was just restating old ground rules which, incomprehensibly, had come to be seen by many other men and women over the previous quarter-century as intrusive and sometimes racially suspect dictates. Two members of Congress actually reprinted the column in the Congressional Record. Reactions, in sum and simultaneously, were stunning and absurd, illustrating most of all how far we had fallen.

If I were to expand on the column today, I would only need to imagine and then transcribe what almost all hard-working parents would surely tell their own children as they approached maturity and first jobs: work hard, be respectful, smile regularly, put a permanent hold on new tattoos and body piercings, recognize that middle-class values and below-butt pants don't mesh—you get the not terribly complicated or unreasonable idea.

At the risk of irritating Joe again, I might describe him as a "compassionate conservative." The term is not used as frequently as it was early in George W. Bush's administration. But even when it was mentioned then, it usually wasn't in a complimentary way, almost regardless of the politics or disposition of the writer or speaker. Democrats and liberals routinely saw compassionate conservatism and its main policy vehicle, Bush's Faith-Based Initiative, as a chintzy and inadequate way of helping Americans in need; a sacred-sounding subterfuge enabling government to weasel out of morally incumbent responsibilities. They also warned of how the tack threatened to rumble through and crumble the wall separating church and state. As for Republicans and conservatives, they often denigrated the modifier "compassionate" as a redundant and insulting prefix, as it implied (or so they charged) that basic brands of conservatism are insufficiently feeling and kind. Injury over and above insult, they seemed to dislike the term even more than they disliked his father's decision to talk about a "kinder and gentler America" in the immediate aftermath of the Reagan administration.

Very much in contrast, I've always liked the term compassionate conservatism for a number of reasons, starting with the full-bodied and compelling way Bush explained it during a campaign speech in Indianapolis as early as July 1999. "Often when a life is broken," the president-to-be said, "it can only be rebuilt by another caring, concerned human being. Someone whose actions say: 'I love you. I believe in you. I'm in your corner.' This is compassion with a human face and a human voice. It is not an isolated act—it's a personal relationship and it works."

A moment later he said:

*In the past, presidents have declared wars on poverty and promised to create a great society. But these grand gestures and honorable aims were frustrated. They have become a warning, not an example. We found that government can spend money, but it can't put hope in our hearts or a sense of purpose in our lives. This can only be done by churches and synagogues and mosques and other charities that warm the cold of life, a quiet river of goodness and kindness that cuts through stone.*

As understood both by Bush and its seminal theoretician, Marvin Olasky, compassionate conservatism is anything but a limp or evasive way of helping people, as both its mandate and means are face to face, hug to hug, and heart to heart. The very roots of the word "compassion," as Olasky is fond of pointing out, are "to suffer with." Yet while intensely personal and personally demanding, compassionate conservatism (again as proposed by Bush) doesn't let any level of government off any legitimate hooks.

I've long been of the mind that, as a society, the only way of adequately serving fellow citizens in distress is by taking greater advantage of our religious institutions and traditions while, needless to say, exquisitely respecting the Constitution and American variety. Failing to avail ourselves of such resources is the equivalent of tying a uniquely powerful and benevolent arm behind our backs. The Bush administration's Faith-Based Initiative never got more than a few yards off the ground for various reasons, starting and essentially ending with 9/11 and its subsequent distractions. To understate matters, this was unfortunate. Also to understate matters, unless and until we find politically viable ways of better tapping our spiritual strengths, too many people will suffer needlessly.

A quick word about education before moving on to a giant cause of poverty in the United States, as well as the single biggest obstacle to its significant reduction: the deinstitutionalization of marriage in many communities.

It wasn't all that long ago that a higher proportion of young people in this country graduated high school than almost anyplace else. The same held true for the proportion of Americans going on to college. Times have changed, though, and a significant number of other countries now do better than we do in both categories. Such rankings are troubling, but several indicators are positively grim in regards to many students of color.

Calculating graduation (and dropout) rates is a much more difficult—as well as artful and politicized—exercise than people assume. Hence, numbers can be all over the place. But there seems to be an emerging and rough consensus that only about 72 percent of young Americans overall are currently graduating high school in four years, with rates much lower for African Americans, Hispanics, and American Indians. I suspect that Minneapolis school officials can point to other, more encouraging data, but as recently as 2002, in a study published jointly by the Minneapolis Chamber of Commerce, the Minneapolis Foundation, and the Minneapolis public school system itself, four-year graduation rates for the Class of 2000 in city public schools were found to be 58 percent for "White Americans"; 47 percent for "Asian Americans"; 31 percent for both "African Americans" and "Hispanic Americans"; and 15 percent for "American Indians." Obviously, life-stunting education rates like these are inseparable from life-stunting poverty rates. Yet this is neither the time nor place for education reform litanies—with one exception.

Without in any way unfairly beating up on public schools and the good people who work in them, and acknowledging that far too little attention is generally paid to how many students rarely break a conscientious sweat, research clearly shows that inner-city students tend to graduate at higher rates from private schools than public ones. This being the case, it would seem we are morally obliged to at least experiment with voucher and tax-credit programs. (For those of you whose first instinct just now was to scream "NO" for whatever ideological or other reason, please ask yourself this one simple question: Would you be eager to send your own children or grandchildren to an average inner-city public high school any place in the United States, including the Twin Cities?)

When talking about marriage, I always try to make three caveats early and clear.

First, the *only* kinds I've ever advocated are healthy, non-violent, low-conflict, and equal-regard marriages. Each one of these descriptions refers to something essential.

Second, in no way is my intention to single out or gang up on single moms, as I've always sought to make it clear that I respect and empathize with the very large number of unmarried women who are, in fact, raising their children successfully, even heroically, under often very hard circumstances. I also always try to acknowledge that life is inescapably messy; a fact I was steeped in even before Governor Palin became a grandmother. I'm quick to point out, for instance, that my wife and I are each in our second (and last) marriage—not that she likes the locution. Diane was a single mom for a long time after her divorce and before we met.

And third, even though fatherlessness increases the odds against children doing well, it does not inevitably consign them to troubled lives. Many kids growing up with only one parent at home (or in other "non-traditional" arrangements) are doing very well, while many other kids, growing up with both their biological parents, are not doing well at all. But in the main—and the point is central—growing up without both a father and mother at home, especially in tough neighborhoods, invites big-time trouble.

With such cautions in place, and with the demonstrable virtues of MicroGrants notwithstanding, a paramount question remains: Is it possible to make more than marginal progress against poverty and too-small incomes, as long as immense numbers of households are led by single parents—both men and women, but overwhelmingly the latter—who are poorly educated, with few job skills, weak job histories, and who are understandably preoccupied with raising young children alone or nearly so? Calamitously, it's not the least bit possible. Just two national numbers: Almost 40 percent of all American babies come into this life outside of marriage, with the proportion rising to about 70 percent for African Americans. (The latter rate, I'm afraid, is much worse in Minneapolis.)

Granted, bringing a child into this world outside of marriage doesn't necessarily mean that biological fathers are uninvolved; or that second wage earners aren't part of "single-parent" households; or that some number of women don't eventually marry, be their husband the birth father of one or more of their children, or a stepfather. Yet even so, particularly when compounded by the fact that the United States has the highest divorce rate in the industrial world, ending poverty, simply and sadly, is not fathomable given the near-evaporation of marriage in large swaths of Minnesota and the nation.

Somehow, marriage as an institution, particularly in inner cities, must be revived. Somehow, we must fix, not just policies or economies, but our very culture. I have a few ideas about how to do this, albeit none equal to the task—with one exception, which applies to the nation as a whole: Perhaps someday soon, enough people will figuratively grab their heads and exclaim, "My God, we're hurting our kids, we're hurting ourselves, we're hurting our country, and we simply can't continue this way anymore."

*Mitch Pearlstein is founder and president of Center of the American Experiment in Minneapolis. A former editorial writer for the* St. Paul Pioneer Press, *he holds a doctorate in education from the University of Minnesota, and his newest book is* Riding into the Sunrise: Al Quie and a Life of Faith, Service & Civility *(Pogo Press).*

# MicroGrants, Poverty and the Liberal Voice of Conscience

## A commentary by Tom Fiutak, EdD

*"How does the 'liberal voice of conscience' help people I love and care about who need help now?"*

*— Paul Wellstone*

### THE CALL FROM THE LEFT

The call from Paul Wellstone was not one of desperation, but a challenge to those who he was certain knew the answer. The bottom line cynicism of the conservative right, measuring the individual's worth according to a withering calculus medicinally prescribed by those who have, was and is a failed meter. The failure becomes institutionalized if the calculus creates a mote of protection for those whose conscience would other wise move them to act. Once acknowledged, the thinning of the veneer between those who have and those who have not, demands a response comparable to the courage shown by those who survive despite the manipulated odds of life without a safety net.

Faceless poverty does not confront one's conscience. Instead, what quacks our consciences are the voices in this book that confirm the dignity by which those in poverty sustain themselves.

I was struck by the following comment in the introduction to this book from one of the "haves" who instructed Joe Selvaggio, "If I can't see it from my office on the 49th floor of the IDS Center, I don't want to fund it." What can one see from the 49th floor? A thriving community engineered to produce value and worth to be both exported and integrated back into the rich mix of interests and natural conflicts, or a yearning to control what you can see without the emotional demands of having to touch. This is a cry from the other side of the mote, literally and figuratively, from the high ground.

What's our choice? One choice is to stay on the 49th floor and, guaranteed, you will not be provoked by tears of the third-time mother in her early 20's having to make the daily gut-wrenching decision to feed the children, or gamble what money she has on uncertain car repairs needed to get to work. Or by the parched poet who dreams of melting the shackles of isolation that separate him from his nurturing community by proclaiming his vision of hope to those whose solitary confinement of poverty is even greater than his. From the low ground, the 49th floor is as far as the moon.

Somewhere, uninvited, often unnoticed, Joe Selvaggio steps out of the moonlight and into the lives of those staggered by poverty. He has made the choice to bridge the void of these two worlds, one small miracle at a time. With each MicroGrant, a statement is made on behalf of hope and compassion with little regard for whether this one recipient will "do the right thing" according to rules imposed by those on the high ground. The rules of the road and the street corner, while often arbitrary, have consequences. Once more in the words of Wellstone:

*Organizing is difficult where there is no expectation for social change, and where the assertion of dignity often leads to retaliation.*

That is the danger for the liberal. If the individual is the ultimate unit of worth, and the commonwealth is the confluence of the individuals involved, as soon as those who govern are estranged from the governed, this basic building block of a liberal democracy, or a liberal republic, itself becomes a commodity. Human capital becomes atomized because then the individual pieces are more malleable to the degree that the natural cohesion among the units that form the "wealth in common" is fractured.

Where are the needed social controls if the individual arrogantly steps out of his assigned role? And who is in control of what choices may open to which unit of wealth? The individual? Then there is anarchy! Compassion? Then there is empowerment!

Throughout the seventy plus snapshots of courage addressed in this book, the common thread is an awakening to power. The power flows to those riveting individuals vividly captured on these pages, from those donors who as the antiphonal choir, are cast in the shadows, off stage, chanting encouragement, celebrating both the successes and failures of the actors whose fates they soon realize are not wholly in the hands of the giver or the receiver, the governed or the governors, the haves or the have nots. The power of the MicroGrant is not in the giving of resources but in the glimpse of control that comes with the warming of one's self esteem.

Joe learned from the 1% club that those who have money and wish to affect the lives of those in poverty in our community, prefer to give it to people rather than programs. Simple enough. So Joe finds those in need of a financial and spiritual lift in our community in order to provide those who have the means, the spiritual and moral opportunity to do noble deeds. Joe is the surrogate for the people who wish to use their money to benefit individuals they do not know. He gives voice to the voiceless and sight to those who have the insight to their own blindness. He is the trusted medium among these distant tribes. In a nutshell, Joe brings the Liberal's bottom line, authenticity, to life.

Authenticity is the coherence among the intent, the behavior, and the values that drive the intent. It's a circle. If the behavior is in conflict with the intent, the value of the behavior is inauthentic and disingenuous.

By way of example, in 1996 I found myself in Asyut, Egypt, in a photo shoot with the chief administrator of one of its communities. As we shook hands, I handed him a University of Minnesota "M" pin as a sign of good will and friendship from my institution to his. After the cameras stopped, he looked at the back of the pin, looked me straight in the eye, and with more irony than rebuke, asked why I would give him a pin representing my State and University when it was made in Taiwan. A crisis of authenticity stopped me in my tracks. The behavior belied the intent, and the value of the exchange and the relationship, if even ceremonial, was listing to port.

So the authenticity trap faced by the well-meaning conservative right has found its antidote in the MicroGrant structure, and in Joe Selvaggio's discernment. Rather than risk the awkwardness of the inherent inauthenticity when the behavior and intent lose value by virtue of ambiguous intent, hyper-administrative expenses, or poorly masked faith based agendas, a simple exchange of $1000 for a promise, works.

The reason MicroGrants lifts the souls of its recipients is that the intent, value, and behavior are inseparably authentic. It's not the money. It's the ontological springboard that propels those heroes in this book to do more, do good, or just try again. The cash will run out, but the residual echo that ripples into their communities will not. The result is the unfettered joy that comes when, one by one, each existence is ratified.

No predictive test administered, no cobbled formula applied, just the simple truth that the worth of their struggles deserves support despite their failures.

The deepest peace of the liberal voice of conscience comes from the abiding certainty that cost/benefit analysis is, in its human incarnation, irrelevant.

## Why MicroGrants Work

I find myself being cautious when attempting to convey why I believe MicroGrants work. It would be more comfortable to fall back to the structural argument that leans on the "how" of success, the miraculous geometry that connects those who have to those who are in acute need. We have the advantage of peering beyond the individual case and tying the threads that appear to lead to several common effects stemming from uncommon lives. And from that vantage point, we are fools if we fail to accept that our conclusions and analysis limp badly. Not because the attempt was callous, but because any attempt to understand the core of another's satisfaction, by the very act, appears arrogant.

The concept of MicroGrants works, not because it is liberally based or conservatively structured. It works because of its authenticity and because of its ability to speak to the needs and wants of those whose lives are at the crossroads. The stories in this book are reflections on the path each took after Joe called them aside and had them question how their lives and those around them can be better with a little help.

The tendency of the conservative voice would be to measure worthiness as an individual trait before administering the help. The liberal voice of conscience assumes one's worth unconditionally, and gauges what support is appropriate based on the more complex and meaningful potential for integration of that individual back into the community as a whole. This is not a pure liberal perspective where government's role is to protect and defend against individual shortfalls. In the MicroGrants schema, government is not even in play. It provides neither its aegis of legitimacy nor its beneficence.

MicroGrants works because it fulfills the needs of the human spirit with no pretense to satiate the agenda of the giver. Money is given; multiple paths to support are identified; and the individual is left to deal with her or his own conscience as to what constitutes fulfillment.

When Joe first sent me the draft of the multiple stories in this book, my plan was to either skim several pages and start this brief piece or randomly choose a half-dozen examples as a sample from which to work. But as I began reading the clipped glimpses into the lives of these heroes, I realized that in order to honor the collective sacrifice and wisdom these stories represented, I felt bound to move from one expression of despair and hope to another, until the individual, disparate voices began to feel like part of the chorus I could too easily silence.

Each story is an incomplete autobiography. We see a glimpse of lives that are in some way, shape, or form in turmoil. The contexts may be foreign or alienating, but the psychological frames nudge our own realities because they dwell in our community. The voice of conscience forces us to keep reading deeper into each scene. On one level, it is difficult to turn away, yet on another it has been all too easy to turn away. What appears to be a redundancy, a litany, of failures, ambushes, and just bad luck, becomes a re-discovery of the same layers of life that constitute the "slings and arrows of outrageous fortune" that form us all.

Without the call of conscience, each story remains an isolated, impersonal scene. If I deny my inner voice, I need to maintain that cliff until those less fortunate than I can meet me on my terms. If fear pervades my life, and politics, I will "conserve" my resources for fear that I will not have enough; I will "conserve" the processes by which people raise themselves up, lest those I deem undesirable should prosper; I will "conserve" the definitions of fulfillment and success, including expressions of interpersonal love and devotion, in fear that my own shortcomings will be revealed.

The MicroGrants process is not fear-based. There is no hint of guilt laid on the recipients. No doubt there is personal pressure to succeed—a common thread that runs through each story. Some handle that well, while others succumb to such a test of personal responsibility. Instead, the process succeeds because it lifts people from their fear without demanding that they deny its existence. Satisfaction becomes legitimate in each case because it acknowledges its transitory nature. Instead of an unattainable fable, satisfaction can be defined as simply a hope regained.

While satisfaction is not fulfillment, it is a taste, nevertheless. Rather than a commodity whose value expands through its conservancy, fulfillment to the liberal manifests itself most profoundly in the "commons." The term commonwealth means just that; to be able to leapfrog past the forced scarcity of the market driven conservative point of view and into the realm of joined worth. Satisfaction becomes a condition of the community that is measured by the degree to which those in need are supplied with hope that their future will be more satisfactory than their past, and the progression from one to the other is the responsibility of us all.

In my work as a mediator, I gauge our chances for reaching a durable agreement according to the degree each party can independently reach satisfaction, substantively, procedurally, and psychologically. These are not absolute measures but relative expressions that each party has to confront. Commonly for people in conflict, what may appear to be a real condition of satisfaction is often an apparent standard that shifts as the context of the negotiation shifts. How one moves towards acceptance and why some find satisfaction and others do not, is a very idiosyncratic phenomenon. From the mediator's point of view, delving too deeply into why someone has come to accept an agreement will often put the negotiated agreement in peril. So with those caveats established allow me to go deeper into the "why" of the MicroGrants success.

Substantively, the satisfaction comes from a grant of $1000 without strings. This amount is of relative value for several reasons. Many of the recipients used the money to accelerate a dream, whether it was to finish school, or to take a step closer to opening a business. Others, whose safety net had all but disappeared, used the money to stave off the hunger of a child or to put a few more miles between themselves and the demons that were on the chase.

More sustaining is the satisfaction that comes from a process that is rooted in social justice. Life may not be fair, and the lives of those who have received these grants may be examples of compounded unfairness to the point of despair. Yet, the serendipitous process that brought them to Joe will stand as a billboard on their life's path that they cannot deny. While they may have been dealt a tough hand, this grant confirms that this community may be treating them more fairly than they had recognized. The final measure of this procedural satisfaction is whether this investment in them produced the courage to step into the lives of others who have found it even harder than themselves to hope. Procedural satisfaction opens the curtain to the effects of social justice.

Deeper still is the satisfaction that comes from increasing the security, social status, self esteem, and emotional connectivity of those whose lives make this book come to life. How does $1000 make one more safe? The psychology of security had more to do with understanding how individuals judge the risk that bends the options in their own lives. A new sign for the business increases the number of customers, and that reduces the risk of having to move to a new location. I believe, however, that MicroGrants increases the security of the grantees more by providing them with control over their whereby they can determine for themselves how that most personal sense of security will be shaped.

Social status is that psychological attribute that comes when those within a community acknowledge and respect one another. It is a social vehicle to move up the ladder or laterally to a platform of greater hope and respect from those within their community. As an external expression of respect, it empowers a person to take action towards the actualization of one's worth and individuality. For example, some of the people presented in this book used their MicroGrant to buy new clothes for themselves or their loved ones in anticipation of an upcoming job interview. This is an affirmation that they have the right and responsibility to present themselves as "authentic" to their community. When their actions, intent, and values coincide, their image within the community is transformed from mere appearance to that of self-confidence as a worthy member of society willing and able to contribute to the commonwealth.

Often the hardest shift is the challenge to love yourself. Self-esteem is the quotient of one's inner peace. To the grantees in this book, the positive effect was most telling when you consider the vibrant references the student authors used to reflect the initial energy they perceived on first meeting the many recipients. Furthest from the idea of pure substantive satisfaction, the promotion of self-esteem within these individuals constitutes the pinnacle contribution of the liberal voice of conscience. It is the most sustaining, durable, and productive measure when analyzing why MicroGrants is a success. At its core, self-esteem gives us permission to love, and allows us to accept the love from others.

And finally MicroGrants is an undeniable expression, a tangible display, of an emotional connection to a community that cares and is capable of compassion and love. So here may be the answer to Paul's challenge.

Is there any one argument that adequately answers the question of why MicroGrants has succeeded? No, and there never will be. Each of us has been called into this incredible process of grant-giving by a different path, some from high places, others from low, some from no particular place they can call home. But this experience has brought me to a deeper appreciation of what one man, Joe Selvaggio, can do by stepping into each of our paths and reminding us, conservatives and liberals alike, that the voice of conscience without authentic action, rings hollow.

Thank you, Joe.

*Tom Fiutak*
*January 1, 2009*

# An Entrepreneur's Perspective: Moving MicroGrants Forward

## Commentary by Betsy Buckley

I was 50 before I became an entrepreneur, even though I'd definitely sought out entrepreneurial-like experiences for more than 25 years before finally starting my first company. What I now can look back on that fueled both my appreciation for—and resistance to—founding and running a business was the realization that it was all up to me.

That resistance—finally!—was overcome by understanding that challenge. Accepting the blessing—and the risk—of being what I knew in my heart I was meant to be, in spite of any fear and apprehension. The single-minded resolution that silenced all doubt and pushed against all odds to turn from "I'd like to" to "I want to" to "I will."

I see that same spirit in the stories of these micro-grantees and in the wisdom behind the micro-grantors. I see a belief system that's different from the traditional grant awards world, one that is less patriarchal and more about self-sufficiency. A philosophy that's all about possibility and accountability. An approach that shows that small steps can stimulate more small steps that ultimately stretch and become as broad and deep as your vision takes you.

So, I write as an entrepreneur today for three reasons:
- To celebrate the courage and the commitment of these grantees;
- To congratulate the contributions and the confidence of these grantors; and,
- To challenge the rest of us, as we read these tales of triumph, to understand how we can play a part on spreading opportunity, possibility

and hope.

I know the MicroGrants program is about more than helping people start businesses. It is not exclusively designed to serve entrepreneurs like Shegitu, Molly and Marie. In my view, however, the matching of people of means who want to make solid investments with people of possibility is in itself exprepreneurial. Those possibilities are just as important when a $1000 grant is awarded to help someone stay and grow in a job working for someone else as when $1,000 supports the starting or continuation of an entrepreneurial venture.

My perspective is that the overall program works as well as it does because the grantees share the best characteristics of entrepreneurs, because the grantors understand and embrace those values and because the founder, the amazing Joe Selvaggio, is the most entrepreneurial philanthro-pest I've ever known.

Entrepreneurial-like grantees. Let's start with what makes a great entrepreneur. It's really only been in the last 15-25 years that the study of entrepreneurs has come into vogue, largely because business leaders had begun viewing entrepreneurship as the way to revitalize America's dormant productivity and scholars felt a need to explore how that all happened. Just over five years ago, I was at The Hudson Institute of Santa Barbara, doing advanced coaching work. I decided to do my major paper on how non-entrepreneurial organizations (think big corporations, big government) became exposed to and adopted the best traits of entrepreneurs. And how, in doing that, they added creativity, which in turn increased competitiveness, higher sales and greater profits. In addition to doing a significant amount of secondary research, I embarked on a series of interviews and focus groups to determine what those traits were, and how they could be applied. Essentially, I found that most successful entrepreneurs:

• Demonstrate an expectation that they can take control of their own life and their own future and yet graciously accept support (being more gracious when the strings were fewer).

• Exhibit an ability to take risks, realistically balancing the potential gains against losses.

• Consistently display a gift for "moving things forward," even if it means two steps backwards at some points.

• Understand their own weaknesses, learn from their own mistakes,

capitalize on their strengths and exhibit a strong work ethic.
- Display resilience, integrity and intellectual honesty.

Aren't those the same characteristics of the people featured in this book? How noble their stories, how firm their commitments, how entrepreneurial their choices.

## ENTREPRENEURIAL-LIKE GRANTORS

The "philanthropy" concepts behind MicroGrants are far different than traditional foundation grant awards. Certainly, an investor in Micro-Grants takes a more personalized and more imaginative approach towards social change. The relationship emphasis is on individuals, not institutions. The giving is towards a change in one person's life, not towards a program or service that touches many. And, the ROI is defined, upfront, by the vision of the grantee—a more stable work environment, a chance to increase self-sufficiency and be a great parent at the same time, an opportunity to get yourself and your children successfully through school.

MicroGrants' investors have an experience that bears little resemblance to traditional philanthropists. Their gifts are small by intent—yet their impact is large. The costs for the management of the overall program are, by intent, minimal. Through creative relationships with non-profits, potential grantees are vetted; equally creative is the partnership with colleges and universities, where "free" resources analyze and maximize the outcomes of the program. MicroGrants has held costs down—and benefits up. This is a short-turn around, fast moving initiative. A very self-sufficient, move it forward entrepreneurial approach.

A truly entrepreneurial founder and Executive Director. Those who have ever been approached by Joe Selvaggio would easily say he demonstrates these characteristics:
- The willingness to lead, often into unchartered territories
- The ability to see connections between disparate concepts, and in putting them together, solve a significant problem
- A resiliency of body, mind and spirit

He used these talents first as he conceived of and launched Project for

Pride in Living, a now 37-year-old non-profit that has helped thousands of lower-income Twin Cities residents achieve greater self-sufficiency through housing, employment training, support services, and education. Next, Joe went on to found the One Percent Club, through which more than 1000 people have committed to contribute at least 1% of their net assets or 5% of their income to the causes of their choice, effectively bringing at least $100MM of additional assets to support important causes in our community. Is it any wonder than he moved on from that to MicroGrants?

With such an entrepreneurial spirit, it's no wonder Joe has stimulated new thinking about how to address the issues of our times, bringing all people together.

## Where can the rest of us fit?

In 2004, social change agent Mark Desvaux wrote a piece describing the next generation of philanthropists, calling them "philanthropreneurs", and defining them as people who *"devote their time and effort along with their entrepreneurial skills to ultimately benefit others and the world at large."* His key point was that there's a philanthropic shift going on, from a group of people who give generously in their later years, after amassing large amounts of money, to people who can give some money and much entrepreneurial spirit and business acumen to good causes earlier in life.

The celebration around MicroGrants first million dollars of investments marks milestone one. The grantees highlighted in this work and the grantors who made this all possible can stand proudly at this celebration. And, there is room for so much more.

How can this spirit spread? Like any good entrepreneur, I have a few ideas. And, I offer them with the hope of stimulating many, many more.

• FIND SOME FRIENDS. If Joe was able to motivate 100 people to invest $4000 apiece a year, why can't each one of us try for 10 people for $400 apiece, pooling resources? Or 100 for $40? Or? I'm asking myself: What could I do? Who do I know who could work with me? We may not yet be at the age (or status or life experience) where we've amassed large amounts of money, but we are definitely at the "give back" philosophical time of life. Want to join me in being creative in exploring another way to be part of this trend?

• USE YOUR CONNECTIONS. MicroGrants has had enormous success, in part because of the partnerships it's forged. Recognizing that spending money on referral checks, processing grant applications and other types of time-intensive administrative work would be better done by groups in daily connection with potential grantees, MicroGrants forged extraordinary partnerships with groups like WomenVenture, Train to Work , PPL, Summit Academy OIC , Twin Cities Rise! Prism, Midtown Global Market and the African Chamber of Commerce, to name a few.

MicroGrants has cemented relationships with the organizations and staff people closest to their prospective grantees to make sure that the opportunities are connected quickly and efficiently, so that when people of potential are ready to ask, answers can be given. Many of us have well-established relationships with those organizations—and others. This is the time to step back, explore who we know and consider how we can use those connections to help further this process.

• STEP UP, STEP OUT. Come all you venture capitalists, come all you government executives, come all you accountants and lawyers, come all you entrepreneurs. Come, join in the possibilities. There are millions of creative ways—from a percentage of your product sales, to a two-hour-a-week donation of your time, to using a contribution to MicroGrants as a Father's Day or holiday gift, to sponsoring a social event and encouraging grantcontributions.

I am sure there are more. And, I believe you would not be reading this if you didn't think just as I do. With more ideas. More possibilities. And more positive outcomes.

Want to be a part of this movement? Call me. Spread the word. Let's move this forward, together.

*Betsy Buckley*
*May, 2009*
**Betsy Buckley is CEO and Founder, What Matters**
**Call 651-603-0441 when you want growth**

# Women of Color and the Tragedy of Trickle-Down

## Commntary by Laura Waterman Wittstock

Grants of $1000 to women of color and American Indians will be a useful tool to help them in their climb to economic self-sufficiency. The utility of micro-grants has not been fairly tried in the United States, but efforts such as Joe Selvaggio's will establish a model for others to follow.

Women of color and American Indians in the United States are part of the general population of women who are deeply affected by poverty or touched by an inability to rise above a salary and wage limit that effectively keeps them out of economic prosperity. Seemingly, there are few answers to the question of women and poverty, just as there is an apparent widespread acceptance of poverty in America. One answer could lie in discontinuing the term "color" except to refer to culture or community. Race is a continuing term that effectively separates people by making comparisons based on skin color.

No matter how much race training takes place, the barrier of color is always present. On the other hand "culture" generally is a neutral term describing how different groups celebrate their histories, foods, and fashions. It breaks down the term "white" into communities that are different based on culture and it breaks down black, Asian, Latino, and American Indian into the hundreds of cultures within those artificial labels. True appreciation of culture can emerge from its hiding place behind the term "race" when groups celebrate their heritage and others can see how valuable this is to the larger population. For example, an Indian can be singled out as a person of the red race when she is wearing western clothes, but when she is dancing in a powwow, she is seen as a member of a culture others want to know more about. Sans "race," she gains the cultural tag as an ongoing positive.

In the United States, there are different histories for each category of "color," a term imposed primarily by the British when they reigned as a world power. Since all humans dispersed throughout the world from Africa, the division of white and color is highly prejudicial and based entirely on armed might and colonization. Color is incidental and simply an indicator of geographic region, yet for centuries the white north has successfully imposed a meaning attributable to lack of pigment as a sign of superiority. Yet the white north is a very slight variation of one closely related type; the only diversity of human life exists in Africa. A worldwide epidemic that might wipe out the north would leave life to begin again where it started millennia ago: in mother Africa.

African American women were brought to America as slaves against their wills and almost entirely by brute force., although a few came ashore as free people. Asian women came as immigrants or indentured servants. Latina women came into the country as legal and illegal immigrants, in some cases as slaves, and in many cases as American Indians who spoke Spanish as their colonial language. These women paid an enormous price for coming here. Cut off from their mother cultures, they eventually adapted and were left with a designation of "race" rather than the rich cultures of home.

An example is the term "Latina" or "Hispanic," which has come to mean a huge population of many cultures. They speak Spanish, but they are just as colonized as women of color and American Indians who speak English in the United States, or French in Canada. Because they are grouped together regardless of culture, little attention gets paid to women from Oaxaca or the rich Puerto Rican culture in New York City.

Asian women, particularly Chinese and Japanese, came as "picture" brides of the men who toiled on the railroads, in the fields, sugar cane fields of Hawaii, and in the cities of the coastal areas of the U.S. Separation from family life, and from its norms and customs, not only made life difficult for these women, they suffered changes in social behavior as their husbands moved toward a looser, less attached married life. Generations forward, in such places as the State of Hawaii, it was painful to know that grandparents and great grandparents had been forced into heavy labor, never able to leave company "towns," as they were pressured into leaving their home cultures behind.

In 1942, President Franklin D. Roosevelt signed Executive Order 9066 and assigned Dillon S. Myer to open several Japanese "relocation" camps. He did so, and by the end of 1942 the camps were in operation. Japanese nationals as well as U.S. citizens were put into the camps in an unconstitutional act based on national hubris. Despite the fact that Presidents Roosevelt and Eisenhower and the Secretary of Interior called them "concentration" camps, the euphemism "relocation" camps danced around any similarity to the death camps in Europe. With a formal apology in 1992, the U.S. distributed $400 million in reparations to living Japanese. It was a small token for the lives and property lost when President Roosevelt felt he, not Congress, could suspend habeas corpus over the (unfounded) fear of Japanese military action against the United States by these people. For perhaps the only time in history, U.S. Census secrecy was broken to reveal the names and addresses of Japanese people. The whole affair was one of America's deepest affronts to its own Constitution.

There can be no doubt that current culture in the African American communities across the U.S. reflects the early days of slave transport and life in the fields and plantation houses. A powerful combination of guilt and the practice of false superiority has prevented the country from coming to terms with deep prejudice and making real steps toward understanding African American cultures. Even whites willing to learn still feel they are of a different race than their southern cousins. On the other side is an American African culture passed down from generation to generation with a robust cuisine, subtle notes on childcare, relations with whites, and the development of a powerful kinship with other Africans acculturated to America. The remnants of fierce segregation, the ghetto and poor health, have created an inescapable experience of pain and fear for African American women and their children.

American Indian women, although frequently grouped with all others who are not white, actually were never women of color but members of sovereign nations located within the United States. Greed for land made them part of the "red race." Their ancestors were in the North American continent when everyone else came, and they suffered military defeats in dozens of vicious slaughters. In particular, Women and children were killed and wounded by U.S. military forces, singled out for rape and mutilation. Highly organized civilizations and societies gave Indians no advantage against brutes with steel. In fact, in many cases they suffered more from those wielding bayonets, rifles, and the ability to burn or starve out native villages and co-located hunting communities. Unable to move as fast as their male relatives, they stayed behind and attempted to hide their children or younger siblings from the coming military. They were not valuable chattel, so they died with children in their arms. Little was known of how these women earned their living in countries without a currency base. The soft science of anthropology has attempted reconstructions of Indian life, but lacking evidence, with very little accuracy because of the wholesale slaughter by American troops or militias and frontiersmen.

In modern-day America, one thing brings women of color and American Indians in poverty together: sub-rosa commerce in fragile cultural economies. Producing food is particularly common in small, poor economies. Some of the best, most culturally expressive and unregulated foods in the country are to be had in areas where opportunity and vending find each other. Women are adept at producing income for their families when opportunity and demand come together. Few outside of cultural communities are able to taste these genuine foods. The legal, regulated foods available are mass-produced, sanitized, and made for white American tastes, despite claims of truly representing various cultures of color.

Other unregulated items traded by women of color and poor white women include stolen goods, liquor, cigarettes, and numbers (an unorganized gambling racket). Women are less likely to be involved in these areas than men because they are less successful at forming effective relationships to safeguard a larger network to support these illegal enterprises. In some areas of the country, sub-rosa economies make up significant parts of a community's income.

There are areas where women of color and poor women are victimized: gang activity, prostitution, sales and use of drugs and alcohol, rape, and the transport of stolen or other illegal items, such as international drug transport. Young women and children under the age of 18 are likely to be victimized and in the control of adult males. To maintain an illegal economy, it is the duty of some of the males to prowl the streets looking for young females to be forcibly enlisted or "turned" into these illegal trades. Once brought into the activity, it is very difficult for these children and young women to escape and go on to lead normal lives. They lead short, dangerous lives, mostly invisible to general society. Compared to other parts of the sub-rosa economy led principally by women, this sector makes an even larger income, primarily for males, but the revenue does not stay in the communities. Excessive consumption sees income flowing out of the community.

Larger still external sources, particularly in prostitution and drugs, take in the revenue and under those circumstances victimize males and females alike. The United States particularly is a huge consumer of drugs, just as it leads the world as a consumer of other goods and services. The 2009 U.S. budget for drug control is $14.1 billion. The United Nations Drug Control Program estimates that total drug sales are worth $400 billion per year, equivalent to 8% of world trade.

Most American Indian women and women of color involve themselves in none of these activities, but instead try to improve their life circumstances to meet the expectations of the lifestyle portrayed as the "American dream." These expectations are seen every day on American television in soap operas, quiz shows, and advertising. The relentless message is: all Americans can expect and should expect greater earnings and improved outlooks for their children. But along with that comes debt from car and home ownership loans. Until recently, the American dream was sold regularly on credit to families who clearly did not earn enough to pay down the debt while struggling to meet daily living costs and other consumer costs associated with credit cards which were far too easy to obtain. Crippled by debt, the outlook for women of color has become even more precarious.

Of course there are women of color who never had the chance to take on monstrous debt because they live in public housing—Section 8 housing—and are on the government-imposed five-year lifetime limit for public support. The outlook is bleak, yet daily television still sends out its relentless depiction of the American dream. Though they face impossible hurdles, poor women of color try to provide the best life for their children they can. Although the sub-rosa market is open to them and they use it as a normal part of their lives, in poor society moving up to the middle class, the hurdle becomes more difficult as time goes by. A young woman of color who had a child when she was under the age of 18 has only a small chance of obtaining the education she needs to make a lifetime income significant enough to support retirement. Poor women have to work as long as possible, after which they succumb to a relatively early death from chronic or debilitating diseases. Conditions among the poor that impinge on the U.S. average lifespan of 78.11 years include obesity, lack of exercise, tobacco use, high alcohol consumption, stress on muscles and the skeleton, and poor diet.

In poor countries, the nonprofit organization Kiva has experienced some success by connecting Americans who want to loan small amounts of interest-free capital to individual entrepreneurs. The loans help finance small equipment and supplies to start retail enterprises. The small, $1,500 loans are not expected to be effective in the United States, but $10,000 loans are being considered. Micro-loans, for essentially retail efforts, will not work well in a market downturn and may not work well in the U.S. in a prospering market either. Upping loans to $100,000 may work, but the debt load would create a burden too difficult to bear for the entrepreneur. In other countries, there are studies underway that question the success of micro-loans in such countries as Uganda.

Another example is Grameen Bank, which has a foundation that solicits funds for micro-loans and uses micro-loans to help eradicate poverty in developing nations. The lending program was created by Muhammad Yunus, a Bangladeshi economist who won the 2006 Nobel Peace Prize for developing the bank.,

The bank has now offered loans to American women in Queens, New York. Loans average $3,000 to $5,000, small amounts given U.S. costs of living. But there are some applicants who are happy with the loans and feel they will help to lift them out of poverty eventually. Even with this early success, it will take some time to evaluate how well these loans work and to determine if Greeman can be successful in other U.S. cities.

American Indians and women of color as entrepreneurs have a long history in the Western Hemisphere, but the marketplace has changed, as has the role of women. Today, many women are solely responsible for raising their children. The number of single mothers is higher than it has ever been. Whether these women can continue to sustain their households and enter into entrepreneurial efforts to increase income is a question well worth asking. An unknown number of women already do this, but they often function in the sub-rosa market.

Political pressure against abortion and even birth control has hampered the ability of poor women to gain economic independence. In the U.S. women have babies early and if there is a second child within two years, the chances of economic independence plummet. Economic threats are not the only issue. Prolonged health problems are also present.

Whether legitimate or sub-rosa, American Indians and women of color find life difficult as American riches trickle down to them. Their investment in their children and their struggle to partake in some way in the rich American life creates a huge challenge that some women will overcome, but most will not. The investments of Greeman and Kiva will be helpful, but other efforts are needed as well.

A former model, the National Welfare Rights Organization (NWRO), started in Boston and was joined by George Wiley, who brought the effort to national status and showed that organizing could work with poor women. The model has been criticized, but no large-scale organizing effort has been found to replace it. The women's feminist groups by and large have left American Indians and women of color out of leadership rolws and have not had poor women's issues on their main agenda

New organizing efforts such as micro loans may be a good strategy for general social improvements as programs like Kiva and Grameen take a turn at helping American women of color. But if the efforts are trickle-down, the question is open as to whether women will rise to participate in the American Dream they see every day on television.

Another model, now underway is the MicroGrants' program of giving $1000 grants to low-income women of color. Although tiny given the cost of living in the U.S., there is reason to be optimistic about trying these out. They are not connected to the sub-rosa economy, and they leverage greater independence for the women who use them to better their lives.

The United States is a huge consumer in the world. The American Indians and women of color who live in the country are swept along on a tide of debt. A MicroGrant that can buy tools, raw materials, or a course of learning can be a paddle to traverse the tide.

*Laura Waterman Wittstock*
*May, 2009*

*Laura Waterman Wittstock is the President and CEO of Wittstock and Associates.*

## YALE INTERNSHIP PROGRAM

The Yale student interns deserve a great deal of gratitude for the tireless and professional-quality work they performed for MicroGrants and the publication of this book. Without their conscientious efforts there would be no book. The interns were part of a national Yale program that matches the school's students with for-profit companies or non-profit corporations in nine cities across the U.S. to serve and to learn. In the Twin Cities of Minnesota the ten-week program is called "Bulldogs on the Lakes," and the students are housed in the Danebo building on the western side of the Mississippi river.

Andrew Dayton
Class of 2007, Law

James Kallestad
Class of 2010, Am. Studies

Daniel Geoffrion
Class of 2010, Economics

Catherine Bader
Class of 2008, Law

Berit Johnson
Class of 2010, History

Winnie Tong
Class of 2011, Psychology

Sarah Hill
Class of 2011, Poli. Sci.

Gregory Korb
Class of 2010, History

Steve McLachlan
Class of 2011, History

## COLLEGE VOLUNTEERS

Brett Burns
Valderbilt University
Class of 2008, Law

Nick Nhep
University of Wisconsin at River
Falls, Class of 2010
Business Administration
Management Information Systems

## THANK YOU NOTES TO MICROGRANTS

Dear MicroGrants,

Thank you very much for selecting me as a recipient for the Micro-Grants funding! Receiving assistance to reach my goal of being an Equine Assisted Growth Therapist is amazing. It makes my dreams seem that much more tangible. Half of my grant will go to my credit card company since I paid for my $450 Level 1 course with that card. As soon as my Level 1 is complete this June, I will use the remaining funds to pay for my Level 2 course in 2010. Thank you again for making my dreams a reality! I am truly grateful!

Sincerely,

Jenny Gustavson-Dufour

Dear Joe,

Yesterday I received a check for $1000.00 as a micro-grant, and I was moved to tears. This has been a difficult year, and I thank you so much for helping us help others!

Sincerely,

Bernice Johnson

Thank you for providing me with the money that allowed me to go to school to become a Certified Nursing Assistant. I recently found out that I passed the Minnesota Nurse Aid Exam. I am very grateful for the money and the opportunity to become a Certified Nursing Assistant.

Sincerely,

Lydia Williams

## Index of Grantees

We promote equity,

not debt

We encourage savings,

not borrowings

We fund opportunities,

not daily needs

We partner with People

of Potential


And, It's Working!!!


**Contact MicroGrants at**

**1035 East Franklin Ave**
**Minneapolis, MN 55404**
**Telephone: 612.823.2077**
**Fax: 612-455-5101**
**Email: joe@microgrants.net**